First Certificate
Masterclass

Student's Book

Simon Haines
Barbara Stewart

OXFORD

Contents

Exam factfile

The First Certificate in English corresponds to Level Three in the Cambridge ESOL five-level system. It also corresponds to the Association of Language Teachers in Europe (ALTE) level 3 and Council of Europe level B2 Vantage.

The examination consists of five papers. Each of these papers is worth 20% of the total. A, B, and C are pass grades, D and E are fail grades, and U is an unclassified result.

Paper 1 Reading

This paper consists of four parts and takes 1 hour and 15 minutes.

Each part contains a text and a comprehension task of some kind. There are thirty-five questions in total.

The texts are taken from newspaper and magazine articles, advertisements, brochures, guides, letters, fiction, messages, and reports.

Part	Task type	Number of items	What do you do?	What does it test?	Exam techniques
1	Multiple matching	6 or 7	Match headings or summaries with paragraphs	Your ability to identify the main points in paragraphs	page 80
2	Multiple choice	7 or 8	Answer each question by choosing one option from a set of four	Your understanding of detailed points in a text, including opinions and attitudes	page 54
3	Gapped text	6 or 7	Choose sentences or paragraphs to complete gaps in a text	Your understanding of how texts are structured	page 108
4	Multiple matching	13–15	Answer questions by identifying information in short texts	Your ability to scan and locate specific information in a text	page 28

Remember!

- Read and follow all instructions carefully.
- Read each text through quickly before doing the related tasks.
- You will not have time to read all texts in detail, and it isn't necessary. Skim and scan texts for answers where possible.

Paper 2 Writing

This paper takes 1 hour 30 minutes and consists of two parts.
In Part 1, you must answer the question, which is always a letter.
In Part 2, you must choose one of four questions. These may include articles, discursive compositions, informal letters, letters of application, reports, or stories.

Part	Task type	Number of words	What do you do?	What does it test?
1	Question 1 Formal or informal transactional letter	120–180	Read the context and task instructions and write your letter	Your ability to identify key information and then write a letter for a particular purpose, e.g. requesting an action, giving information, and in an appropriate style for the reader
2	Questions 2–4 A selection of three from these task types: article, discursive composition, informal letter, letter of application, report, or story. Question 5 Two tasks,(a) and (b), from the list above related to the set books for FCE.	120–180	Choose one from Questions 2–5. Read the task instructions and write your answer	Your ability to put together ideas on a topic and express them clearly for the reader within the format of the task

In *First Certificate Masterclass*, examples of each Paper 2 question type can be found in the *Writing Guide* pages 162–172.

Remember!

- Spend a few minutes making a simple plan for each piece of writing. Decide on an appropriate style, layout and organisation. Think about the content of paragraphs and the language you will use, e.g. verb tenses. Keep your plan in mind while writing.
- Don't spend more than half the time on your first answer.
- Make sure you answer all the points in the question appropriately.
- Check your writing by reading it through. Try to hear your own voice and 'listen' for mistakes. Check grammar, spelling, and punctuation.

Paper 3 Use of English

This paper consists of five parts and takes 1 hour 15 minutes.
You will be tested on your knowledge of grammar and vocabulary.

Part	Task type	Number of items	What do you do?	What does it test?	Exam techniques
1	Multiple-choice cloze	15	Choose one word or phrase from a set of four options to fill a gap in a text	Your accuracy with vocabulary, including differences in meaning between similar words, and how words fit with the grammar of a sentence	page 95
2	Cloze	15	Think of a single word which best fits in each space in a text	Your accuracy with grammar and vocabulary in context	page 66
3	Key word transformations	10	Read a prompt sentence, then complete a second sentence with between two and five words, including a given word	Your accuracy with a wide range of structures, as well as phrasal verbs and lexical phrases	page 120
4	Error correction	15	Decide if each line of a text contains an unnecessary word and identify it	Your ability to identify the kind of grammar mistakes you might make in your writing	page 17
5	Word formation	10	Use a given root word to form another word which fits in a text	Your accuracy in word-building, including compound words and the use of prefixes and suffixes	page 43

Remember!

- Spend about ten minutes on each task. This will allow you at least twenty minutes to check your answers and to go back to parts you found difficult.
- If there's a question you can't answer, don't waste time worrying about it. Go on to something else.

Paper 4 Listening

This paper consists of four parts and takes about 40 minutes.

The recorded texts may include the following:
Single speakers: answerphone messages, commentaries, documentaries, instructions, lectures, news, public announcements, advertisements, reports, speeches, stories, talks.
Two or more speakers: chats, conversations, discussions, interviews, quizzes, radio plays, transactions.

The speakers will have a variety of accents. Background sounds may be included before the speaking begins to provide contextual information.

Part	Task type	Number of items	What do you do?	What does it test?	Exam techniques
1	Multiple choice	8	Listen to eight short unrelated extracts. For each one, you answer a question by choosing one option from a set of three	Your understanding of general ideas or detailed points in a text, including opinions and attitudes	page 41
2	Note taking, blank filling or sentence completion	10	Listen and complete the spaces with the missing information	Your ability to select information and take notes while listening	page 93
3	Multiple matching	5	Listen to five related extracts and match them with given prompts	Your understanding of general ideas or detailed points in a text, including opinions and attitudes	page 15
4	Selecting from two or three possible answers	7	Listen and select Yes/No, True/False, Multiple choice, or decide which speaker said what.	Your understanding of general ideas or detailed points in a text, including opinions and attitudes	page 68

Remember!

- Listen carefully to the instructions on the cassette.
- Try to predict as much about the recordings as you can from the question paper.
- Don't panic if you don't understand everything the first time.
- Answer all the questions.

Paper 5 Speaking

This paper consists of four parts and takes approximately 14 minutes.
There are normally two candidates and two examiners. One examiner assesses, while the other gives instructions and talks to the candidates.
In certain circumstances, three candidates may sit the test together, which takes approximately twenty minutes.

You will be assessed on
• accurate use of grammar
• range and use of vocabulary
• pronunciation
• communication
• successful completion of tasks

Part	Task type	Timing (minutes)	What do you do?	What does it test?	Masterclass example
1	Interview	3	Answer the examiner's questions about personal information	Your ability to give basic personal information about yourself	page 19
2	Individual long turn	4	Speak individually for one minute without interruption about two colour photographs	Your ability to organise your thoughts and ideas and express yourself coherently	page 57
3	Two-way collaborative task	3	Talk together and work towards making a decision based on a visual stimulus	Your ability to interact with another speaker, give and ask for opinions, and work towards completing the task	page 79
4	Three-way discussion	4	Discuss the topic introduced in Part 3	Your ability to give opinions about everyday situations and current events in full but natural answers	page 94

Remember!

• At first the examiner will ask you a few general questions about yourself. This is to help you relax.
• In Part 2, when you are given the pictures, don't spend too long talking about physical details. Move on to the theme of the pictures.
• Don't dominate the conversation. Allow your partner the opportunity to talk.
• In all parts of Paper 5, try to show how good your English is. This means speaking correctly and fluently with good pronunciation, using a range of vocabulary and communicating successfully.
• Above all, keep talking and stay calm.

The sexes

Introduction

1 Work in pairs or small groups. Choose two of these photographs and discuss what they have in common and how they are different.

2 Discuss these questions.

Which of the images of men and women do you find the most normal? the most shocking? the funniest? the most unrealistic?

How are the roles of men and women changing in your country? Do you think these changes are for the better?

If you had the choice would you speed up this process of change or slow it down?

What do you think the situation will be fifty years from now?

Reading

1 Read the extract from a newspaper article on the right. How do you react to the idea of an all-female spaceship crew?

2 What problems might a single-sex crew face on a forty-three-year space journey?

3 Why might a mixed-sex space crew be a better idea? Read the article below to check your ideas.

No role for men in space exploration

WOMEN will set sail for the stars in as little as fifty years, Nasa scientists have predicted. Men will not be needed; the all-female crew will have children by artificial means.

The spaceships will carry the first interstellar travellers to Alpha Centauri at a tenth the speed of light. The journey will take forty-three years.

DISTANT SPACE TRAVEL BETTER AS FAMILY AFFAIR

'Forget the kind of macho astronauts you are used to seeing in films – space travel to faraway solar systems will probably be a family affair conducted by married couples and their kids,' says
5 US anthropologist, John Moore.

'The family has the kind of natural organisation to deal with the tensions likely to characterise space trips of 200 years or longer to settle remote planets,' says Moore. 'We
10 are less likely to go crazy in space and more likely to accomplish our missions by using crews that are organised along family lines.'

'Whenever colonisation is done on Earth, it is always by people looking for a better life. All
15 of the colonisations that I know about have been done by families, especially young couples.'

In the past, astronauts had to be specially trained and physically very fit to survive in very small space capsules, but spacecraft size is no longer a constraint,
20 making it possible to take ordinary people such as midwives, electricians and cleaners. For a space crew that is going to colonise space and reproduce for many generations, these kinds of people will be just as important as space technologists.

25 Starting with a population of childless married couples also works best on board a spaceship because it will give the initial crew a few years to adjust to their new surroundings without the distraction and responsibility of caring for children.
30 People may be horrified at the idea that children will be living and dying in space, with their only images of Earth coming from pictures and videos. But, says John Moore, parents have always made choices affecting their children's lives.

35 'We change jobs, we move to another town, we emigrate to a foreign country. If we educate our space kids properly, I think one day they might say, "Gosh, I'm sure glad I'm on this spaceship and not back on dirty old Earth."'

According to Moore, a starting population of 150 40 to 180 would best sustain itself at the same rate over six to eight generations. Every person would have the opportunity to be married – with a choice of at least ten possible spouses within three years of their age – and to be a parent. 45

Ideally, the group should share social and cultural values. 'Having some people accustomed to monogamy and others to plural marriages would create some confusion when it becomes time for the 50 sons and daughters of the first generation to marry,' says Moore. 'Designing morals for people on such a fantastic voyage is problematic because people on Earth would have little influence once the crew is on its own. If the 55 space crew decides on a system of slavery for some and privilege for others, there is little the planners on Earth will be able to do to prevent it.'

Thinking about these issues is not as far-fetched as you might think. Experts predict that such a space 60 mission will take place within the next hundred years.

> "Gosh, I'm sure glad I'm on this spaceship and not back on dirty old Earth."

4 Read the article again. For questions 1–5, choose the answer (A, B,C or D) which fits best according to the text.

1 What makes families especially suited to long-distance space travel?
   A They are good at organising.
   B They are naturally better than other groups of people.
   C They will be able to cope with the stress of space travel.
   D They can settle down better in new situations.

2 Why will more ordinary people probably go on space flights in the future?
   A Space travellers will no longer need to be specially trained.
   B There will be a greater need for people with useful abilities.
   C Space travellers will not need to be especially fit.
   D Modern spacecraft will be much bigger than spacecraft in the past.

3 Why is it better for the first crews of space flights to be childless couples?
   A Childless couples are more responsible than couples with children.
   B Childless couples work harder than couples with children.
   C Crews need to get used to their environment before having children.
   D Couples with children would always put their children first.

4 Why is it difficult to design morals for space travellers?
   A People on earth will be unable to affect the behaviour of space travellers.
   B No one knows what is the correct way for space travellers to behave.
   C Space travellers may have different ideas and values.
   D Travellers may be confused by their experience in space.

5 The article suggests that long-distance space travel
   A is a theoretical possibility.
   B will probably start within the next century.
   C could be a disaster.
   D will be a fantastic adventure.

over to you

Would you like to be a space traveller setting out to colonise another planet? Why? Why not?

What kinds of people would be most suitable for this role? Make a list of specific personal qualities they would need.

5 Group nouns are singular nouns which can be followed by singular or plural verbs. Complete sentences a–f with the correct word.

audience   class   crowd   jury   staff   team

a In my first year at school, there were thirty children in my _____.
b The _____ found the man guilty of theft, and he was sent to prison for two years.
c I was always good at sport. I used to play for the university football _____.
d The company is having a hard time. About half the _____ are going to lose their jobs.
e It was a brilliant concert, but only a small _____ was there to hear it.
f After the match, the police found it difficult to control the _____ – they were so excited.

What other group nouns do you know?

Grammar and practice

The future

1 There are many different ways of talking about the future in English. Match these future sentences a–g with the appropriate meaning 1–7 below.

a The space rocket *blasts* off in precisely forty-eight hours.
b The crew *is meeting* to discuss final preparations on Friday evening.
c My sister *is going to have* a baby. It's due in three weeks.
d The astronauts *are going to send* regular reports back to Earth.
e The journey to Alpha Centauri *will take* forty-three years.
f That's the phone. *I'll get* it.
g Space travel to faraway solar systems *will* probably *be* a family affair.

1 an action or event that has been arranged
2 a prediction or expectation
3 an offer of help or an instant decision about the immediate future
4 a scheduled or timetabled event
5 a prediction based on evidence or knowledge
6 a future fact
7 an intention or plan to do something

◀ GRAMMAR REFERENCE PAGE 174 ▶

2 Read this letter. Fill spaces 1–12 with the appropriate form of the verbs in brackets.

On Friday we 1_____ (break up) for the holidays. My friends and I have got a great weekend planned. On Friday evening we 2_____ (have) a party to celebrate the end of the college year. Then we 3_____ (start) our mini adventure – on Saturday morning we 4_____ (get up) early – that's the plan anyway – to drive to Dover to catch the ferry to France. The boat 5_____ (leave) at 9.30.

When we get there, I expect we 6_____ (stop) at a café for something to eat, and then we 7_____ (drive) straight to Paris. We're not sure how long it 8_____ (take). There's a rock concert there that evening which we 9_____ (probably go) to.

We 10_____ (catch) the Tuesday morning ferry back to Dover. I 11_____ (send) you a postcard if I have time.

Hope you have a good summer. 12_____ (you do) anything exciting?

Love, Sue

PS By the way, this is an all-girls trip. We all want a break from our boyfriends!!

3 How would you respond in the following situations? Use appropriate future forms in your answers. Write your answers or make conversations in pairs.

a You think that your boyfriend / girlfriend may be secretly going out with someone else. Tell a friend what you plan to do about it.
b A college friend invites you to go on holiday with them. Apologise and tell them that you have already arranged to visit relatives.
c One of your friends is having a party this evening. They haven't got time to do everything themselves. Think about all the things that need doing, then offer to help.

d Someone asks your age on your next birthday. Give your answer.
e Predict how your personal life will be different in five years' time.
f It has been raining all day. Suddenly the temperature drops to zero. Make a prediction.

Future continuous and future perfect

4 The *will* future can also be used in the continuous or the perfect form. Match examples a–c with their meanings 1–3.

a People may be horrified at the idea that children will be living and dying in space.
b By the year 2100, people will have visited other planets.
c This time next year, we'll be living and working in the USA.

1 to refer to actions or events which will be in progress at a specific time in the future.
2 to predict future trends, developments or tendencies.
3 to refer to actions or events which will be completed by a particular time in the future.

◀ GRAMMAR REFERENCE PAGE 174 ▶

5 Look into your own future. Complete these sentences with your own ideas and then compare ideas with a partner.

a This time next week I'll be ...   c This time next year I'll be ...
b By this time next year I'll have ...   d In five years' time I'll have ...

Cloze

6 Read the text below and think of the word which best fits each space 1–15. Use only one word in each space. There is an example at the beginning.

RACE TO SAVE WORLD'S ONLY WOMEN'S LANGUAGE

Experts have called 0____*for*____ efforts to save a language used only 1_____ women of an ethnic group in central China's Hunan Province. The language, used among women of the Yao ethnic group in Hunan Province, 2_____ believed to be the world's only women's language.

Some experts believe 3_____ the language is related to inscriptions 4_____ animal bones from more 5_____ 3,000 years ago, but no conclusions have 6_____ reached on when the language originated.

The Central-south China Institute for Nationalities in Hubei Province began 7_____ study the language in 1983. So 8_____, about 2,000 characters have been identified.

However, as the small number of women 9_____ use the language die off, it draws closer 10_____ extinction. Yang Huanyi, 93, and He Yanxin, in her sixties, 11_____ among the few women who 12_____ read and write the language.

13_____ is believed that the language was handed 14_____ from mothers to daughters. For unknown reasons, men seem 15_____ to have been interested in learning it.

Vocabulary

1 Read these statements about boys and girls.
Do you think any of them are true?

Boys grow their fingernails long because they're too lazy to cut them.
Girls grow their fingernails long so they can dig them into a boy's arm.

Most baby girls talk before boys do. Before boys talk, they learn how to make machine-gun noises.

Girls turn into women. Boys turn into bigger boys.

Personality

2 Which of these adjectives do you associate with boys and which with girls?

adventurous   competitive   confident   co-operative   emotional
generous   independent   lazy   materialistic   optimistic   possessive
self-centred   sensitive   sincere   sociable   stubborn

3 What are the nouns related to these adjectives?

EXAMPLE *confident – confidence*

4 Write a description of a young boy or girl. It could be your younger brother or sister, or it could be you when you were younger. Use some of the personality adjectives and nouns above.

Confusing verbs: *lay / lie*

5 Match the verbs in italic in sentences a–c with the correct definitions 1–3 below.

a He didn't look at me while he was speaking. I'm sure he was *lying*.
b As soon as he *laid* his head on the pillow, he fell asleep.
c For the first three days of the holiday, she just *lay* on the beach reading and sunbathing.

1 put or place something in position
2 be in a flat resting position
3 the opposite of telling the truth

6 Complete these sentences with the correct form of the verbs in 5.

a I'd had a hard day. All I wanted was to _____ down and go to sleep.
b She knew he was upset, so she just _____ her hand on his shoulder and said nothing.
c When police officers broke down the door, they found three people _____ on the floor.
d I couldn't get to sleep last night. I just _____ on my back and stared at the ceiling.
e I know you _____ to me last night! Now I want to know the truth!
f When we were kids, my sister and I took turns to _____ the table and wash up.

7 Work with a partner. Compare your answers to these questions.

a What is your favourite sleeping position?
b Have you ever lied to protect someone's feelings?

Exam techniques • LISTENING PART 3

dos and don'ts

- Read the instructions and the six options carefully. Don't forget – one option is not needed.
- The first time you hear the recording, listen for general understanding. Note key words and make a first choice of answers.
- The second time you hear the recording, listen for words associated with the options.
- Make your final choice of answer, using any notes you have made. Don't leave any spaces.

1 You are going to hear five people talking about bringing up children. For questions 1–5, choose which opinions A–F each speaker expresses. Use the letters only once. There is one extra letter which you do not need to use. Use the *Dos and Don'ts* above to help you.

A Bringing up children is difficult and needs two people.

B Men are incapable of looking after children successfully.

C Fathers who look after children were considered unusual.

D Mothers and children have a special emotional relationship.

E Women can't take on the role of fathers.

F Men get less practice than women at looking after children.

Speaker 1	1
Speaker 2	2
Speaker 3	3
Speaker 4	4
Speaker 5	5

Phrasal verbs with *bring* 2 Replace the words or phrases in italic in sentences a–g with the correct form of *bring* and one of the particles from this list.

back   about   up   round   in   down

a *Raising* children is far too hard a job for one person to do.
b It took doctors an hour to *make her conscious again* after the accident.
c Most of the damage to the houses was *caused* by the recent storms.
d I hope she doesn't *mention* the embarrassing subject of money again.
e The government *has introduced* a new law banning smoking on public transport.
f Visiting Spain again *made me remember* lots of happy childhood memories.
g They'll have to *reduce* the price of cars. Nobody's buying them at the moment.

Vocabulary

Formal and informal language

1 Which types of letters would you write in a formal style and which in an informal style? Make a list of each type. Then, compare your list with a partner.

2 Read the two short letters below and answer these questions for each.
   a What kind of letter is each one?
   b What is the purpose of each letter?
   c What is the relationship between the writer and the reader in each case?
   d How are the two letters different? Think about the information they contain and the language the writers use.
   e Why is the second letter so much longer than the first?

Hi Rachel,

Sorry about last night. The thing is I was held up at work and didn't get in till half six. I got changed and had a bite to eat, then I tried to get you on your mobile, but it was switched off, so I texted you just to let you know I was going to be late. I know you didn't get it, 'cos by the time I got to the club you'd obviously given up and gone home. Sorry!!! Hope you're not too cross with me.

Love you!!

Tim

Dear Ms Shaw,

I am writing to apologise for yesterday evening. Unfortunately I was delayed at work and I did not arrive home until 6.30. I changed, had a snack and attempted to contact you on your mobile phone, but it was switched off. I therefore sent you a text message to inform you that I was going to be late for our meeting. I realise that you did not receive my message, because by the time I arrived at the restaurant you had decided I was not coming and returned home. I do apologise.

Yours sincerely,

James Wood

3 Which words or phrases are used in the second letter instead of these informal words and phrases in the first letter?
   a a bite to eat   e to let you know
   b tried   f 'cos
   c so   g gone home
   d I texted you   h Sorry!

4 Phrasal verbs are more common in speech and informal writing than in formal writing.
   • Read lines 1–2 of the first letter and underline the two phrasal verbs.
   • Read lines 1–3 of the second letter and underline the phrases used instead of the phrasal verbs.

5 Replace the verbs in italic in these sentences with the correct form of a phrasal verb from this list.

back down   bring up   bump into
call off   go on   put (someone) down
put up with   split up   work out

   a My boyfriend refuses to *admit he's wrong* even when he knows I'm right.
   b Even after Tom and his wife *separated*, they still *continued* working together.
   c I wish people wouldn't smoke in the office. I just can't *tolerate* it.
   d I wish you wouldn't *criticise* me in public, it's really embarrassing.
   e *Quite by chance I met* someone I was at school with yesterday.
   f Have you heard about Tim and Jan? They've *cancelled* their wedding!
   g My grandparents *raised* five children on a very low income.
   h I've been trying to *calculate* how long we've known each other.

Meanings of *get*

6 *Get* has many meanings in informal English. Underline the examples of *get* in the first letter. Find the more formal equivalents in the second letter.

> **dos and don'ts**
> - Read the text carefully sentence by sentence. Think about the grammar and the meaning.
> - Read the text again, line by line. Look for unnecessary words and underline them. Remember there is never more than one extra word in a line. Tick (✓) any correct lines.
> - Read the text to check it makes sense.

1 For questions 1–15, read the text below and look carefully at each line. Some of the lines are correct, and some have a word which should not be there. If a line is correct, put a tick in the space. If a line has a word which should not be there, write the word in the space. There are two examples at the beginning. Use the *Dos and Don'ts* above to help you. Look particularly for these kinds of extra words:

Verbs	He ~~has~~ arrived last week.
Prepositions	He's done more ~~of~~ than me. / Are you going ~~to~~ home?
Articles	He climbed ~~the~~ Mount Fuji.
Pronouns	The restaurant you're looking for ~~it~~ has closed down.

At home with Mamma

0	Gianluca Vinti has been a teaching job at an Italian university,	*been*
00	a car, fashionable clothes and a mobile phone. But in reality,	✓
1	Vinti is a Mamma's Boy, who is still living at the home at 33 and	_____
2	unashamed of it. 'It's true that life at home is easier than,' he	_____
3	says. 'I have fewer expenses and my mother still brings me	_____
4	coffee in bed each morning. But I choose to stay because of	_____
5	my relationship with my family it is excellent. Until I see a valid	_____
6	reason for leaving, I'll stay.' Vinti's not being alone: according to	_____
7	recent figures, the number of boys between the ages of 18 and	_____
8	34 who living with their parents has reached 58.5 per cent, up	_____
9	from 51.8 per cent seven years ago. The main reason the boys	_____
10	are at home long time after they've become men is financial,	_____
11	but the mother-son relationship remains as strong as ever. In	_____
12	Italy, leaving from your parents' home at an early age before	_____
13	you getting married can lead other people to suspect that	_____
14	there something is wrong in the family. The normal time to move	_____
15	out of your parents' house is when you start to your own family.	_____

> **over to you**
> At what age do young people leave home in your country?
> Is it the same for boys and girls?

Listening

Lead in

1 🎧 Work in pairs. Time yourselves to see how long it takes to work out these problems.

   a *The day before yesterday I was eighteen, but next year I'll be twenty-one.* What is the date of the speaker's birthday? What date was this statement made?

   b Two friends on the beach are sharing a personal stereo. They work out that they will each be able to listen for forty-eight minutes in the time they have. Then, four more friends arrive. Now the six friends agree to share the stereo for an equal length of time. How long will each person be able to listen for?

2 Do you think men or women are better at solving mathematical puzzles?

Multiple choice

3 🎧 Listen to the recording about a TV programme called *Just for Fun* in which contestants try to solve mathematical problems.

   a Are your ideas supported by any of the speakers?
   b Do you find the ideas convincing or not? Give your reasons.

4 🎧 Listen to the second part of the recording again. Answer these questions by writing M for Men, and W for Women.

   a On *Just for Fun*, which group starts with more confidence?
   b Which group gets more problems right on the programme?
   c Which group tries to answer the questions more quickly in the first place?
   d Which group panics when they're being watched?
   e Which group doesn't like taking risks?
   f Which group takes longer to answer the questions?
   g Which group seems to be naturally better at maths?

over to you

Are there any skills or abilities that men or women are particularly good at? Consider music, sports, science, politics, languages, cookery, economics, child-rearing, teaching, painting.

Do you think it is true, as someone says in the recording, that 'women don't like to take such big risks as men'?

Speaking

1 Have you ever had a penfriend? If you have, tell a partner about

where they lived	what they looked like
their job / school	how long you kept in touch with them

2 Fill in this application form for a penfriend scheme. Then, compare what you have written with a partner.

Personal details	Your preferences
Name _____	Would you prefer a male or a female penfriend?
Address _____	_____
_____	What nationality would you like your penfriend to be?
Male / Female _____	In what language do you wish to write?
Age _____	
Occupation _____	What are your main interests or hobbies?

3 What information would you want to find out about a new penfriend? Write a list of questions that you might ask in your first letter.

Giving personal information

4 🎧 Listen to two FCE candidates answering questions in Part 1 of the Speaking test. Make a note of some of the questions asked by the interviewer in the table below.

Topics	Questions
Family	_____
House and home	_____
Leisure	_____

5 Did the interviewer ask any of the questions you thought of for your penfriend?

6 🎧 Listen to these extracts in which the candidates give extra information, and answer these questions.

Extract 1 Why doesn't Yasko live with her brother?
Extract 2 Why does Sun like where he lives?
Extract 3 What kind of book does Sun enjoy reading?
Extract 4 Why did Yasko become interested in playing the piano?

7 Work in pairs. If possible, work with someone you don't know well. Ask your partner the questions you heard in the Part 1 recording. Remember to give explanations and examples where appropriate.

tip!

In Part 1 of the Speaking paper, it is important to give full answers to the questions. Don't just answer with a few words or single sentences.

Writing

Informal letter

1 Read this example of a Part 1 task and answer the questions.

   a Make a note of the information that should be included in the letter.

   b What style will the letter be written in? Why?

> Your friend has sent you a wedding invitation, telling you the time and place of her wedding. She has also sent a note, asking you to pass on an invitation to Nicky, a friend she has lost touch with. Read the information and write a suitable letter to Nicky. Write between 120 and 180 words in an appropriate style. Do not write any postal addresses.

Alice Blakemore
and
David Jeremy Simmons

invite you

to join them in celebrating their marriage

on Saturday 29th June at 3 o'clock in the afternoon

at St. Michael's Church, Rochester, Kent

RSVP

Hi Chris

Could you let Nicky know about the wedding? We'd love to see her if she can come. She can bring a friend.

Alice

xxxxx

PS - You can find our wedding list on the Internet.

Alice and David's Wedding Present List

Coffee Maker   Ok
Kitchen Clock   No - boring
Contemporary painting – large   Don't know what they'd like
Flower vase   Boring
Wine glasses   Ok

2 Read this letter written in answer to the task. Is the relevant information included, and is the style appropriate?

Hi Nicky,

Guess what - Alice is getting married! She's sent me an invitation and she has requested that an invitation be passed on to you. She'd love you to come, but she does not know how to get in touch with you.

The wedding's at 3 o'clock in the afternoon in Rochester. Alice says you can bring a friend if you like.

I thought we could buy Alice and Dave a present between us. I've looked at their Wedding List on the Internet and I've come up with a few ideas. A number of the items are rather boring, like the kitchen clock. They'd also like a modern painting, but I think that's the kind of thing they should choose themselves. What about purchasing a coffee maker or a set of wine glasses? They're not too expensive.

Anyway, let me know if you can come, and tell me what you think about the present ideas. Look forward to seeing you.

Yours sincerely,
Chris

3 Answer these questions with F (formal) or INF (informal).

Which kind of writing is more likely…
a to have short sentences?
b to have an impersonal tone?
c to use contractions (shortened verb forms)?
d to include polite phrases?
e to use passive verbs?
f to use phrasal verbs rather than single-word verbs?
g to leave out certain words such as pronouns?
h to use very simple words or slang?

4 How many of the informal features from the list a–h above can you find in the sample answer? Read the letter again and check.

Think, plan, write

5 You are going to write a letter. First, read the task below and decide what style – formal or informal – would be appropriate.

> A British penfriend has sent you a letter to tell you that they are coming to stay in your town with their boyfriend / girlfriend. Read the letter, on which you have made some notes. Then using all the information in your notes, write a suitable reply. Write your letter in 120–180 words. Do not include any addresses.

fantastic!

Tell them!

Is camping a good idea? Could stay with me …

say what they can do and visit

take them to …

We're coming when our exams are over – that's in mid-June. We'll probably stay for two weeks before moving on.
The most important thing really is a good place to stay. What will the weather be like in June? We'll have tents with us, so camping's possible.
Is there anything interesting happening around that time? It'd be great if you could suggest a few places to visit while we're there.
Of course, we must get together with you sometime.

6 Decide in detail what information you can give about your town.

7 Here is a paragraph plan:
Paragraph 1 Greeting / react to penfriend's news.
Paragraph 2 Tell them about the weather and possible accommodation.
Paragraph 3 Make suggestions about things to do and places to visit.
Paragraph 4 Respond to your friend's suggestion about meeting.
Remember to end the letter appropriately.

8 Finally, read through your letter, checking grammar, spelling and punctuation.

◀ WRITING GUIDE PAGE 164 ▶

Overview

1 Some of the lines in this text contain an unnecessary word. Write the unnecessary words in the spaces at the ends of the lines. Tick any lines that are correct. There are two examples at the beginning.

Maya Angelou

0	In 1970, Maya Angelou who became the first	*who*
00	African-American woman to have a non-fiction book	✓
1	in the bestseller lists. It was one the first volume of	_____
2	her autobiography and was called as *I Know Why*	_____
3	*the Caged Bird Sings*. The book which is about	_____
4	Maya's childhood in Arkansas in the 1930s. She	_____
5	grew up in a rural town called Stamps, where in the	_____
6	black and white communities were strongly divided.	_____
7	At the age of eight, she was been attacked by her	_____
8	mother's boyfriend. When he was murdered, she	_____
9	blamed herself for and didn't speak for five years.	_____
10	Before she turning to writing, Maya was an actor, a	_____
11	singer, a dancer and a cook. She also worked with	_____
12	the civil rights leaders such as Martin Luther King and	_____
13	Malcolm X, who they fought for equal rights for black	_____
14	people in America. As well as her any autobiographical	_____
15	books, Maya Angelou has published out several	_____
	volumes of poetry.	

2 Complete the sentences using the correct form of a phrasal verb with *bring*.

a Jim was _____ to believe that stealing things was wrong.

b Hearing old pop songs often _____ memories of my younger days.

c Paramedics sometimes use strong smells to help to _____ unconscious accident victims.

d Giving up smoking can _____ a tremendous improvement in your health.

e Sarah embarrassed her boyfriend when she _____ the subject of his driving difficulties.

3 Replace the *get* phrases in italic in these sentences with more formal equivalents.

a Why didn't you just phone me and explain? I don't *get it*.

b Can I *get* you a drink? You look worn out.

c What did you *get* your girlfriend for her birthday?

d We *got* a bus to the airport and *got* there with plenty of time to spare.

e I must be *getting* thinner. My jeans are really baggy on me.

2 Compulsion

Introduction

1 Work in pairs or small groups. Look at the photographs and discuss these questions.

What are the people in the photographs doing?

Which of these things do you do?

How much do you enjoy doing these things?

Which statement best describes your attitude to them?
  a This doesn't interest me at all.
  b I do it every now and then.
  c I really enjoy it.
  d I'm hooked. I'd like to cut down.

2 Discuss these questions.
  a Why and how do people become addicted to certain substances and activities?
  b Are addictions always bad? For example, is it bad to be a workaholic?
  c What can people do to overcome their addictions?

Listening

Whether you are a keen skater or just a keen gamer, Pro Skater 4 is an essential addition to your collection. The controls provide a realistic feel to the game. As a result you can now do bigger and better stunts with ease. However, don't imagine that this is an easy game to play. It will take a true professional to complete all the challenges.

The graphics are highly impressive, the characters move realistically, and the locations are varied. The skater creator mode lets you build your own individual character in great detail from hair colour to clothing.

Lead in

1 Why are games like the one described above so popular?

2 🎧 You will hear the first part of a radio phone-in programme.
a What is the programme about?   b Who will be answering questions?

Sentence completion

3 🎧 Listen to the second part of the programme and answer these questions.
a What advice does each speaker give to the caller?
b Whose advice do you most agree with?

4 🎧 Listen to the second part again. Complete these sentences with one, two or three words.
a Marion gave her son a games console because it was _____.
b Adam is absolutely exhausted after he has _____.
c Adam plays games for more than _____ hours at weekends.
d When Adam's sister told him it was lunchtime, he _____ her.
e According to the child psychologist, eleven-year-old boys are _____.
f The headteacher thinks Adam could damage _____ or brain if he continues to play his games so much.
g According to Oliver Newton's research, children who spend a lot of time playing games are capable of _____ faster.

over to you

Have you ever played games like the ones described by the worried mother? How often?

What advice would you give to parents who are worried about their children's obsessions?

Moods and attitudes

5 These twelve adjectives all describe moods or attitudes. Put them into four groups according to their meaning. There are three near synonyms in each group.

abusive   assertive   depressed   determined   exhausted   fed up
impolite   overtired   rude   sleepy   stubborn   unhappy

6 Discuss these questions in pairs.
a In what situations do you feel *sleepy*? What makes you *exhausted*?
b Are you ever *impolite*? In what situations? Has anyone ever been *really rude* to you?
c Can you be *stubborn* if you want to be? What kinds of situations make you feel *stubborn*? How is being *stubborn* different from being *determined*?
d What makes you *fed-up*? How is being *depressed* different from being *unhappy*? Why are so many people *depressed* these days?

Grammar and practice

Habits

1 Which of these sentences refer to habits, routines or generalisations in the present? Which verb forms and other words tell you this?

   a We bought him a new Playstation for his birthday last month.
   b He always gets so involved in the games that, when I ask him to stop, he doesn't even hear me.
   c He tends to be very rude, especially when he's been playing a difficult game.
   d Sometimes he just refuses to stop playing.
   e He used to get on so well with the rest of the family.
   f They'd get into arguments or fights with other children.
   g They usually develop improved powers of observation and reaction.
   h He spent much more time with us before we bought him the game.

2 Which sentences refer to habits, routines or generalisations in the past? Which verb forms and other words tell you this?

   ◀ GRAMMAR REFERENCE PAGE 175 ▶

3 *Always*, *sometimes* and *usually* are frequency adverbs. What other frequency adverbs do you know?

4 How do people, including you, behave in situations a–c below? Think of three different answers for each situation.

   EXAMPLE   *When people are* tired and sleepy, *they tend to forget things, get bad-tempered and fall asleep in the middle of doing things. Sometimes they drop things or lose things.*

   a When people are *fed up*, …
   b When people are *nervous* or *embarrassed*, …
   c When people are *excited*, …

Repeated actions

5 The present continuous can also be used with *always* to refer to repeated actions. How do you think the meaning of this structure is different from the present simple with *always*?

   EXAMPLES   *He's always losing his temper and behaving in an aggressive way.*
   I'm always losing my glasses – it's very frustrating.

6 Make sentences using *always* to answer these questions. Then, compare your answers with a partner.

   a What do you find annoying about people you know? Think about your acquaintances, friends and family.
   b What do other people find annoying about you? What annoys you about yourself?

7 Match sentences a–c with the meanings in 1–3 below.

a I'm *getting used to* doing my shopping in the evenings and at night.
b I *used to* go shopping on Saturday mornings .
c I'm *used to* shopping in supermarkets.

1 This is a past action which no longer happens.
2 This is a present situation.
3 This is a present situation which is changing.

◀ GRAMMAR REFERENCE PAGE 175 ▶

8 Complete these sentences with the correct form of *be used to* or *get used to*.

a No matter how hard I try, I _____ (never) driving on the right.
b Before children start school, they _____ (not) sitting still for long periods of time.
c When British people come to my country, they have to _____ eating at unusual times.
d Before some people get married, they _____ (not) sharing things.
e I feel really sleepy. I _____ getting up later than this.

9 Compare aspects of your life ten years ago with aspects of your life now. Think about these situations and write sentences. Then, compare your answers in pairs.

EXAMPLE *Holidays* *I used to get up early and play with my friends. Now I stay in bed and watch TV.*

a How you spend your money   c Your taste in music
b Your favourite food and drink   d How you travel around

Cloze

10 Read the text below and think of the word which best fits each space. Use only one word in each space.

strange hobbies

People have the strangest hobbies, don't they? Take my brother, for example. When he was nine or ten years old, he ¹_____ to be a train-spotter. At weekends and during school holidays, he often used to spend whole days on the platform of our local railway station, watching and ²_____ photographs of trains. Sometimes he went train-spotting in London.

Basically train-spotting involves collecting train numbers. Train-spotters simply write ³_____ the numbers of all the trains they see in a little notebook. ⁴_____ is even possible to buy books with lists of numbers ⁵_____ train-spotters can underline.

If you walk along the platform of any station in Britain ⁶_____ a Saturday afternoon, you will see them, in groups ⁷_____ alone. Dressed in practical but unfashionable clothing, they wait ⁸_____ the next train. But most of these train-spotters are ⁹_____ nine-year-old boys, but teenagers and even men ¹⁰_____ their twenties or thirties!

In Britain, train-spotting ¹¹_____ regarded as the most obsessive hobby there is. In fact, ¹²_____ word 'train-spotter' and their favourite item ¹³_____ clothing, the anorak, have become associated with 'obsessive' and 'ridiculous' people. And train-spotters themselves are looked down on ¹⁴_____ the rest of the population as boring individuals who can't think of ¹⁵_____ better to do with their free time than stand in the rain and write down numbers.

Vocabulary

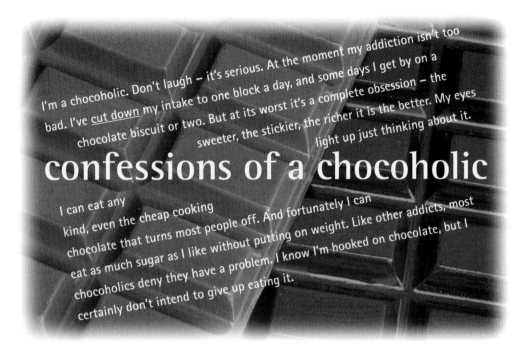

I'm a chocoholic. Don't laugh – it's serious. At the moment my addiction isn't too bad. I've <u>cut down</u> my intake to one block a day, and some days I get by on a chocolate biscuit or two. But at its worst it's a complete obsession – the sweeter, the stickier, the richer it is the better. My eyes light up just thinking about it.

confessions of a chocoholic

I can eat any kind, even the cheap cooking chocolate that turns most people off. And fortunately I can eat as much sugar as I like without putting on weight. Like other addicts, most chocoholics deny they have a problem. I know I'm hooked on chocolate, but I certainly don't intend to give up eating it.

Lead in

1 How does the writer of this text feel about their addiction?

2 Are you addicted to these or any other foods? Discuss your ideas in pairs.
chocolate   cheese   chips   hamburgers   coffee   sugar   chilli peppers

Phrasal verbs

3 Underline six phrasal verbs in the text. Replace the phrasal verbs with the correct form of a word or phrase from the list below.

EXAMPLE   *I've* reduced *my intake to one block a day …*

disgust   gain   shine   survive (on)   reduce   stop

4 Match these phrasal verbs with *give* with the meanings in 1–7. Some verbs have more than one meaning.

a give away	1 surrender or admit you can't do something
b give back	2 distribute things to people
c give in	3 stop being involved with a person because they
d give out	disappoint you
e give up on	4 reveal secret information
	5 return something to its owner
	6 let a person have something without paying
	7 hand work to a teacher

5 Complete these sentences with the correct form of a phrasal verb with *give*.

a I've been playing this CD ever since Rachel lent it to me. I really ought to _____ it _____ to her and buy it for myself.

b I feel like _____ James – he never does what he says he's going to do.

c One of the supermarkets in town is _____ free samples of a new kind of non-addictive chocolate. You ought to try it.

d No thanks, I haven't had a cigarette for three days, and I'm not going to _____ now.

e All over town there are people _____ leaflets about how to stop smoking.

- Read the questions quickly to find out what information you are looking for.
- Read the texts for general understanding. Make a note of any answers that you find.
- Look at the questions again. For each question, identify the key words, then read the part of the text where the information is mentioned. Don't read everything again.
- Go on to the next question if you can't find the information quickly.
- Make a sensible guess if you can't find the answer. Don't leave questions unanswered.

1 You are going to read a newspaper article in which people talk about their smoking habits.
For questions 1–15, choose from the people A–H. The people may be chosen more than once.
Where more than one answer is required, these may be given in any order.
There is an example at the beginning. Use the *Dos and Don'ts* above to help you.

Which person

has never tried to stop smoking?	0	*B*	1		2	
doesn't believe in the harmful effects of passive smoking?	3					
is in a minority in their profession?	4					
was shocked when someone they knew died of cancer?	5					
found smoking helped them get over a personal tragedy?	6					
was punished after they had stopped smoking?	7					
admits to having smoking-related health problems?	8		9		10	
started smoking as a student?	11		12			
found the effects of giving up smoking unacceptable?	13		14			
had special treatment to stop him or her smoking?	15					

Discuss your reactions to these statements in pairs.

Smoking should be banned in all public places, including restaurants, bars, trains and cinemas.

Everyone has the right to smoke.

People who continue to smoke when they are ill should be refused medical treatment.

Employers should provide a place where people can smoke.

the EVIL WEED

A Ambrose Huxley – Editor

I refuse to employ non-smokers. They always gang up and try to stop everyone else from smoking. Anti-smokers are so bossy. There's nothing to prove that passive smoking causes cancer. Actually, I gave up recently because I was wheezy and very short of breath, but it won't last. I tried to stop once before. I had electric shock treatment, which was extremely expensive, and I stopped for three months, but then I went back to it.

B Ann Gore – Journalist

I started when I was at university. Everyone else seemed to be doing it. I only realised I was hooked when I discovered I'd run out late one night and walked for miles through the pouring rain to find a shop that was still open. I tell people that I smoke about thirty cigarettes a day, but it can be much more. When I'm on a story, and existing on two hours' sleep a day, I smoke non-stop. I don't even enjoy it.

C Rowena Taylor – Novelist

There's no point giving up. Smoking will soon be considered good for us, and people with dirty, wasted lungs will have more resistance than people with fresh, tender lungs. That's my excuse anyway. I did stop once for forty-eight hours after visiting a local shop. The owner, who always had a cigarette in her mouth, had died of lung cancer. That upset me a lot because it was someone I knew. Actually, I'm a bit suspicious of people who don't smoke. I suppose I think they're rather cowardly.

D Graeme Ashbury – Actor

In twenty-six years I probably haven't gone without a cigarette for more than six hours, except when I'm asleep. I smoke the second I wake up and would be uncertain how to approach the day without one. No, I've never tried to give up. In New York anti-smokers are very aggressive – people gesticulate at you in the street. But in England, I've only been subjected to exaggerated waves of the hand in restaurants or to whispered comments. I certainly hope that our six-year-old daughter won't smoke.

E Adrian Daniels – Dancer and choreographer

I retain an old-fashioned image of smoking. I see it as attractive and rebellious, and I was a pre-ten-year-old smoker. A lot of dancers smoke. It's the hanging around and tension that get to you. I'm sure I'd notice a difference in my dancing if I stopped, but I've never tried. I don't doubt the health risks. Most of my friends smoke, and my partner does too. I suppose I might be more self-conscious about it if they didn't.

F Joanne Archer – Freedom Organisation for the Right to Enjoy Smoking Tobacco

It's not the best thing you can do for your health, but if you have an introverted personality and suffer from stress, cigarettes can become your best friend. When my husband died last year, I would have been utterly lost without cigarettes. The mood against smokers is openly hostile. There should be restricted areas for smokers in all public places. I've tried to give up twice due to chest problems, but I'm not happy with my personality as a non-smoker.

G Julian Carter – Doctor

Most doctors don't smoke. There are only about 8% of us who still do, but two years ago I replaced my cigarette habit with cigars. My wife forced me to give up. I was on around 15 a day. It all started when I was at university. There was a lot of hanging around and talking, and smoking was very much a part of that. Now I limit myself to two cigars a day. My views are changing. Now I believe that smoking is anti-social.

H Kate Clements – Model

I started to smoke at boarding school when I was fourteen but gave it up pretty quickly. Two weeks after I'd quit, the headteacher found an empty packet in my drawer, and I was suspended from school for two weeks. I thought, 'If I'm going to be suspended anyway, I might as well smoke.' Now I get through ten to fifteen a day. At the end of each photographic shoot, I'll light up. I've tried to give up, but I put on weight and became so bad-tempered that I started again. Even at twenty-one I'm short of breath, have chest pains and feel lousy until I've had my first cigarette.

Vocabulary

SUPERSTITIONS

Do you believe that you'll be <u>luckier</u> if you do certain things? Do you avoid doing something because it may bring you bad luck? I worry about some things, like Friday 13. But a lot of people are worse than me – my sister, for instance, refuses to walk under ladders or open her umbrella inside the house, and my brother, who is one of the least superstitious people I know, often touches wood for luck. He doesn't even realise he's doing it. Some people might think that in the twenty-first century we shouldn't be as superstitious as we were in the past, but I think superstition is one of the most natural human characteristics. The fact we still believe in these things in the age of computers is fantastic. It shows that we haven't lost the more mystical side of our nature.

Lead in

1 Do you do believe in any of the superstitions mentioned in this article?

2 Compare your ideas about superstitions in pairs.
How superstitious are you?
Do you agree that being superstitious is a natural human characteristic?

Comparison

3 Underline the six comparison expressions in the article. The first one has been underlined for you.

4 What are the comparative and superlative forms of these adjectives and adverbs? Think of other examples of each type.

a long/short
b large/late
c flat/thin
d heavy/funny
e important/independent
f clever/narrow
g good/bad
h easily/carefully

◀ GRAMMAR REFERENCE PAGE 176 ▶

5 These phrases are used with comparative adjectives. Which refer to things that are very different, and which refer to things that are almost the same?

a bit   far   a little   a lot   much   slightly

6 Complete these sentences with the correct form of the adjective in brackets.
a Helena is one of _____ (unlucky) people I've ever met.
b In general, motorbikes are far _____ (dangerous) than cars.
c The weather was much _____ (hot) today than anyone expected.
d People say I've got _____ (bad) handwriting they've ever seen. I'll have to learn to write _____ (neatly).
e I have to admit that my _____ (young) brother is a lot _____ (clever) than me.
f David may be _____ (short) student here, but he's also _____ (intelligent).

7 Write a parapraph comparing yourself with someone you know well: a friend, someone in your family or another student in the class.

Speaking

Lead in

1 Do you support a particular sports team? If so, how keen are you? To what lengths would you go to support the team?

2 Do you have a favourite singer or pop group? Have you ever seen them? How far would you travel to see them?

Long turn

3 Compare and contrast photos 1 and 2 and say why you think sports fans and pop fans enjoy looking the same and behaving in a similar way.

4 Compare and contrast photos 3 and 4 and say what kind of people you think prefer to do activities on their own.

tip!

In Part 2 of the Speaking paper, say what you think is similar and different about the two photographs. Don't describe each picture separately. Use comparing and contrasting expressions such as:

Both photographs show ...

The main difference between the photos is ...

Writing

Article

1 Read this Part 2 task and answer the questions.

  a In what situations do people read magazine articles?
  b Why do people choose to read or not to read a particular magazine article?
  c What would be an appropriate style for this kind of article?

> An English-language magazine for students is running a series of articles entitled 'I'm just crazy about …' in which young people write about their personal interests. Write an article for the magazine in 120–180 words about an activity you are enthusiastic about.

2 Read this article and answer the questions.

  a How does the writer try to interest the reader?
  b How interesting do you find the article?
  c How would you describe the style? Formal or informal? Personal or impersonal? Serious or humorous?
  d In which paragraph does the writer describe a personal experience?
  e What descriptive language does the writer use?

I'm just crazy about rock climbing

You may be wondering how anyone can be **crazy** about something **dangerous** like rock climbing? To be honest, I'm not sure why I'm so keen on it. It isn't because I'm good at it – I'm only a beginner.

I've come up with some reasons that non-climbers might understand. There are practical reasons. For example, climbing keeps you **fit**, and you meet lots of new people with the same interest as you.

In addition to this, there are reasons that only experienced climbers would give. The main one is that climbing is **scary** – it gives you a fantastic **thrill**. I'll **never** forget my first climb – it was terrifying. Once you've got over the **fear**, you feel great because you've achieved something.

I must admit that sometimes I feel annoyed with myself because I can only do easy climbs. I feel **terrible** if I can't finish a climb and have to give up half-way.

So, **why** do I carry on? I don't really know. It's just something I have to do.

Creating interest

3 Which of these are essential features of an article title?
a It should attract your attention.
b It should make you want to read the article.
c It should tell you exactly what the text is about.
d It should give you an idea of what the text is about.
e It should be short.

4 Which of these titles would make you want to read an article about sky-diving? Give reasons.

a Sky-diving for beginners.

b No, I'm not completely mad.

c So you'd like to try sky-diving.

d A complete history of sky-diving.

5 Which of these opening sentences would make you want to continue reading? Give reasons.

a Sky-diving is a relatively recent sport.

b Have you ever wondered what it would be like to fall out of an aeroplane?

c Sky-diving isn't for everyone.

d The best thing about sky-diving is that anyone can do it.

Think, plan, write

6 You are going to write a magazine article. First, read the task.

> An English-language magazine for students of your age is running a series of articles entitled 'I've always wanted to …' in which young people write about an activity they'd be keen to try. Write your article for the magazine in 120–180 words.

7 Decide on an activity to write about and note down some key ideas. If possible, choose an activity you would really like to try.

8 Plan your article. Make brief notes as you work through these stages.
a Work out a paragraph plan. Think particularly about what you will write in your first and last paragraphs. How many other paragraphs will you need? Remember to plan a new paragraph for each main idea.
b Think of a suitable title and an interesting first sentence.
c Who is going to read this article? Think about people of your own age: what kind of thing interests them?
d Can you include your own opinions and any personal anecdotes?
e What style and tone would be appropriate – informal? personal? humorous?

9 Write an article based on the notes you have made. Don't forget to check your grammar, spelling and punctuation.

◀ WRITING GUIDE PAGE 166 ▶

Overview

1 Read the text below and think of the word which best fits each space. Use only one word in each space. There is an example at the beginning.

What is a shopaholic?

In recent years, shopaholics have come to the public attention 0 _*on*_ television and in newspaper and magazine articles. While 1_____ media sometimes uses the word casually, shopaholics suffer 2_____ a real, and sometimes very frightening, lack 3_____ self-control.

Without a doubt, we live in a 'spend-happy' society. Most people live beyond their means and are 4_____ debt. Many people, whatever their level of income, think of shopping 5_____ a hobby. They take weekend-long shopping excursions, spend money 6_____ do not have, and often regret their purchases the next day. 7_____ this mean that they have a problem? 8_____ necessarily.

True shopaholics 9_____ they can't help it. They go on buying things long 10_____ they are heavily in debt. They shop when they are feeling depressed, and use spending as a way of coping 11_____ the world. They do not shop because they enjoy it, or because they are buying things they need. They buy things because they feel they have to. A shopaholic is 12_____ of control.

Two pieces of advice given 13_____ shopaholics are these. Firstly, 14_____ you go shopping, only take cash. Leave your credit cards and chequebooks at home. And secondly, if you see something that you want to buy, don't 15_____ yourself buy it on the spot. Instead, give yourself a 'waiting period'. If you still want the item in a few days, then you can go back and buy it.

2 Match a first sentence from a–e with a continuation 1–5.

a I'm used to getting up early.
b He's always making excuses for being late.
c I tend to reply to emails when I get them.
d I am gradually getting used to not smoking.
e When I first got my mobile, I received a huge bill.

1 I must admit, I feel a lot healthier than I used to.
2 I do it every day, so it isn't hard for me.
3 I used to spend hours talking to my friends.
4 Otherwise, I completely forget.
5 I find it very annoying!

3 Complete these sentences with a word from the list. There are two words you do not need to use.

assertive   depressed   determined   exhausted
fed-up   rude   sleepy   stubborn

a Max is taking his driving test again. He's absolutely _____ to pass.
b I didn't mean to nod off. I'm not really tired – just a bit _____.
c The tourists were so _____ with the terrible weather that they cut their holiday short and went home.
d My dad is incredibly _____ – once he's made his mind up he refuses to change it.
e When I asked whether there were any letters for me, the receptionist was quite _____ – she told me not to bother her.
f I admire _____ people – too often these days people don't stand up for their rights.

3 Talents

Introduction

1 Work in pairs or small groups. Look at the photographs and discuss these questions.

   a What talents or qualities do you need to be able to do these jobs or activities well?

   b Which of these talents are people born with and which are learnt?

   c What talents have you got? How do you use them?

   d How important do you think talent is in success?

Reading

Think ahead

1 What do you know about Will Smith?
Why do think he has been so successful?

2 Read this article about Will Smith quickly
to check your ideas, ignoring the gaps.

Will Smith

0 *H*
Will Smith was born Willard Smith in
Philadelphia on 25 September 1968. He
grew up in a multicultural, lower middle-
class neighbourhood, where his father, a
5 former US Air Force sergeant, ran a
successful refrigeration business and his
mother worked for the local school board.

1
The second oldest of four children, Will
excelled at school – particularly at maths,
10 which remains a passion – and seems to
bear few scars from the attentions of a
disciplinarian father. 'I grew up in a
military household,' he says. 'We had to
roll our underwear up in the drawers, along
15 with our socks, and put them in neat little
lines. Learning that level of discipline and
a commitment to doing things right is
going to help you to win.'

2
In his teens, his mother managed to get
20 him an interview at the world-renowned
Massachusetts Institute of Technology, but
Will was born to perform. He began
performing at parties with his friend Jeff
Townes while the pair were still at school.
25 Signed up by Jive Records in 1986 as DJ
Jazzy Jeff and the Fresh Prince, the pair
became an instant international success,
enjoying a string of hits. By twenty, the
lanky, jug-eared rapper was a millionaire.

3
30 Then he very nearly blew it. 'What did I
know?' Smith reflected a few years later. 'I
was running around with all this money
and these girls chasing me and just having
a great time.' But the after-hours shopping
35 trips to Gucci and the trans-continental
partying caught up with him. 'I had six
cars but I wasn't able to afford the gas,' he
admitted.

4
Then, when he was still only twenty-one,
40 came the offer to star in a sit-com. The
Fresh Prince of Bel-Air, which ran on US
TV for six years from 1990, was the
remaking of him. After a shaky start, he
revealed himself as a talented comedian
45 and, crucially in a country as racially
divided as the US, one who appealed to
both black and white audiences. The Fresh
Prince of Bel-Air was a surprise hit, and it
provided the perfect platform for Smith to
50 move into the movies.

5
With credits that include Independence
Day, Men in Black I and II, Wild Wild West,
and Ali, Smith is not just the most
successful black actor in the world but
55 also one of the most successful actors,
period. Meanwhile his musical career
gathered pace. To date, he has sold over
twenty million records in a rap career
which shows no sign of slowdown.

6
60 Even if his next film is a flop, Smith is
prepared. 'Hollywood,' he once said, 'is a
tough town. I look at it like when you're
driving on the highway and it's raining, and
there's that one car broken down on the
65 side of the road. "One day that's gonna be
you. One day you're gonna be that car
broken down on the side of the road."'

7
But not today, not tomorrow and probably
not for the rest of his life. The above quote
70 is not really typical of Smith. The following
is: 'I don't know if I'm arrogant, but it's a
plus to me that people are lazy. I take
comfort in knowing that even if someone's
more talented, a better rapper or actor
75 than I am, they're not going to put in the
hours I do. I have this psychotic drive. I
can't sleep, I can't eat until what I've
started is finished to the best of my
ability.'

3 Read the article again. Choose from the list A–I the sentence which best summarises each part (1–7) of the article. There is one extra sentence that you do not need to use. There is an example at the beginning (0).

A Making his name as a singer
B Determination and hard work
C Demonstrating his talent
D Order was all important
E Ready for the worst
F Just an ordinary childhood
G Spend! Spend! Spend!
H No working-class kid
I Combining two careers

over to you

Do you think you need to be talented to become famous?

What would you most like and most dislike about being famous?

4 Match the phrasal verbs a–g with their meanings 1–7.

a Will Smith says, 'One day you're gonna be that car that has *broken down* on the side of the road'.
b When do schools *break up* for the summer in your country?
c Fighting *broke out* between the opposing groups of supporters when a penalty was given in the last minute of the game.
d The burglar *broke in* through the bathroom window.
e I was surprised to hear that Sandra and Joseph *had broken up*.
f The prisoner managed to *break out of* his cell while the guard was asleep.
g As she was describing how the accident had happened, she *broke down*.

1 close for a holiday (of an educational institution)
2 escape from a place of imprisonment
3 start suddenly
4 collapse in tears
5 stop and not start again (for vehicles, machinery, etc.)
6 separate (of couples)
7 force entry into a building

Grammar and practice

Can, be able to

1 *Can* and *be able to* are often interchangeable. Rewrite these sentences using the other form.

a I *can't* eat, I *can't* sleep until what I've started is finished.

b I had six cars, but I *wasn't able to* afford the gas.

2 Why is it impossible to use *can* in these sentences?

a *To be able to* make people laugh, you need to have a special talent.

b He *has been able to* appeal to both black and white audiences.

3 Rewrite these sentences using *can* or *could*, making any other necessary changes.

a He's *able to* run 100 metres in just over twelve seconds.

b When I was younger, I *was able to* climb a mountain without getting out of breath.

c They had eaten such a big breakfast that they *weren't able to* finish their lunch.

d He *would* probably *be able to* touch his toes if he lost weight.

e Even if I'd been stronger, I *wouldn't have been able to* lift those heavy weights.

4 *Could* or *be able to* are both possible in sentences (a) and (b). Why is *could* not possible in (c)?

a Before Dave started smoking, he *could / was able to* hold his breath for three minutes.

b The doctors *couldn't / weren't able to* save the woman's life.

c After five hours, the fire-fighters *could / were able to* put out the fire.

◀ GRAMMAR REFERENCE PAGE 178 ▶

Other ability structures

5 In sentences 4b and c, *can* and *be able to* forms can be replaced by *manage* and *succeed*.

EXAMPLE
After five hours, the fire-fighters succeeded in putting out / managed to put out *the fire.*
Why is it not possible to rephrase 4a in the same way?

◀ GRAMMAR REFERENCE PAGE 178 ▶

6 Complete these sentences with the correct form of the verb in brackets and another verb. You may sometimes need to use the negative. There is an example at the beginning.

a He *managed to win* (manage) the election despite strong opposition.

b Although they searched for several hours, the rescue party _____ (succeed) the climbers.

c He did his best but he _____ (be able to) all his work before the boss got back.

d Daniel was thrilled when he _____ (succeed) his driving test first time.

e Although there were several people in the house, the burglar _____ (manage) and steal the video without being seen.

f Melanie _____ (be able to) three lengths of the pool when she was William's age.

g Paul's interview was this afternoon. I wonder if he _____ (manage) the job.

h I was so tense that I _____ (be able to) asleep, despite being tired.

i Although he didn't have a corkscrew, he _____ (succeed) the bottle.

j _____ you _____ (manage) any weight since you started your diet?

7 Which sentences could be rewritten using *could* or *couldn't*?

8 Complete the text at the top of page 39 with the correct forms of these verbs and verb phrases. Use each word or phrase only once. Add any other necessary words, such as verbs and prepositions.

can   able to   learn how   be good   manage

Juggling

I am often asked whether it takes a long time ¹_____ juggle and whether you need to be especially dexterous. The answer is simple. Anyone who ²_____ a ball in the air with one hand and catch it with the other can be a juggler. The mistake that most people make is that they try to run before they can walk. Remember, if you want ³_____ something, it takes patience and practice. So don't be overambitious. Start off with just one ball. Keep in mind that you ⁴_____ juggle with three balls until you can manage with two or even one. Another tip is to practise in front of a table when you start. That way, if you don't ⁵_____ the balls, you won't tire yourself out picking them up off the floor. Give yourself three half-hour sessions to get the hang of it and another hour and a half to practise, and you should be ready to perform in public!

9 Think of something you can do or used to be able to do. It could be a sport or an activity like juggling. The other students will ask you questions to find out what it is. Answer only *yes* or *no*. Here are some suggested questions.

Can you still do it?
Did you learn how to do it?
Do you need special equipment to do it?
Did someone teach you how to do it?

Can anyone do it?
Do you need special skills?
Is it easy to do?

Cloze

10 Read the text below and think of the word which best fits each space. Use only one word in each space.

Muhammad Ali – The Greatest

Muhammad Ali, possibly the most famous athlete ¹_____, is certainly one of the most recognisable faces in world history. Ali, ²_____ proclaimed himself the 'Greatest of All Time', started fighting under the name of Cassius Clay. When he converted to Islam, he changed his name ³_____ Muhammad Ali.

Ali became world heavyweight boxing champion ⁴_____ the age of twenty-four and went on to become the first man ⁵_____ win the heavyweight title three times. Both arrogant and charismatic, people ⁶_____ loved him or hated him. His refusal to serve in the United States army during the Vietnam War, saying that ⁷_____ was against his religious beliefs, made ⁸_____ unpopular with the authorities. He ⁹_____ arrested, stripped of his heavyweight title and not allowed to box ¹⁰_____ three years, ¹¹_____ many feel were his peak years.

Ali was once asked on a TV show ¹²_____ he would have done with his life given a choice. He replied that he ¹³_____ not think of anything other than boxing. That is all he had ever wanted or wished ¹⁴_____. He couldn't imagine doing anything ¹⁵_____.

Vocabulary

1 What kinds of stunts do stuntmen perform in films? Which do you think they least like to do?

2 Read the text to check your ideas.

The 'car chase' is an integral part of many of today's blockbuster films. The reason why is obvious: if well done, it is spectacular and hugely entertaining. But while some actors insist on doing their own stunts, others rely upon their stunt doubles to do them. Staging a fight, falling off a horse, flipping over cars, crashing through glass and jumping from a great height are the most basic stunts a stuntman has to do. The most unpopular? Falling under a moving train.

Film vocabulary

3 Discuss these questions.

a How many other jobs do you know related to the film industry?

b How many film genres can you name? For example, *romantic comedy*.

c What are your favourite types of film?

4 Complete these sentences with the correct words from the list.

acting   animated   cast   ending   plot   script
soundtrack   special effects   stars   subtitles

a The film was in French, but it had _____ in English so we were able to understand it.

b The _____ was unconvincing. The performances were very amateurish.

c I always find the _____ of spy films complicated. I'm never sure what's going on.

d The film _____ is available on CD from all good record stores.

e The _____ used in science fiction films have improved because of new technology.

f Why do almost all Hollywood films have a happy _____?

g _____ films like Walt Disney's *Snow White* are still popular with children today.

h Epic films like *Ben Hur* required a _____ of thousands. Nowadays, because of computer graphics, they don't need so many actors.

i What the actors say is very important. It's essential to have a good _____.

j The film *Ali* _____ Will Smith in the leading role.

---

over to you

What is your favourite film of all time?

Who or what do you think is most responsible for a film's success?

Do you prefer to see foreign films in the original language or dubbed into your language?

Do you prefer to watch films at the cinema, on pay-per-view TV, on video or on DVD?

Exam techniques • LISTENING PART 1

dos and don'ts

- Read and listen carefully to the first question and the options.
- As you listen for the first time, mark the options which you think are possible.
- As you listen for the second time, check your ideas and make your final choice.
- Follow the same procedure for each question.
- Don't think about the last extract – remember to read and listen carefully to the next one.

---

1 ⬤ You will hear people talking in eight different situations. For questions 1–8, choose the best answer, A, B or C. Use the *Dos and Dont's* above to help you.

---

1 You hear a woman talking on the radio about an actor. Why does she think he is so popular?

A because he is very attractive
B because he is a very good actor
C because of the parts he plays

[1]

2 You overhear a woman talking in a café to a friend. What does she want him to do?

A get her a part in a film
B arrange a meeting with the director
C introduce her to an actor

[2]

3 You overhear a man telling his friend about a film he has seen. What is his opinion of it?

A It was too long.
B It was excellent.
C Parts of it were good.

[3]

4 You overhear a man phoning a cinema box-office on his mobile. What does he want them to do?

A change his tickets
B change his seats
C refund his money

[4]

5 On local radio you hear some people discussing plans for an old cinema. What does the speaker want to do?

A knock it down and build a new one
B make alterations and modernise it
C turn it into a conference hall

[5]

6 You overhear a telephone conversation between a man and his son. Why is the man angry?

A His son has forgotten to buy some tickets.
B His son has lost some tickets.
C His son has bought the wrong tickets.

[6]

7 You hear part of a radio documentary about the making of a film. What are the director and producer talking about?

A changing an actor
B filming a scene again
C cutting a scene

[7]

8 You hear part of a radio interview where a woman is talking about a famous actress. How does she know her?

A They went to the same secondary school.
B They went to the same university.
C They went to the same drama school.

[8]

---

over to you

Do you think acting is a natural talent or an acquired skill? Can it be inherited?
Why do children of famous people often follow their parents into the same profession? Does this just happen with famous people?

Vocabulary

Lead in

1 Who are the highest earning sportsmen and sportswomen in your country? What sports do they compete in?

2 Do professional sportsmen and sportswomen deserve the money they receive?

Noun suffixes

3 Which of these adjectives describe qualities needed to be successful in each of the sports related to the photos above? Add any others which you think are important.

accurate   aggressive   ambitious   arrogant   athletic
brave   determined   fair   fit   honest   intelligent   reliable

4 Use these suffixes to form nouns from the adjectives in 3, making any necessary spelling changes.

-ion   -ence   -ance   -ry   -ism   -ness   -ity   -y

5 Which words are these nouns formed from? Say whether these words are nouns or verbs.

EXAMPLE   separation *is formed from* separate (*verb*)

adulthood   friendship   actor   teacher
disagreement   justification   occurrence

6 Underline the suffix used in each case. Make a list of other nouns which end this way.

7 Complete these sentences with a noun made from the word in brackets. Then, discuss the statements in pairs.

a _____ (participate) in a sporting competition is just as important as winning.
b _____ (child) should be a time for playing games or playing with toys, not playing a sport competitively.
c Sport _____ (sponsor) should not come from tobacco companies.
d Football _____ (support) who get into trouble at matches should be banned for life.
e Top sports personalities have an _____ (oblige) to behave well at all times.
f Professional sportsmen and women who take drugs to enhance their _____ (perform) should be banned for life.

dos and don'ts

- Read the text quickly to get a general idea of the topic.
- Read the text again, using the words on either side of the space to help you decide what kind of word is missing, e.g. noun, verb, adjective.
- Change the word in block capitals into the word you need by adding a prefix or suffix, or by making some other change. For example, if the missing word is a noun, think of typical noun endings and choose the one that sounds best. Remember some words may be negative.
- Read the completed text to check it makes sense.
- If you are not sure, make a sensible guess. Don't leave any spaces empty.

1 Read through the text quickly and decide which of these titles best describes what the text is about.

   a   Men still at top of earnings league

   b   The price of fame

   c   Million dollar kids

2 Read the text below. Use the word given in capitals at the end of each line to form a word that fits in the space in the same line. There is an example at the beginning (0). Use the *Dos and Dont's* above to help you.

Nowadays, although prize money for women tennis 0 _players_ is still	PLAY
less than men receive, top women players' 1_____ in a fortnight	EARN
are more than those of a 2_____ company director's in a year.	SUCCESS
But most 3_____ earned by both male and female players does not	COME
come from official prize money. Instead, it comes from 4_____	SPONSOR
contracts with fashion and sportswear companies.	
These massive deals have turned some of these stars into 5_____	MILLION
at a very young and vulnerable age. It is 6_____ surprising then that	HARD
some sports stars have been 7_____ to cope with the pressure that	ABLE
goes hand in hand with being 8_____, and have consequently become	FAME
victims of their own success.	
Possibly brilliant careers have ended in cases of personal 9_____	FAIL
and 10_____ trauma for more than a few.	PSYCHOLOGY

over to you

Why do you think women tennis players earn less than male tennis players? Is this fair? Do you know any sportsmen or sportswomen who have become victims of their own success?

Listening

Lead in

1 Think about your childhood and discuss these questions in pairs.

a Did your parents encourage you to take part in any activities outside school, such as sport or music? Did you enjoy them?

b Should parents expect their children to be succesful? Can this be a bad thing?

True or false?

2 🎧 You will hear a radio interview with a child psychologist. Decide whether these statements are True or False.

Some people disagree with Dr Taylor's views. | 1 |

Dr Taylor's book tells parents how to develop a child's talent. | 2 |

Dr Taylor sympathises with today's parents. | 3 |

Dr Taylor says most parents today are competitive. | 4 |

Dr Taylor believes parents have the right motives. | 5 |

Dr Taylor thinks parents need to organise more activities for their children. | 6 |

Dr Taylor believes parents should be realistic about their children's talents. | 7 |

over to you Do you think today's society is too competitive?

Confusing verbs:
rise, arise, raise

3 Match each of these nouns with the appropriate verb, *rise*, *raise*, or *arise*.

EXAMPLES   *prices* rise   raise *a child*   *an opportunity* arises

a child   a problem   a situation   an opportunity   someone's hopes
money   prices   unemployment   the alarm   the sun

4 Complete these sentence with the correct form of *rise*, *raise*, or *arise*.

a It seems to me that _____ a child is anything but easy these days.

b Problems can _____ where parents invest an awful lot of their time and money in their children.

c Unemployment _____ by 5% last year.

d If the opportunity _____, I'd take it if I were you.

e Her parents died when she was young, and she _____ by an elderly aunt.

Speaking

Lead in

1 Discuss these questions in pairs.

   a If you could do any job, which would you choose?
   b What qualifications and skills would you need?
   c What personal qualities would you need?
   d What would be the advantages and disadvantages of having this job?

Two-way task

2 What jobs are represented in these pictures?

3 Work in pairs. Imagine that a friend has asked you for some advice about their career. Talk to each other about the abilities and personal qualities needed to do these jobs. Then, say which two jobs you would find the most difficult.

tip!

In Part 3 of the Speaking paper, give some ideas about each of the options before finally making a decision

Discussion

Is money the most important consideration for you when choosing a job?
What other considerations are important?
How could employers improve working conditions?
What are the advantages and disadvantages of working from home?

Writing

Letter of application

TOUR GUIDES

- Do you speak English?
- Are you interested in the history of your town?
- Are you good at organising?
- Are you reliable?

If the answer to these questions is 'yes', then you may be just the person we are looking for.

We require tour guides in most towns in Italy during the summer season.

One, two or three-month contracts are available.

No experience or knowledge necessary (training will be given).

Interested applicants should apply in writing to:

The Director,
Tour Guides in Italy,
58 Black Street, Blackwell

Punctuation

1 Read this Part 2 task and answer the questions.
   a Would you be interested in applying for the job? Would you be suitable?
   b How will you begin and end your letter?
   c Will you write in a formal or informal style?
   d What information will you include?

> You have seen this advertisement in a local newspaper. Write your letter of application in 120–180 words. Do not write any addresses.

2 Read this letter of application and answer the questions.
   a Is the format and style what you had predicted?
   b Have the questions in the advertisement been answered?

> Dear Sir or Madam
>
> I would like to apply for the job of tour guide as advertised in *The News* on Monday 13 January. I have just finished my second year at university, and I am looking for summer employment. I would be available to work for three months from the end of June.
>
> With regard to your requirements, I believe I meet all of them. I have been studying english for five years and can speak it well. I have been told that I am a reliable person and good at organising activities, last summer I assisted at a youth camp, where I was responsible for organising sports and games. The course leader said 'he would be happy to employ me again'.
>
> Although I have not studied the history of Palermo. I am interested in learning about it. I have a good memory for facts and would enjoy passing on information to others.
>
> I look forward to hearing from you and wish to advise you that I am available for interview at any time.
>
> Your's faithfully,
>
> Giovanna Rinaldi

3 Underline any phrases which will be useful when writing any letter of application.

4 Find and correct six errors of punctuation in the letter.

5 There is a punctuation mistake in each of these sentences. Correct it and say what kind of mistake it is. The first one has been done as an example.
   a I have just seen your advertisement in the daily news, and I am interested in applying for the job of tour guide. (*Daily News* should be in capitals)
   b I worked as a guide for your company last year. But I had to leave after a week because I broke my leg.

c My spoken English is very good, I can speak a little French and some Italian as well.

d If you require me to come for an interview I am available any day.

e The only day I will not be able to come for an interview is Wednesday when I attend college.

f I have shown groups of visitors around my school although I have never worked as a tour guide before.

g I am a twenty two year old Japanese student.

h I am studying tourism at Palermo University. So this would be valuable experience for me.

i Will you require any references.

j My previous employer is willing to be one of my referee's.

Think, plan, write

6 You are going to write a letter of application. First, read the task and think about what the job requires.

> You have seen this advertisement in an international magazine.
> Write your application in 120–180 words. Do not write any addresses.

CAMP USA

We are looking for helpers to organise sports and other activities at our American summer camps for children.

You must be 18 or over and able to work for at least 9 weeks, starting June 15.

You should also be fit, enthusiastic and responsible.

Accommodation, food, pocket money, medical insurance and return travel are all provided.

Apply to: Camp USA, Box 104, Bath

7 Plan what you are going to write, using these questions to help you. You can invent as much information about yourself as you like.

Age	How old do you think the ideal applicant would be?
Availability	When would you be available?
Sports	What sports are popular with children? What sports are you good at? Do you play any team games?
Other activities	What activities could you be asked to organise? Do you have any experience of these activities?
Qualities	How could you indicate that you are physically fit? How could you show your interest and enthusiasm? In what ways could you demonstrate that you are responsible? Have you any experience of looking after children?

8 Follow this plan. Remember to write in formal English.

Paragraph 1   Say why you are writing and where you saw the advertisement.

Paragraph 2   Give relevant details about yourself and your availability.

Paragraph 3   Say what skills and experience you can offer. Be convincing!

Paragraph 4   End your letter in an appropriate way. Refer back to the model if necessary.

9 Finally, read through your letter, checking grammar, spelling and punctuation.

◀ WRITING BANK PAGE 168 ▶

Overview

1 Read the text below. Use the word given in capitals at the end of each line to form a word that fits in the space in the same line. There is an example at the beginning.

Madonna

If any 0 _musical_ artist of our times could truly be called a phenomenon,   MUSIC

it would have to be Madonna. ¹_____ three decades after her debut, she   NEAR

remains the most ²_____ female pop artist of all time. An all-round   SUCCESS

performer in the truest sense – singer, ³_____, actor and executive – it   COMPOSE

seems there is nothing she cannot do. But it isn't simply her ⁴_____   ORDINARY

list of achievements that has earned her status as one of the most ⁵_____   INFLUENCE

artists of our time. It is her ⁶_____ commitment to excellence, her   PASSION

involvement in every ⁷_____ aspect of her art, and what can only be   ESSENCE

called a stubborn ⁸_____ to settle for anything less than the best.   REFUSE

Madonna is a chameleon. In her music and acting career she has ⁹_____   INVENT

herself many times so that the Madonna of the 80s bears little ¹⁰_____   RESEMBLE

to the artist she is today.

2 Complete these sentences with the correct forms of *can, be able to, manage* or *succeed*.

a _____ you speak Italian before you went to live in Italy?
b We _____ (not) to persuade Charlotte to come.
c After ten minutes of manoeuvring, I finally _____ in parking my car.
d I'm sorry but I _____ (not) to contact Gill yet. She isn't answering her phone.
e _____ you whistle? My brother taught me how to.
f We _____ (not) swim to the shore because of the strong currents.
g You _____ win the race if you really wanted to.
h Instead of calming the situation, he only _____ in making it worse.

3 Choose the correct word to complete the phrasal verbs in these sentences.

a Emily broke *up/down* when she heard the sad news.
b We break *in/up* in July and don't go back to school till September.
c Fights break *out/down* every time the team loses a match.
d I didn't know that Amy and Darren had *broken up/out*. I thought they were still together.
e The lift isn't working. It's broken *down/out* again!
f A burglar had broken *down/in* and stolen the video.
g During the riot, twenty prisoners managed to break *down/out of* the jail.

4 Appearances

Introduction

1 Work in pairs or small groups. What can you tell about a person from their face? Look at the faces on this page and discuss these questions.

Who would you like to be friends with?
Which people look the most interesting?
Who looks happy or unhappy?
Who looks fashionable or unfashionable?
Who would you trust or mistrust?

2 Read this short extract from an article and discuss the questions.

We've all been taken in by appearances more often than we'd like to admit. Let's face it, we've all allowed innocent-looking sales-people to separate us from our money or been conned into voting for a politician just because he or she looks sincere. But research suggests our brains are programmed to react this way.

- Can you remember an occasion when you have been tricked by someone you thought you could trust?

- Have you ever been put off someone by their appearance and changed your opinion later?

Listening

Lead in

1 Many people wear different clothes for different situations. For example, children sometimes wear a uniform for school but wear jeans and a T-shirt the rest of the time.

 a How many kinds of clothes have you got for different occasions? Which kind of clothes do you prefer wearing?
 b Have you ever had to wear a uniform? What was it like? Did you enjoy wearing it?

Multiple matching

2 🎧 You will hear five people talking about clothing or fashion. Choose which subject A–F each speaker 1–5 talks about. Use the letters only once. There is one extra letter which you do not need to use.

A my general appearance	Speaker 1	1
B the pros and cons of my lifestyle	Speaker 2	2
C where my creative ideas come from		
D clothes I have to wear	Speaker 3	3
E clothes for small children	Speaker 4	4
F buying something fashionable	Speaker 5	5

over to you

Apart from clothes, what other aspects of their appearance do people change for different situations?

What do you think your appearance says to other people?

Confusing adverbs

3 Some pairs of adverbs look similar but have different meanings.

EXAMPLE

So far I've flatly refused to pay more than £30 for trainers. (flatly means completely)
He tripped and fell flat on his face. (flat means spread out in a straight position)

Choose the correct adverb in each of these sentences.

1 a In some countries, old people travel *free / freely* on the buses.
  b There's no one listening, so we can talk quite *free / freely*.
2 a Some people work *hard / hardly* and get paid very little money.
  b Other people do *hard / hardly* any work and are paid a fortune.
3 a Where's Gloria? I haven't seen her *late / lately*.
  b Don't worry, she's coming. She always arrives *late / lately*.
4 a It is *wide / widely* known that the President is about to resign.
  b At the dentist, you have to open your mouth *wide / widely*.
5 a Be careful not to drive too *near / nearly* the edge of the cliff.
  b A colleague of mine *near / nearly* had a terrible accident last week.
6 a In most big cities, there are poor people sleeping *rough / roughly*.
  b Parents don't treat their children as *rough / roughly* as they used to.

Vocabulary

Lead in

1 Who would wear boots like the ones shown in the photograph?

2 What are your favourite shoes for everyday wear?

Multiple-choice cloze

3 For questions 1–15, read the text below and decide which answer, A, B, C or D, best fits each space. The first one is completed as an example.

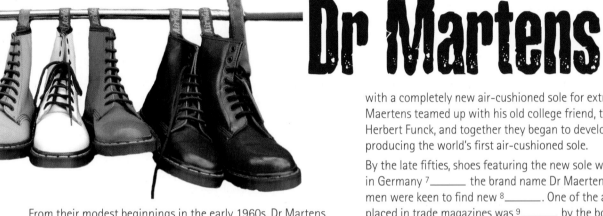

Dr Martens

From their modest beginnings in the early 1960s, Dr Martens boots have become 0__C__ all over the world. Numerous groups of young people have 1_____ the Dr Martens brand as a 2_____ of their identity, from the Skinheads of the 1960s and the grunge music fans of the 1990s to the most recent twenty-first century revival.

To discover the beginnings of the Dr Martens brand, we must travel back in time to 1945 and the little German town of Seeshaupt, 3_____ Munich. A German medical doctor, Klaus Maertens, 4_____ his foot while skiing in the Bavarian Alps. As he was recovering, he 5_____ up with the idea of making a shoe

with a completely new air-cushioned sole for extra 6_____. Dr Maertens teamed up with his old college friend, the engineer Dr Herbert Funck, and together they began to develop the idea, soon producing the world's first air-cushioned sole.

By the late fifties, shoes featuring the new sole were selling well in Germany 7_____ the brand name Dr Maertens, but the two men were keen to find new 8_____. One of the adverts they placed in trade magazines was 9_____ by the boss of the English shoe manufacturer, R. Griggs & Co. Bill Griggs's company had been making footwear 10_____ the beginning of the twentieth century but were looking for something new. Bill bought the 11_____ to use the Dr Maertens sole and started work 12_____ developing a range of shoes and boots to use it.

It was the new company which developed features such as the famous yellow stitch and the 13_____ sole pattern. On 1 April 1960, the first pair of boots rolled off the 14_____ line in the Northamptonshire village of Wollaston in England. The rest, as they 15_____, is history.

0	A	celebrated	B	distinguished	C	famous	D	renowned
1	A	bought	B	adopted	C	taken	D	imitated
2	A	signal	B	symbol	C	brand	D	symptom
3	A	close	B	by	C	near	D	beside
4	A	injured	B	spoiled	C	wounded	D	harmed
5	A	brought	B	gave	C	took	D	came
6	A	ease	B	comfort	C	relief	D	relaxation
7	A	by	B	under	C	from	D	in
8	A	shops	B	businesses	C	markets	D	commerce
9	A	noticed	B	watched	C	recognised	D	looked
10	A	for	B	since	C	by	D	until
11	A	rights	B	permission	C	permit	D	consent
12	A	to	B	in	C	on	D	while
13	A	alone	B	unique	C	singular	D	particular
14	A	company	B	factory	C	manufacturing	D	production
15	A	inform	B	speak	C	say	D	tell

Grammar and practice

Modal verbs of obligation

1 Read these sentences from the recordings and underline the verbs which express obligation, necessity, or absence of necessity.

 a You don't have to worry about what to put on in the mornings.
 b Pupils must wear ties at all times.
 c Children must not wear earrings in class.
 d You must come and see my new collection.
 e You don't need to/needn't write if you don't want to. You can phone if you prefer.
 f I have to lose a couple of kilos to stand a chance of getting that job.
 g You mustn't let the press attention go to your head.
 h I need to get right away from the business.

2 Which sentence or sentences express

 a a necessity?
 b a strong suggestion, a piece of advice or an invitation?
 c a rule, law or prohibition with authority?
 d an obligation imposed on the speaker?
 e an absence of necessity or obligation?

3 What are the past and future forms of sentences 1a–h above?

4 Read the guidelines on the right about preparing for a job interview. For questions 1–11, choose the correct modal verb, or say where both are possible.

5 Think about your own past and discuss in pairs what you *had to do* or *didn't have to do* in these situations:

 • as a secondary school student
 • if you went out for the evening under the age of sixteen
 • if you wanted to get extra pocket money from your parents
 • to keep on the right side of your parents

 ◄ GRAMMAR REFERENCE PAGE 179 ►

didn't need to/needn't have

6 What is the difference in meaning between these sentences? In which sentence did the speaker hurry?

 a I didn't need to hurry. There was plenty of time.
 b I needn't have hurried. There was plenty of time.

 ◄ GRAMMAR REFERENCE PAGE 179 ►

Appearances count!

First of all clothes. You ¹ *must/need to* look smart. You ² *needn't/mustn't* wear your most formal clothes, but it ³ *must/mustn't* look as if you've just got out of bed.

Arrive on time. You ⁴ *need to/must* allow more time than you think. There may be unexpected hold-ups.

You ⁵ *have to/should* do everything you can to prepare thoroughly. Find out about the company. You ⁶ *must/should* think of a few questions to ask your interviewer.

The job advertisements normally say that you ⁷ *must/should* provide references when applying for a job. If you haven't already sent these, take them to the interview. You ⁸ *have to/should* also have extra copies of your CV with you.

If you are offered the job, you ⁹ *must/have* to try to find out anything you ¹⁰ *need to/needn't* do before you start. For example, you may ¹¹ *need to/have* to have a medical examination.

7 Complete these sentences with *didn't need to* or *needn't have* and the correct form of the verb in brackets.

a I went to the airport to meet him. Unfortunately he was ill and had to cancel his trip, so I _____ (drive) all that way.

b I was about to go shopping, when Dad arrived home with everything we needed, so I _____ (go) after all.

c The car was really dirty, but then it rained for a couple of hours, so I _____ (wash) it.

d I carried my umbrella round all day, but it didn't rain once. I _____ (take) my umbrella.

e Last year my father won one million pounds. He _____ (work) any more, so he gave up his job.

f That was a lovely meal, but you _____ (go) to so much trouble.

be allowed to / can't

8 Read the information in the chart. Write some sentences describing what young people in Britain are allowed to do using *can*, *can't* and *be allowed to*.

EXAMPLE *When you're eighteen, you're allowed to have a tattoo.*
You can't have a tattoo until you're eighteen.

Age	12	13	14	15	16	17	18
buy pets	✓						
get a part-time job		✓					
go into a pub			✓				
drink alcohol in a pub							✓
leave school					✓		
buy cigarettes					✓		
vote in elections							✓
become a soldier					✓		
drive a car						✓	

9 Make a similar chart like this for your country. Compare charts with other students.

◀ GRAMMAR REFERENCE PAGE 179 ▶

Error correction

10 Read the text and look carefully at each line. Some of the lines are correct, and some have a word which should not be there. If a line is correct, put a tick (✓) in the space. If a line has a word that should not be there, write the word in the space. There are two examples.

She's jealous of me!

0	My mother is always saying ~~me~~ I think too	*me*
00	much about myself, though, in my opinion	✓
1	I don't be think about myself nearly as much	_____
2	as she does. She's always telling to me not to	_____
3	be so much fashion-conscious. She says I'm	_____
4	too fussy about my appearance. But most of	_____
5	people at school think I'm scruffy and untidy.	_____
6	I am think she is jealous, but actually she's	_____
7	quite a pretty herself, and I must admit she	_____
8	often buys me the nice clothes. How can I	_____
9	make her to see that all my school friends	_____
10	will wear make-up and spend a lot of time	_____
11	looking at themselves in the mirror. She	_____
12	thinks I'm unusual. My brothers make a fun	_____
13	of me as well as, and that's quite upsetting	_____
14	because I feel they should at least take the	_____
15	trouble to understand me why I am like this.	_____

1 You are going to read a magazine article about two people who shared a flat. For questions 1–7, choose the answer (A, B, C or D) which you think fits best according to the text. Use the *Dos and Don'ts* above to help you.

THE perfect FLATMATE

WHEN I was twenty-one, I came to live in London. I shared a damp basement flat with a beautiful ex-art student from Brighton. Her name was Sam. She had long brown hair and a slim figure that I was madly jealous of. She ate three chocolate
5 bars for breakfast every morning.

I used to lie in bed looking at her eating and getting dressed, wondering how she could possibly consume so much sugar without losing her teeth, her figure or her complexion. She'd put on her make-up in under a minute, throw on whatever
10 clothes happened to be lying around the room, and rush off to work looking like a model on the cover of a fashion magazine. Like me, she was just an art teacher in a secondary school.

ON the other hand, I used to put on weight if I even smiled at a bar of chocolate. I'd already lost several upper teeth, my face was
15 spotty, and I looked like a heavyweight boxer whatever I wore.

MY morning reaction to Sam was always the same. I'd shut my eyes, pull the blankets up over my head and force myself back to sleep. I knew that I really ought to get up too and make use of the early start to have a shower, iron my blouse, polish my shoes,
20 paint my nails and eat something for breakfast.

BUT I have never been what you'd call a morning person. The teaching job I was doing at the time was the only period of my life, thank goodness, that I've had to be anywhere by 8.30 a.m. Anyway, I needed a few extra comforting dreams after the
25 shock of seeing Sam looking so beautiful. Going back to sleep to shut everything out, and using my bed as a favourite means of retreat became an addiction – my worst habit.

OF course, I overslept and was late for work every single day of the week. Eventually I was told if things didn't improve I
30 might be given the sack. So I gave up my job, and soon after I got married. I blame it all on Sam and her beauty.

1 The writer of the passage wished

A she had Sam's job.

B she was called Sam.

C she looked like Sam.

D she was an art student.

2 In the mornings Sam used to

A take a long time to put on her make-up.

B get ready for work very quickly.

C choose her clothes carefully.

D lie around before going to work.

3 The writer went back to sleep in the mornings because

A she couldn't face the day ahead.

B she was always tired.

C she always went to bed late.

D she had no reason to get up.

4 The writer got to work late because

A she always had a big breakfast.

B she spent a long time getting ready.

C she wasn't keen on her job.

D she didn't get up in time.

5 Eventually the writer left her job because

A she wasn't very good at teaching.

B her employer dismissed her.

C she got married.

D she knew she couldn't get to work on time.

6 The writer felt that Sam was

A too tidy for her.

B a very fortunate person.

C a good person to share a flat with.

D unsympathetic towards her.

7 What do we find out about the writer of the passage?

A She didn't get on with her flatmate.

B She lacked self-confidence.

C She paid great attention to her appearance.

D She was a well-organised person.

 over to you If you wanted to share a flat with another person, what sort of person would you choose?

Would you be an easy or a difficult person to get on with? Why?

Phrasal verbs with *put*

2 Complete these sentences with the correct form of a phrasal verb from the list.

put across   put forward   put (someone) off
put (something) off   put on   put (someone) out

a Only two people could come to the meeting, so they've _____ it _____ until next week.

b He's very intelligent, but unfortunately he isn't very good at _____ his ideas _____ to other people.

c Thanks for offering to take me to the station. I hope I'm not _____ you _____.

d The government are _____ plans to improve public transport in London.

e They're supposed to be coming for the weekend. I hope the bad weather doesn't _____ them _____.

f The food at the party was fantastic – I must have _____ at least two kilos.

3 Match the phrasal verbs with *put* with the meanings in a–f.

a discourage someone from doing something

b inconvenience or make things difficult for someone

c communicate information and opinions

d delay until later

e suggest an idea or proposal

f gain (weight)

Vocabulary

Parts of the body

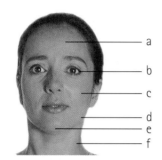

1 Label the parts of the body shown in these photos.

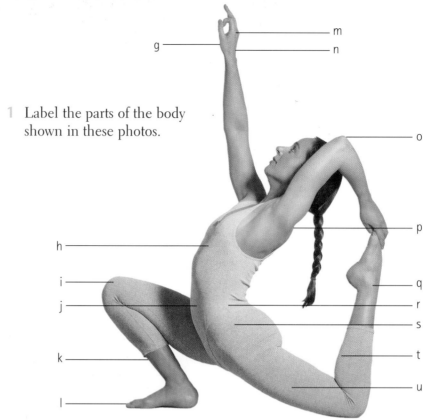

2 Complete these sentences with the correct parts of the body.

a When I asked her the time, she just shrugged her _____s and said she didn't know.

b As I went upstairs last night, I stubbed my _____ on one of the stairs.

c Some fortune-tellers read people's _____s.

d I always wear my watch on my left _____.

e Babies crawl around on their hands and _____s.

f He sat with his _____s on the table and his head in his hands.

Seeing verbs

3 Complete these sentences with the correct form of a verb from the list. More than one answer may be possible.

gaze   look   notice   see   stare   watch

a She _____ exactly like my sister. I couldn't take my eyes off her. She must have wondered why I was _____ at her.

b Many teenagers spend more time playing computer games than _____ television.

c _____! There's a fantastic rainbow in the sky.

d He's my greatest hero, but, when I tried to get his autograph, he didn't even _____ me.

e The couple _____ lovingly at their new-born baby. They couldn't believe he was theirs.

f I could just about _____ the station through the fog.

4 The eyes in some paintings appear to follow the viewer around the room. How do you think artists achieve this illusion?

When you have discussed this, turn to page 161 for an explanation.

Speaking

Lead in

1 The buildings in these photographs are all thought to be among the ugliest in Britain. What do you think of these buildings?

2 Tell a partner about a building you particularly like or dislike.

Long turn

3 🎧 You will hear Part 2 of an FCE Speaking test in which you are asked to compare and contrast two photos. Make a note of what else the examiner asks the candidate to do by completing the paragraph.

> tip!
>
> In Part 2 of the Speaking paper, listen carefully to what the examiner asks. Try to answer both parts of the question in the time you have.

> Here are your two photographs. They show places where people might live and work. I'd like you to compare and contrast these photographs and say how you think the appearance of a city _____ .

4 How would you answer this question?

5 🎧 Listen to a candidate answering the question.
   a Did she compare and contrast the photographs?
   b Did she talk about all she was asked to talk about?
   c Did she have similar ideas to you?

6 Work in pairs (Student A and Student B). Turn to page 161 and follow the instructions next to the photos on that page.

Turn to page 161

over to you

What do you like and dislike about the town or city you live in?

Desmond Morris, the British biologist, said 'The city is not a concrete jungle, it is a human zoo'. What do you think he means? Do you think you live in a concrete jungle or a human zoo?

Writing

Report

1 Read this example of a Part 2 task and answer the questions below.
   a Who is going to read the report?
   b How formal or informal should the style be?
   c What information is it essential to include in the report?

> Your town would like to attract more foreign visitors, especially young people. The local council has asked students to write reports suggesting how the town might update its image to attract more young visitors. Write your report in 120–180 words.

2 Read this report and answer the questions.
   a Is it written in an appropriate style?
   b Does it contain everything that is asked for in the task?
   c What features of the layout make this report clear to follow?
   d What is wrong with the clause in blue?

Introduction
The aim of this report is to recommend ways in which *the town could update its image* to attract more young people from other countries.

Recommendations
I have discussed the question at school and most people think that the following ideas should be considered by the local council if it really wants to attract young people from abroad.
1 Organise a summer music festival. Local and national pop and rock groups could be invited to play.
2 Invest in the Water Sports Centre. This is already popular with local young people but is not known to foreign visitors.
3 Build a new International Centre where accommodation could be provided at reasonable prices for young people.
4 Encourage local cafés and clubs to make themselves more attractive to young people. They could play modern music or serve fast food.

Conclusion
All these recommendations would be popular with young visitors from abroad. However, the most important thing is publicity. The town needs to be advertised more actively. We suggest a new website showing what the town has to offer.

Impersonal language

3 The passive may be used in reports to express ideas in an impersonal way.
   a Underline all the uses of the passive in the answer above.
   b The words in italic in the introduction to the answer are too informal. Rewrite these words using the passive.

4 Rewrite these sentences using the passive to make them more appropriate for a report. The beginnings of the new sentences have been given.

   a We should replace the old-fashioned hotels with youth hostels.
      The old-fashioned hotels _____.

   b The town should provide better sports facilities for foreign visitors.
      Better sports facilities _____.

   c We could put adverts in the local papers asking for host families where foreign students could stay.
      Adverts _____.

   d Lots of foreign students come to our language schools. We could open more of these.
      More language schools _____.

   e The town should get someone to design an up-to-date website.
      An up-to-date website should _____.

Think, plan, write

5 You are going to write a report. First, read the task and decide

   a who is going to read the report?
   b what information is it essential to include in the report?

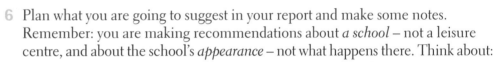

The director of the language school you attend is considering making improvements to the general appearance of the school. He/She has asked you to write a report making your recommendations on how this might be achieved. Write your report in 120–180 words.

6 Plan what you are going to suggest in your report and make some notes. Remember: you are making recommendations about *a school* – not a leisure centre, and about the school's *appearance* – not what happens there. Think about:

   a the approach to the school, the entrance and the reception area.
      Are these areas warm and welcoming?
      Is there always a receptionist to welcome visitors?

   b the classrooms.
      Are they light, spacious and well-decorated?
      Are they comfortable to work in?
      Are they well equipped with learning aids, like a video machine, computers, etc.?

   c other areas.
      Is the café or dining room a pleasant place to spend time? Are the menus interesting?
      Are the notice boards kept up to date? Is it easy for students to find the information they need?

7 When you write, don't forget to include all the information required in the task. Make sure the layout and style are appropriate.

8 Finally, when you have finished, check your grammar, spelling and punctuation.

◀ WRITING GUIDE PAGE 169 ▶

Overview

Error correction

1 Read the text below and look carefully at each line. Some of the lines are correct, and some have a word which should not be there. If a line is correct, put a tick (✔) in the space. If a line has a word that should not be there, write the word in the space. There are two examples.

The Body Shop

0	On her travels south of the equator, Anita Roddick,	✔
00	who was born in 1942 noticed that many of women	*of*
1	cared for their skin and hair are using traditional, natural	_____
2	methods. On her return to England, she opened a	_____
3	small shop called *The Body Shop*, by selling cosmetics	_____
4	based on a natural ingredients. To keep costs down	_____
5	and reduce unnecessary waste, Anita was packaged her	_____
6	cosmetic products in cheap enough plastic containers, and	_____
7	encouraged her customers to bring them back to be	_____
8	refilled. Today there are being over 1,400 branches of	_____
9	*The Body Shop* in the forty-six countries throughout the	_____
10	world. The company is committed to a social and	_____
11	environmental changes, and does all business with	_____
12	needy communities in developing and industrialised	_____
13	countries. In all of its products, it makes uses ingredients	_____
14	which they have not been tested on animals. Through	_____
15	*The Body Shop*, Anita Roddick she became one of Britain's	_____
	most successful businesswomen.	

2 Complete these sentences using the verb in brackets and the negative form of a modal verb from the list.

have to   must   need

a Children in Britain go to school from Monday to Friday, but they _____ (go) on Saturdays.
b These tablets are very strong. You _____ (take) more than eight a day.
c I wish I'd known the train was going to be late. I _____ (hurry).
d You _____ (tire) yourself out. You've got a busy day tomorrow.
e I had just turned on the computer when she phoned, which meant that I _____ (send) her an email.

3 Choose the correct phrasal verb with *put* to complete these sentences.

a I'd love to go and see the match, but the thought of the huge crowds *puts me off / puts me out*.
b She got sunburned at the beach because she forgot to *put in / put on* any sun-block.
c The opposition party is *putting across / putting forward* a proposal to cut taxes by 10%.
d I'd like the chance to *put across / put in* my point of view at our next meeting.
e Unfortunately, we're having to *put off / put out* our holiday until next year.

5 Foreign parts

Introduction

1 Work in pairs or small groups. Look at the photographs and discuss these questions.

a What similarities and differences are there between the eating styles? the forms of transport?

b How has your country been influenced by other cultures? Think about:
language   customs   dress   food   transport   music

c Are these changes positive or negative in your opinion?

d What are the benefits of travelling to other countries and experiencing different cultures?

Reading

Think ahead

1 You are going to read the true story of how Nigel Hughes flew to Brazil by accident. How do you think this could have happened?

2 Read the article quickly, ignoring the spaces, to check whether your prediction was correct.

Settling into my seat on the plane, I felt tired and ready for a drink. I was really looking forward to getting home. As I sipped a glass of lemonade and pushed my seat back, I remember thinking, 'Only a couple of hours and I'll be home.'

5 I'd phoned my girlfriend, Georgina, from Copenhagen before the plane took off to tell her I was on my way. 0 _*I*_ . I'd make my own way home.

After another drink, I snoozed until I heard a flight attendant announce, 'We will shortly be landing at Heathrow. 1_____. And 10 that was it. I honestly don't remember another thing until I woke up again later on.

For a couple of minutes I sat wondering sleepily if we were still on our way down to Heathrow. Then I began to realise something funny was going on. The two seats next to me had been empty 15 when I fell asleep. 2_____. There'd been a little girl in front, who'd kept grinning at me over the back of her seat. She had gone. And weirdest of all, the lights were off and everyone seemed to be asleep.

Slowly it began to dawn on me what had happened. The plane 20 must have landed at Heathrow, let off some passengers, taken on others and set off on the next part of its journey. And I knew where that was to – Rio de Janeiro, in Brazil.

3_____. Georgina would be wondering what had happened to me, and I was stuck on the plane with no ticket. Would they believe it 25 was an accident?

Not knowing what else to do, I went to look for a flight attendant and told her what had happened. I found out it was about 3 a.m. and we were several hours into the eleven-hour flight to Brazil. The flight attendant thought it was very funny and told me not to worry. There wasn't much anyone could do, anyway.

30 We landed in Rio at lunchtime on the Saturday. 4_____. In fact, they took me straight to the departure lounge and told me that I had to sit and wait for the next flight to London, which was at ten o'clock.

The first thing I did was ring Georgina to tell her what had happened. 5_____. So, I slipped out of the airport and jumped into a 35 passing taxi. It was surprisingly easy!

As the driver took me round Rio and down to Copacabana beach, I thought about where I should be – at work. The thought of work reminded me of the valuable contract I knew I had now lost, which depressed me momentarily. But then realising that I couldn't do a 40 thing about it, I decided I might as well make the most of it.

In the late afternoon, I headed back to the airport. I had to confess that I'd sneaked out. The airline staff were not at all pleased and gave me an escort to watch my every move. 6_____. I wasn't going to miss that plane home.

45 Fortunately, there were no problems or delays and we landed at Heathrow at lunchtime on the Sunday. I'd set off from Denmark forty-eight hours earlier, travelled 11,000 miles across the world and back, and landed back home again, tired, but otherwise none the worse for the experience.

50 Georgina recovered from the shock and was able to see the funny side of it, eventually. 7_____.

I FLEW TO BRAZIL BY ACCIDENT

Gapped text

3 Read the story again. Choose from sentences A–I the one which fits each gap 1–7. There is one extra sentence which you do not need to use. There is an example at the beginning.

A I was slightly worried that I might be hauled off the plane and locked up as an illegal immigrant.

B As for me, I still haven't worked out how I slept through a whole landing and take-off.

C I couldn't believe my luck!

D However, I wasn't planning on going anywhere else.

E What on earth was I going to do?

F 'Better get my things together,' I thought.

G Having done that, I decided it would be a shame to be in Rio and not see any of it.

H Now a man was lying across them sleeping.

I She'd said she'd pick me up at Heathrow Airport, but I told her not to bother.

4 Discuss these questions in pairs.

a When did Nigel Hughes discover he was on the wrong plane?

b What had probably happened to the little girl?

c Why were the Rio airport staff angry with Nigel?

over to you

Has anything ever gone wrong when you've been travelling?

What do you most like and most dislike about travelling by air?

Phrasal verbs: travel

5 Match the phrasal verbs in a–g with their meanings 1–7.

a We'll come to the airport to *see* you *off*.

b If they *set off* at seven o'clock, they should be here by eight.

c I can give you a lift to the station. I'll *pick* you *up* at six.

d You don't need to drive me home. You can *drop* me *off* here.

e The plane *took off* on time despite the bad weather.

f We had to *check in* two hours before the plane left.

g On our way to Australia we *stopped over* in Singapore for two days.

1 go somewhere to collect someone in a car

2 register as a passenger at an airport

3 go to a railway station, airport, etc., to say goodbye to someone

4 break a journey to stay somewhere, especially when travelling by air

5 begin a journey

6 stop for someone to get out of a car

7 leave the ground and begin to fly

6 Discuss these questions.

a If your flight was at 6 p.m., what time would you *set off* for the airport?

b After you have *checked in* for a flight, what do you usually do?

c Do you like people to come to the station or airport to *see* you *off*?

d Do you feel nervous when the plane *takes off* and lands?

e Would you *pick* a friend *up* at the airport if they arrived in the early morning?

f Would you prefer to *stop over* somewhere on a long distance flight or fly direct to your destination?

Grammar and practice

Past time

1 These sentences contain examples of the past simple, past continuous, present perfect and past perfect. Name the tenses in each sentence.

  a I'd *phoned* my girlfriend, Georgina, from Copenhagen before the plane took off.

  b We *landed* in Rio at lunchtime on the Saturday.

  c I still *haven't worked out* how I slept through a whole landing and take-off.

  d Now a man *was lying* across the seats sleeping.

2 Which of the verb tenses in 1 is used to describe past events or situations that

  a happened before another past event or situation?

  b happened at an unspecified time in the past and is relevant to the present?

  c happened at a specific time in the past?

  d continued over a period of time?

3 Name the verb tenses in the following pairs of sentences. What is the difference in meaning between the sentences in each pair?

  1 a When we arrived at the theatre, the play *started*.

     b When we arrived at the theatre, the play *had started*.

  2 a I've *bought* some presents to take home.

     b I've *been buying* some presents to take home.

  3 a I *was crossing* the road when I saw Adam.

     b I *crossed* the road when I saw Adam.

  4 a She *filled out* the passport application last night.

     b She *was filling out* the passport application last night.

  5 a He *worked* as a travel agent for two years.

     b He's *worked* as a travel agent for two years.

◀ GRAMMAR REFERENCE PAGE 180 ▶

4 Complete this text with the correct forms of the verbs in brackets, making any other necessary changes.

Have you heard the story about the man whose wife ¹_____ (just have) a baby? He ²_____ (work) in London at the time but he ³_____ (live) in Newcastle, which is in the north-east of England, not far from the Scottish border. As soon as he ⁴_____ (hear) the news, he rushed to King's Cross Station, bought his ticket and jumped on the first train north. He was so excited at the news that he told the woman who ⁵_____ (sit) next to him. She asked him if he lived in Edinburgh as that was where the train ⁶_____ (go) and was surprised when he said that he lived in Newcastle. The man realised he ⁷_____ (make) a terrible mistake when she said, 'But this train doesn't stop in Newcastle. It goes straight to Edinburgh'. Despite the man's pleas and offers of money, the driver of the train ⁸_____ (refuse) to stop, but he did agree to slow the train down to 15 m.p.h. as it went through Newcastle Station so that the man could jump off with the ticket collector's help. Two and a half hours later and the train was approaching Newcastle Station. The ticket collector ⁹_____ (hold) the man out of a window at the front of the train, and the man began running in mid-air. When the platform appeared, the ticket collector gently ¹⁰_____ (drop) the man onto it. Just then, the guard at the back of the train ¹¹_____ (look) out and saw a man running very fast along the platform. Putting his hand out, he pulled the man onto the train. 'Lucky I saw you,' he said. 'You almost ¹²_____ (miss) the train.'

Participle clauses

5 Underline the participle clauses in these sentences.

  a Settling into my seat, I felt tired and ready for a drink.
  b Not knowing what else to do, I went to look for a flight attendant.
  c Having rung Georgina, I decided it would be a shame to be in Rio and not see any of it.

6 Which participle clauses in 5 tell you
  1 why something happened?   2 when something happened?

7 Rewrite the clauses in 5, starting with the words *since*, *as*, *when*, or *after*.

◀ GRAMMAR REFERENCE PAGE 181 ▶

8 Rewrite the time and reason clauses in these sentences as participle clauses, making any other necessary changes.

  a Michael opened the living room door and went inside. But, because he didn't recognise the man immediately, he said nothing.
  b Just as he was opening his mouth to ask him what he wanted, Michael realised who the man was.
  c Because he hadn't seen his brother since he'd emigrated to Canada over twenty years ago, Michael hadn't recognised him earlier.
  d As his brother had grown a beard, he looked quite different.
  e Because Michael was so pleased to see his brother Patrick, he threw his arms around him and hugged him tightly.

Key word transformations

9 Complete the second sentence so that it has a similar meaning to the first sentence, using the word given. Do not change the word given. You must use between two and five words, including the word given.

  1 My cousin lost his job two years ago. **unemployed**
    My cousin _____ two years.
  2 Having peeled the onions, he added them to the soup. **when**
    He added the onions to the soup _____ them.
  3 I last saw Sandra a week ago. **since**
    I have _____ week.
  4 After locking the door of the shop, she left. **until**
    She didn't _____ the door of the shop.
  5 I haven't enjoyed myself so much for a long time. **ages**
    It _____ enjoyed myself so much.
  6 The two seats next to me had been empty when I fell asleep. **sitting**
    There had _____ in the two seats next to me when I fell asleep.
  7 It wasn't difficult to leave the airport, which surprised me. **surprisingly**
    It _____ leave the airport.
  8 I was really looking forward to getting home. **wait**
    I _____ home.
  9 Georgina recovered from the shock eventually. **took**
    It _____ to recover from the shock.
  10 I was tired but otherwise none the worse for the experience. **feeling**
    Apart _____, I was none the worse for the experience.

- Read the text quickly for a general idea of the topic.
- Read the text again. Use the words on either side of the space to help you decide what kind of word is missing, e.g. preposition, pronoun, conjunction. Write in any words you are confident about.
- Read the text again, filling in the remaining gaps.
- If you are not sure, make a sensible guess. Don't leave any spaces empty.

1   Read the text below and think of the word which best fits each space. Use **only one** word in each space. There is an example at the beginning. Use the *Dos and Don'ts* above to help you.

An African village

After several hours we arrived at a village called Kakuma. Tim and I decided to explore the village 0 _while_ John organised lunch. The huts were dome-shaped, about four metres across, and were 1_____ from small branches and long grasses. Groups 2_____ ten or twelve huts were enclosed in a compound. In each hut lived a family of mother, father and two or three children. A woman wanted to show 3_____ her hut. We 4_____ to bend down to enter. Inside, 5_____ was quite dark and surprisingly cool. The part nearest the ground was open 6_____ allow the cooling wind to blow through onto a baby which lay on the dirt floor, wrapped 7_____ a green and orange blanket. The hut did not contain 8_____ furniture, and cooking was done outside over a wood fire. These huts, of prehistoric design, were not unlike my own dome tent: they were 9_____ similar shape, small and simple to erect. But, 10_____ the huts did not contain carpets, sofas, beds, pictures or televisions, they were certainly homes. They were places to love, to rest 11_____ work, raise children, welcome friends and neighbours, and to spend hours talking and laughing. These were 12_____ homes should be like, where the desire 13_____ comfort was not the master. At this stage, these people 14_____ no expectations of owning satellite TV, fridges or carpets, and 15_____ certainly better off for it.

What kind of building is your home? What are your home's best and worst features? Where is it situated? What can you see from the windows?

What mod cons and appliances do you have in your home which you couldn't do without?

Vocabulary

etiquette in other countries

When sitting it is *not wise* unwise to cross one leg over the other with the sole of the foot pointing to one side as it may be pointing to another guest, which is regarded as *not polite*. Make sure your feet are always pointing downwards and the soles of your shoes are never visible. (Gulf States)

It is *not respectful* to hand an object to someone or receive an object from them using one hand. Use both hands. (Japan, Korea)

It is *not advisable* to praise an object in the home of your hosts because they will feel obliged to give it to you. (Pakistan)

A person who gets angry in public is considered ill-mannered and *not educated*. (Vietnam)

The body should be fully covered. Even an unbuttoned shirt is regarded as *not decent*. (The Gulf States)

It is *not considerate* to smoke in someone's house without asking if you can smoke first, even if there are ashtrays visible. (Finland)

Lead in

1 Read the advice about etiquette in different countries. Make the phrases in italic into negative adjectives.

2 Someone is coming to your country for the first time. What advice would you give them on matters of national etiquette?

Negative adjectives

3 Underline the negative prefixes in these adjectives. Then, complete the paragraph.

immature   dishonest   impossible   inadequate   illogical   unavailable   irrational

The most common negative prefix which can be added to adjectives to make them negative is *un-*. Other common prefixes are *in-* and *dis-*. However, *il-* is added to some adjectives which begin with the letter ¹_____, *im-* is added to some adjectives beginning with ²_____ and ³_____, and *ir-* is added to some adjectives that start with ⁴_____.

4 What are the negative forms of these adjectives?

appropriate   comfortable   correct   expensive   important   legal
obedient   patient   moral   responsible   successful   suitable

5 Complete these sentences with an appropriate negative form of an adjective from 4.
a She is quite _____ for the job. She hasn't got enough experience.
b He is a very _____ child. He never does what he is told.
c I'm being as quick as I can. Don't be so _____.
d In Britain it's _____ for a shopkeeper to sell cigarettes to anyone under sixteen.
e Parents who leave young children alone in the house are very _____.
f You don't have to spend a lot of money to have a good holiday. There are many excellent and _____ deals around.
g Thank you for attending the interview. I am afraid your application has been _____.
h It is _____ to end a formal letter with the phrase 'Lots of love'.

dos and don'ts

- Read and listen to the task carefully. You may be asked to choose true/false, yes/no, multiple choice, or identify which speaker said what.
- As you listen for the first time, mark or make a note of the options which you think are possible.
- As you listen for the second time, make your final choice.
- If you are not sure, make a sensible guess. Don't leave any questions unanswered.

1 🎧 You are going to hear a man describing a restaurant he used to go to in Thailand. For each question, choose the best answer A, B or C. Use the *Dos and Don'ts* above to help you.

1 The restaurant was popular because
  A famous people ate there.
  B it was the only restaurant in town.
  C the food was very good.

2 What does the speaker think about the name of the restaurant?
  A It was a good name.
  B It was an unimaginative name.
  C It wasn't a suitable name.

3 What was the speaker's main criticism of the restaurant?
  A It wasn't clean.
  B There was no carpet on the floor.
  C The building was in poor condition.

4 Where was the kitchen?
  A in the building round the corner
  B in an area of the restaurant
  C outside in the back yard

5 How many of the cooks were men?
  A some of them
  B all of them
  C none of them

6 The food was cooked
  A as it was required.
  B on a barbecue.
  C in advance.

7 Where did the owner and his family live?
  A in a room above the restaurant
  B in the restaurant itself
  C in a house behind the restaurant

over to you

Which do you prefer, eating out or eating at home? Why?

What is your favourite takeaway meal?

Describe a restaurant or café you know well.

Vocabulary

Lead in

1 Read this short text and answer these questions.
   a What is it not acceptable to do in the country the writer is from?
   b How is eating similar or different in your country?

In China, the sorts of *plates/dishes* served at the three main meals are pretty much the same – soup, rice or noodles, and meat and vegetables. Each person has their own bowl of rice and a *couple/pair* of chopsticks, but helps themselves to the soup, meat and vegetables directly from the communal plates in the centre of the table. It is perfectly acceptable to reach across the table to take food. To eat the rice, the diner *raises/rises* the bowl to their lips and pushes the grains into their mouth with the chopsticks. The diner must finish all the rice. To leave even a tiny amount is considered bad manners.

Confusing words

2 Choose the correct words from the alternatives given in the text above. What do the other words mean?

3 Here are some more confusing words. Choose the correct word in each pair.
   a That pudding was nice. Can I have the *receipt /recipe*?
   b In some religions, people *fast/diet* for periods of time.
   c Crisps and hamburgers are sometimes referred to as *junk/rubbish* food.
   d Most people prefer bottled water to *tap/ running* water. Some people prefer fizzy water to *flat/still* water.
   e There are two main tastes: 'sweet' like cakes and biscuits, and '*savoury/salty*', like crisps and cheese.
   f Don't you think James is an excellent *cooker/ cook*?
   g Waiter! Could we have another look at the *menu/list* please? And could you bring us the wine *menu/list* too?

Extreme adjectives

4 Which word in the text means *very small*?

5 Here are some more extreme adjectives. What normal adjectives do they correspond to?

hilarious   boiling   delicious   amazed
filthy   huge   terrified   delighted
freezing   exhausted   spotless   furious

◀ GRAMMAR REFERENCE PAGE 181 ▶

6 Complete these sentences with an ordinary or an extreme adjective.
   a I can't drink this coffee. I'll burn my mouth. It's absolutely _____.
   b The swimming pool was very _____. In actual fact, it was more like a large bath than a pool.
   c Her kitchen is so clean you could eat off the floor. It's absolutely _____.
   d Daniel was very _____ when the waiter spilt wine on his new shirt, but we all thought it was absolutely _____ and couldn't stop laughing.
   e Thank you for your invitation. We would be absolutely _____ to come for dinner next Friday.
   f This chocolate cake is absolutely _____. I think I'll have another piece if I may.

over to you

Plan a meal or snack for one or more of the following people:

Friends who are coming to your house to watch a video.

A foreign visitor who would like to try something typical.

Members of your family who want to have a picnic on the beach.

Listening

Think ahead

1 Read statements A–F in 3 below, which give some of the reasons why people go to other countries. Can you add any more?

Multiple matching

2 🎧 You will hear five people talking about reasons why they went to another country.

  a Which country is each person referring to?

  b Was the experience on the whole positive or negative?

3 🎧 Listen again, and match statements A–F with speakers 1–5.

A They got married to someone from that country.

B They went for medical treatment.

C They went on business.

D They wanted to learn the language.

E They wanted a change.

F They were visiting someone.

Speaker 1	1
Speaker 2	2
Speaker 3	3
Speaker 4	4
Speaker 5	5

over to you

Would you ever consider living abroad permanently?

Which country would you choose?

Phrasal verbs with *look*

4 Match the phrasal verbs in a–g with their meanings 1–7.

  a I've got three children to *look after*.

  b I can't remember her number. I'll have to *look it up* in the phone book.

  c George had always *looked up to* his father, until he was convicted of fraud.

  d Could you *look over* what I've written to see if it's OK?

  e The more expensive hotel rooms *look onto* the swimming pool.

  f I'm *looking forward to* going to Paris next week.

  g When we arrived in Malaga, we checked into our hotel and then *looked round* the old part of town.

  1 have a view of

  2 anticipate with enthusiasm

  3 visit a place, e.g. as a tourist

  4 respect

  5 search for information, e.g. in a book

  6 examine or check carefully

  7 care for someone

Speaking

1 Imagine you could take six months off work or college to do something else. How would you spend the time?

tip!

In Part 3 of the Speaking paper, try to reach an agreement with the other candidate. Suggest which options you would choose and say why.

2 Work with a partner. Here are some of the ways of getting to know a country and its culture. Talk to each other about what you can learn from each experience. Then say which two experiences you would most enjoy.

sightseeing

archaeology

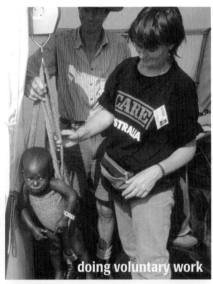
doing voluntary work

having a holiday

learning a language

backpacking

3 Discuss these questions in pairs.

a What do you think is the best way to travel round a country you are visiting?

b Do you think it is better to travel alone or with other people?

c What are the advantages of staying with a host family in the country you are visiting?

d Have you ever done any voluntary work? What kind of voluntary work would you most or least like to do?

e What are the benefits of studying English in an English-speaking country rather than in your own country?

Writing

Informal letter

1 Read this Part 2 task and answer questions a–c.

a Who is going to read the letter?
b What is the purpose of the letter?
c Should the tone of the letter be neutral or friendly?

> Your penfriend in the USA has asked you to describe a traditional festival in your country. Write a letter to your penfriend, describing a festival you celebrate or know about. Write 120–180 words.

2 Read this letter, ignoring the numbers, and answer the questions.

a Does the letter achieve its purpose?
b Is the letter written in an appropriate style?
c Does the letter begin and end appropriately?

Hello Tom!

Thanks for your letter ¹_____. You asked me to tell you something about the festival we celebrate in the spring in my town. I'll be happy to.

I'm not actually sure <u>why</u> we celebrate it, but I can tell you <u>how</u> we celebrate it. In the daytime, there's a procession around the town. Some people wear masks to frighten away the winter ²_____.

The bonfire is lit in the evening, after it gets dark. You can't stand anywhere near ³_____. While the fire is burning, the people in masks dance round and round the flames. ⁴_____

We'll be celebrating this festival again in a few months' time. It would be so nice if you could come. I'm sure you'd love it.

Drop me a line soon anyway. ⁵_____.

All the best,

Agnés Horváth

Creating interest

3 The letter can be improved by making it more personal and adding descriptive detail. Fill the spaces in the letter with these sentences.

a It's quite magical.
b And don't forget to let me know how you're getting on with your exams.
c They're quite scary.
d It was good to hear all your news.
e It's unbearably hot.

4 Which of sentences a–e are intended to show interest in the other person? Which sentences make the letter more descriptive?

5 Read this description of a parade. Make it more descriptive by writing phrases from this list in the spaces.

shiny   enormous   cheering   scarlet and black   crowds of   briskly

The parade passes ¹_____ through the ²_____ people who stand ³_____ on both sides of the road watching it. At the head of the parade is the band, composed of men and boys wearing ⁴_____ uniforms, blowing ⁵_____ trumpets and banging ⁶_____ drums.

Think, plan, write

6 You are going to write an informal letter. First, read the task and answer these questions.

a How are you going to begin your letter?
b What information should you include?

Your British penfriend wants to know how you celebrate an important festival in your country. Write a letter in 120–180 words describing a festival you know.

7 Choose a festival which will interest your friend and note down some details about the celebrations.

8 Write your letter. Here is a possible paragraph plan.

Paragraph 1   Greet your friend and refer to their request.
Paragraphs 2 and 3   Give details about the festival and say how you celebrate it.
Paragraph 4   End the letter in an appropriate way.

9 When you write, remember these features of informal letters.

Your letter should be interesting, so include more description than facts.
You should sound friendly, so ask your penfriend some personal questions too.

10 Finally, read through your letter, checking grammar, spelling and punctuation. Check that you have included features of an informal letter, such as contracted forms and informal vocabulary.

◀ WRITING GUIDE PAGE 164 ▶

Overview

1 Read the text below and think of the word which best fits each space. Use only one word in each space. There is an example at the beginning.

Chopsticks

It is not known when chopsticks first began to be used. 0 _However_ , it is fairly certain that they 1_____ invented in China, 2_____ they have been traced back at least as far 3_____ the third century BC. There are those 4_____ say that the philosopher Confucius, who lived over two hundred years earlier, influenced 5_____ development of chopsticks, with his non-violent teachings. So, knives, which have associations 6_____ war and death were not brought 7_____ the dinner table 8_____ they were in the West. Today, chopsticks are used in other countries such as Japan, Korea and Vietnam as 9_____ as China, making them the world's second most popular method 10_____ conveying food to the mouth. The most popular method is the fingers.

2 Complete the text using the correct forms of the verbs in brackets.

a I couldn't believe it! My alarm clock 1_____ (not ring) and my plane was due to leave in two hours. Hastily, I 2_____ (get) out of bed and 3_____ (rush) downstairs. No time for a shower. Where was my passport? I was sure I 4_____ (leave) it on the table but it wasn't there. Eventually I 5_____ (find) it. It 6_____ (lie) on top of the clothes in my suitcase. I 7_____ (pack) it by mistake.

b If you 1_____ (ever ride) on an elephant, you will know how uncomfortable and scary it is. I was terrified the first and only time I 2_____ (sit) on one's back. It 3_____ (seem) a long way down, and it was.

c The accident 1_____ (happen) while I 2_____ (travel) to Edinburgh for the weekend. It was foggy, and like everyone else I 3_____ (drive) too fast, given the poor driving conditions. One minute I 4_____ (listen) to the radio, the next I 5_____ (lie) in a hospital bed. I 6_____ (crash) into the car in front but had a lucky escape.

3 Complete the phrasal verbs in these sentences with an appropriate word.

a If you don't know what a word means, look it _____.
b On our way to Australia we decided to stop _____ in Hong Kong for a few days.
c Could you pick me _____ from work tomorrow? My car is being serviced.
d After we had checked _____ at our hotel, we looked _____ the town.
e Thanks for the lift. You can drop me _____ at the traffic lights. I can walk from there.
f If your class starts at 9 o'clock, what time do you have to set _____ to get there on time?
g I'm really looking _____ to seeing you again. It's ages since I saw you!
h Look _____ yourself! Take care!

6 The mind

Introduction

1 Read and answer these questions. Which questions do you think test IQ (Intelligence Quotient) and which test EQ (Emotional Intelligence Quotient)? When you have finished, compare answers in pairs. If you have different answers, give reasons for your choices.

1 Decide which of a–e best completes the set on the left.

2 Which of the following is least like the others?

cupboard   bag   pencil   wallet   box

3 Your best friend has just had an argument with her boyfriend. What do you do?

a Tell her to just forget about him. He's not worth it.
b Take her to the cinema to take her mind off it.
c Show that you're on her side by suggesting how she can get her own back.
d Tell her about how a similar thing happened to you and your partner.

4 Which pair of numbers a–e best continues the following series?

1, 30, 4, 25, 7, 20, 10, 15, 13, 10, ?, ?

a 16, 5   b 15, 15   c 15, 10   d 18, 5   e 18, 10

5 Imagine you are selling a student magazine in the city centre. Twenty people have walked straight past you. What do you do?

a Give up and go home – tomorrow you might have more luck.
b Ask yourself whether there is something about your character that is putting people off.
c Next time somebody walks past, try a new tactic.
d Start thinking of a new job you could do instead.

2 Discuss these questions.

a Have you ever taken an IQ test or a personality test? What was it for?
b Who uses these tests and why? How useful do you think they are?
c What other abilities are not tested in either kind of test? How can they be tested?

Listening

Think ahead

1 These factors may determine whether a child will grow up a success or a failure. How could each factor be a positive or a negative influence?

upbringing   wealth   social class   education   intelligence   character

Sentence completion

2 🎧 You will hear part of a radio programme about factors which determine success.

a Which groups of people did Peter Salovey and Martin Seligman use for their experiments?

b What did their experiments and studies seem to prove?

3 🎧 Listen again and complete these sentences.

a The graduates who got high IQ scores at college weren't any more _____ than those who got lower IQ scores.

b When determining life success, other factors are _____ than IQ.

c One of the most important factors for life success is _____.

d The children who didn't eat the sweet would be given _____.

e Approximately _____ of the children couldn't resist temptation.

f The children were retested when they were _____.

g On the IQ test, the group which had resisted temptation got _____.

h Another factor which determines success is _____.

i It is expensive for insurance companies to _____ new salesmen.

j _____ are more likely to leave during their first year in the job.

over to you

If you were in these situations, how much attention would you pay to IQ and to EQ?

a student choosing a private tutor

a university selecting new students

someone looking for a marriage partner

Personal qualities

4 Which of these adjectives describe positive and which describe negative personal qualities? What are the nouns related to these adjectives?

confident   dependable   indecisive   pessimistic   self-reliant

5 Complete these sentences with an appropriate adjective or noun.

a Josie can never make up her mind. She's so _____.

b It's important to believe in yourself and have _____ in your own abilities.

c My grandmother lives alone and doesn't need any help from anyone. She's totally _____.

d James isn't very _____. He doesn't always turn up when he says he will.

e _____ always believe the worst will happen.

Grammar and practice

Gerunds

1 Underline the gerunds in these sentences. Match each example in a–d with a description of its use in 1–4. Some will fit more than one use.

  a Thinking is somehow superior to feeling.
  b If the children could resist eating the sweet, he would give them two sweets.
  c Selling insurance is a difficult job
  d Given the high costs of training, the emotional state of new employees has become an economic issue for insurance companies.

  1 as the subject of a clause or sentence
  2 as the object of a clause or sentence
  3 after certain verbs
  4 after prepositions

◄ GRAMMAR REFERENCE PAGE 181 ►

2 Complete these sentences with a verb in the gerund form.

  a _____ a good memory is seen as an advantage by most people.
  b _____ people's names is an ability which can be developed.
  c _____ the person's name immediately after you have been introduced to them will help you remember it.
  d _____ things down in a diary will jog your memory.
  e _____ where you left your keys is an everyday occurrence for many people.

3 Complete each sentence with a preposition and a verb from each list, making any necessary changes.

at   in   of   for   about
have improve memorise remember remind

  a Some people are better _____ things than others.
  b Some people have such good memories that they are capable _____ hundreds of facts.
  c If you are interested _____ your memory, there are lots of methods you can try which guarantee success.
  d Don't be worried _____ a bad memory. Our capacity for memory is determined by our genes.
  e Secretaries are responsible _____ their bosses about meetings and appointments.

4 How many expressions do you know in English which express how much or how little we like something, e.g. *enjoy, can't stand*? Make a list, then put them in order from extreme liking to extreme disliking.

5 Work in pairs. Tell your partner about your likes and dislikes, using these verbs and expressions. Think about films and TV, music, sports and games, travel, food, other people, duties and obligations.

EXAMPLE
I enjoy *watching horror films*.
I can't stand *people smoking while I'm eating*.

Gerunds and infinitives

6 Some verbs are followed by the gerund, others by the infinitive. Choose the correct verb in these sentences.

  a We just managed *to catch / catching* the bus.
  b We've arranged *to meet / meeting* outside the cinema.
  c Have you considered *to change / changing* jobs?
  d I expect *to be / being* home before nine o'clock.
  e You will risk *to lose / losing* your job if you tell your boss what you think of him.
  f He learnt *to play / playing* golf when he was five.
  g I hope you didn't agree *to lend / lending* her any money!
  h The woman admitted *to drive / driving* over the speed limit.
  i I pretended *to understand / understanding* what he was saying, although I had no idea.
  j We can't afford *to buy / buying* a new car.

7 Some verbs can be followed by either the gerund or the infinitive. In some cases, there is a difference in meaning. Match each pair of sentences with the correct meanings, a or b.

EXAMPLE

1 I've tried taking *the pills the doctor prescribed but I still can't sleep.* (meaning b)
2 I've tried to take *the pills the doctor prescribed but I just can't swallow them.* (meaning a)

   a I've made an effort to do the action.
   b I've done the action as an experiment.

3 I *stopped to speak* to Richard to ask him about the weekend.
4 I *stopped speaking* to Richard after he lied to me.

   a I finished an activity.
   b I interrupted one activity to do another.

5 I *regret to tell* you that I am unable to offer you the job.
6 I *regret telling* her I was sacked from my last job.

   a I am sorry about something I did in the past.
   b I am sorry about something I am doing.

7 He *went on talking*, even after he'd been told to keep quiet.
8 After he'd outlined the problems, he *went on to talk* about his solutions.

   a He continued to do the action.
   b He finished one activity and started another.

9 I *don't remember inviting* him. Are you sure you didn't?
10 I *didn't remember to invite* him. Sorry but I forgot.

   a I didn't do what I intended to do.
   b I have no recollection of doing this.

◀ GRAMMAR REFERENCE PAGE 182 ▶

8 Complete the sentences with a verb in the gerund or infinitive.

   a I hope he's remembered _____ the tickets.
   b UK Air regrets _____ the late arrival of flight UA127.
   c He's tried _____ the window, but it's stuck.
   d Will you stop _____ while I'm talking?
   e She doesn't remember _____ to baby sit.
   f He's tried _____ less but he hasn't lost weight.
   g Do you regret _____ school at sixteen?

Error correction

9 Read the text below and look carefully at each line. Some of the lines are correct, and some have a word which should not be there. If a line is correct, put a tick (✔) in the space. If a line has a word that should not be there, write the word in the space. There are two examples.

A bad memory

0	Having a bad memory can be extremely dangerous. Have you ever left	✓
00	~~from~~ the house without remembering to turn off the gas and almost	*from*
1	have caused a fire? I have. And on more than one occasion as well.	_____
2	Now, even though when I remember to do it, I convince myself I have	_____
3	forgotten. The picture in my mind is so vivid that I rush to home	_____
4	imagining that fire-engines outside my house and flames pouring	_____
5	through the window. But, of course, I find everything in perfect order.	_____
6	Forgetting things can be embarrassing as well. It may seem like	_____
7	incredible, but on one occasion I actually forgot my flatmate's name.	_____
8	We had known us each other for two years, and one day I just	_____
9	couldn't remember what she was called. Naturally, I didn't dare ask	_____
10	her that. She would have thought I had lost my mind, not my memory.	_____
11	Two whole days passed before I had finally remembered. If I'm honest,	_____
12	I have to admit that it was embarrassing both and worrying. However,	_____
13	there are advantages. You can avoid unpleasant experiences like the	_____
14	trips to the dentist simply by forgetting that you have an appointment.	_____
15	Also, as you never remember people's birthdays neither, you save a lot	_____
	of money on the presents that you don't buy.	

Speaking

1 What are some of the negative consequences of stress?

Two-way task

2 🎧 You will hear Part 3 of an FCE Speaking test. Make a note of what the examiner asks the candidates to do by completing these sentences.

> I'd like you to imagine you have been asked to write an article about the best ways to relieve stress.
> First, talk to each other about _____.
> Then, decide _____.

going on holiday

exercise

yoga

having a bath

painting

listening to music

tip!

In Part 3 of the Speaking paper, make sure you give your partner the opportunity to speak. Ask them a question if they don't say anything.

3 🎧 Listen to two candidates answering the question.
   a Do they complete both parts of the question?
   b Did they ask each other questions? What questions did they use?
   c How do they show they are listening to each other?

4 Work in pairs. Answer the same exam question with your partner.

Discussion

5 Discuss these questions.
   a Do you think people today are more or less stressed than in the past? Why?
   b What could companies do to make work more relaxing for their employees?
   c Is it always a good thing to be relaxed? Can you think of any occasions when it might be a bad thing to be too relaxed?
   d What kind of holiday would you find relaxing / stressful?

dos
and
don'ts

- Read the text quickly section by section. Make a note of the main point of each section.
- Read the missing headings or summary sentences carefully. Match the headings or sentences which go with your main points.
- Read any difficult sections again. Try to match these with the remaining headings or sentences.
- If you are not sure, make a sensible guess. Don't leave any spaces empty.

1 You are going to read an article about animal behaviour. Choose from the list A–I the sentence which best summarises each part (1–7) of the article. There is one extra sentence that you do not need to use. There is an example at the beginning. Use the *Dos and Don'ts* above to help you.

A A variety of tricks are used.
B Cheats may be more intelligent.
C This behaviour is familiar.
D Abnormal behaviour is informative.
E Deception proves effective.

F Males cheat more.
G You couldn't fool her.
H There may be problems with research.
I Parental help is requested.

NATURE'S CHEATS

0 *I*

Anna is digging in the ground for a potato, when along comes Paul. Paul looks to see what Anna's doing and then, seeing that there is no one in sight, starts to scream as loud as he can. Paul's angry mother rushes over and chases Anna away. Once his Mum has gone, Paul walks over and helps himself to Anna's potato. 5

1 ____

Does this ring a bell? I'm sure it does. We've all experienced annoying tricks when we were young – the brother who stole your toys and then got you into trouble by telling your parents you had hit him. 10 But Anna and Paul are not humans. They're African baboons, and playing tricks is as much part of monkey behaviour as it is of human behaviour.

2 ____

Throughout nature, tricks like this are common – they are part of daily survival. There are insects that 15 hide from their enemies by looking like leaves or twigs, and harmless snakes that imitate poisonous ones. Such behaviour, developed over hundreds of thousands of years, is instinctive and completely natural. Some animals, however, go further and use 20 a more deliberate kind of deception – they use normal behaviour to trick other animals. In most cases the animal probably doesn't know it is

deceiving, only that certain actions give it an advantage. But in apes and some monkeys the 25 behaviour seems much more like that of humans.

3 ____

What about Paul the baboon? His scream and his mother's attack on Anna could have been a matter of chance, but Paul was later seen playing the same trick on others. This use of a third individual to 30 achieve a goal is only one of the many tricks commonly used by apes. Another tactic is the 'Look behind you!' trick. When one young male baboon was attacked by several others, he stood on his back legs and looked into the distance, as if there 35 was an enemy there. The attackers turned to look behind them and lost interest in their victim. In fact, there was no enemy.

4 ____

Studying behaviour like this is complicated because it is difficult to do laboratory experiments to test 40 whether behaviour is intentional. It would be easy to suggest that these cases mean the baboons were deliberately tricking other animals, but they might have learnt the behaviour without understanding how it worked. So the psychologists talked to 45 colleagues who studied apes and asked them if they

Did you play tricks on your brothers and sisters when you were a child? Do you regret your behaviour now?

Have you ever tried to deceive any of the following people? Why and how did you do it? What were the consequences?

a friend   a customs officer   a boss   a parent   a teacher   a partner

Collocation: verbs and nouns

2 Match each word or phrase in the list with a verb from the article (a, b, c or d).

EXAMPLE *achieve an ambition*

a achieve   b lose   c play   d solve

an ambition   confidence   a crime   a goal   interest   a joke
a mystery   a part   a problem   one's temper   a trick

3 Complete these sentences with an appropriate verb-noun collocation.

a My boss _____ over nothing. The smallest thing makes him explode.

b She had always wanted to win the gold medal. Once she had _____, she decided to retire from professional sport.

c Children enjoy _____ on other people, but they often don't find it funny when someone does it to them.

d Our best player couldn't play for the team because he was getting married that day. We _____ by postponing the match.

had noticed this kind of deception. They discovered many liars and cheats, but the cleverest were apes who clearly showed that they intended to deceive and knew when they themselves had been deceived.   50

5 ____

An amusing example of this comes from a psychologist working in Tanzania. A young chimp was annoying him, so he tricked her into going away by pretending he had seen something interesting in the distance. When the chimp looked and found nothing, she 'walked back, hit   55 me over the head with her hand and ignored me for the rest of the day'.

6 ____

Another way to decide whether an animal's behaviour is deliberate is to look for actions that are not normal for that animal. A zoo worker describes how a gorilla   60 dealt with an enemy. 'He slowly crept up behind the other gorilla, walking on tiptoe. When he got close to his enemy he pushed him violently in the back, then ran indoors.' Wild gorillas do not normally walk on tiptoe. Of course it's possible that the gorilla could   65 have learnt from humans that such behaviour works, without understanding why. But looking at the many cases of deliberate deception in apes, it is impossible to explain them all as simple imitation.

7 ____

Taking all the evidence into account, it seems that deception does play an   70 important part in ape societies where there are complex social rules and relationships and where problems are better solved by social pressure than by physical conflict. The ability of animals to deceive and cheat may be a better measure of their intelligence than their use of tools. Studying the intelligence of our closest relatives could be the way to understand   75 the development of human intelligence.

Vocabulary

1 Work in pairs. Ask each other questions to find out the following information.

How much sleep do you need each night? How much do you normally get?
What happens if you don't get enough sleep?
What do you do before you sleep?
What is your favourite sleeping position?
Do you ever dream or have nightmares?
Do you ever have a siesta?

2 What advice would you give someone who suffers from insomnia?

3 Read this short text ignoring the words in italic. Which of your ideas are mentioned?

> It is difficult to sleep ¹*strongly/soundly* if you are stressed and worried. If your mind races as soon as your head hits the pillow, you need to ²*meet/face* the problem before you go to sleep. It may help to actually write down what your ³*deepest/hardest* anxieties are and try to think of solutions. Reading or watching a video can also help as it distracts you – not TV, as it indicates what time it is. The later it gets, the more anxious you may become.

Collocation

4 Collocations are groups of words which go together. Choose the correct collocation from the words in italic in the text in 3.

5 Choose the adjective which collocates with the noun in each of these sentences. Only one option is correct.

a Susan is a *near/close/main* friend.
b Armed robbery is a *significant/severe/serious* crime.
c Digging is *hard/tough/difficult* work.
d There will be *hard/strong/heavy* rain in the north.
e Truancy is a(n) *important/serious/hard* problem.
f Traffic is usually *heavy/strong/serious* during the rush hour.
g We were almost blown over by the *hard/strong/heavy* wind.

6 The adverbs in this list all mean 'with intensity'. Match each adverb with an appropriate verb.

argue	hard
drink	passionately
listen	attentively
sleep	hard
think	heavily
work	soundly

7 In each sentence, cross out the verb which does not collocate with the noun.

a I'm *sitting / performing / taking* my exam in June.
b We need to *reach / acquire / find* a solution.
c Can I *say / give / express* an opinion?
d The increase in traffic is *causing / creating / making* a problem.

Multiple-choice cloze

8 Read the text below and decide which answer (A, B, C, or D) best fits each space. There is an example at the beginning.

SLEEP

By the time we ⁰ *reach* old age most of us have ¹_____ twenty years sleeping. Yet nobody knows why we do it. Most scientists believe that by resting our bodies, we allow time for ²_____ maintenance work to be done. Any ³_____ that there is can be put right more quickly if energy isn't being used up doing other things.

Sleep is controlled by certain chemicals. These build up during the day, eventually reaching ⁴_____ that cause tiredness. We can control the effects of these chemicals to some extent. Caffeine helps to ⁵_____ us awake while alcohol and some medicines ⁶_____ us sleepy.

By using electrodes, scientists are able to ⁷_____ what ⁸_____ on in people's heads while they sleep. They have ⁹_____ that when we first drop off everything slows down. The heart ¹⁰_____ more slowly, and our breathing becomes shallow. After about ninety minutes our eyes start to twitch, and we go into what is ¹¹_____ REM* sleep, which is a ¹²_____ that we've started to dream. You have dreams every night, even if you don't remember them. There are many theories about why we dream, none of them ¹³_____. A lot of people say they have to have eight hours' sleep every night while others seem to ¹⁴_____ on a lot less. One thing is ¹⁵_____ – we all need some sleep. Going without it can have some very strange effects.

* REM. = Rapid Eye Movement

0	A	arrive	B	reach	C	become	D	get
1	A	passed	B	used	C	spent	D	occupied
2	A	main	B	elementary	C	needed	D	essential
3	A	damage	B	suffering	C	harm	D	hurt
4	A	peaks	B	heights	C	positions	D	levels
5	A	stay	B	keep	C	make	D	maintain
6	A	make	B	cause	C	become	D	affect
7	A	exhibit	B	work	C	study	D	think
8	A	happens	B	goes	C	occurs	D	passes
9	A	seen	B	researched	C	discovered	D	watched
10	A	beats	B	hits	C	moves	D	trembles
11	A	known	B	labelled	C	named	D	called
12	A	clue	B	proof	C	sign	D	signal
13	A	conclusive	B	final	C	concluding	D	definite
14	A	need	B	manage	C	get	D	deal
15	A	fixed	B	decided	C	confident	D	certain

Writing

Short story

1 Work in pairs. Find out what makes your partner feel *bored*, *excited* and *nervous*.

2 Read the Part 2 task and tell your partner about a situation when you got very angry.

> Your language school is running a short story competition. The story must begin or end with the following words:
>
> *I had never been so angry in my whole life.*
>
> Write your story in 120–180 words.

3 The sentences in this answer to the question have been jumbled. Put them in the correct order, ignoring the gaps. The first one has been done for you.

A I returned to the shop and _____ told the shop assistant what had happened. She said I must have washed it in hot water.

B It wasn't until I put it on later that I realised that it had shrunk _____. It was much too small for me now.

C A few days later, after wearing it once, I decided to wash it.

D What could I say? _____, I threw the T-shirt on the counter and left the shop, slamming the door behind me. I had never been so angry in my whole life.

E _____, I repeated that I had followed the instructions exactly. She insisted that I couldn't have.

F I read the washing instructions _____: hand wash in cool water. I decided to use cold water, just in case.

G The bright red T-shirt in the shop window caught my eye. I decided I could just afford it, so I went inside and bought it. *1*

H Nothing makes me angrier than being accused of lying. I demanded to see the manager. 'I am the manager,' the woman said.

4 The following adverbs have been removed from the story. Complete the text by putting them into the most appropriate spaces.

carefully   furiously   noticeably   patiently   politely

Dramatic effect

5 Read this answer to the same question. Make it more dramatic by adding the adverbs in italic at appropriate places in the paragraph.

angrily, casually	I had never been so angry in my whole life. 'That was my parking space. I saw it first!' I shouted. The woman shrugged her shoulders as if it wasn't her problem and walked into the building opposite.
briskly, hurriedly	What was I going to do? I was already late for my interview. I would just have to leave my car illegally parked and hope that I wouldn't get a fine. I picked up my briefcase and walked across the road, straightening my tie as I went.
strangely	I was shown into the interview room. The panel consisted of five people, one of whom looked familiar. My heart sank as I realised it was the same woman I had shouted at earlier. I didn't think I would have much chance of getting the job now.
reluctantly	I got a letter from the company two days later. Opening the envelope, I found to my amazement that I had got the job. Maybe the woman had felt guilty about stealing my parking place after all.

6 Replace the parts in italic in each sentence with more descriptive verbs from this list, making any other necessary changes.

crawl   creep   dash   stroll   whisper   yell

a He *ran* across the road *very quickly*.
b She *told me* the answer *very quietly*.
c The traffic *moved slowly* though the town centre.
d He *walked* upstairs *very quietly*.
e She *shouted very loudly*, 'Look out!'
f They *walked slowly* through the park arm in arm.

Think, plan, write

7 You are going to write a short story. First, read the task.

> Your teacher is organising a short story competition for your class. The best entries will appear in the end-of-year magazine. Your story must begin with the following words:
>
> *I felt so excited when I looked at the envelope.*
>
> Write your story in 120–180 words.

8 Before you write, spend some time thinking of some ideas to include in the story. Use the questions below to help you. Choose one of the answers given or use your own.

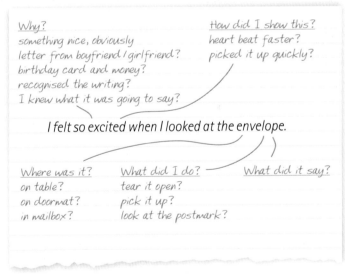

Why?
something nice, obviously
letter from boyfriend / girlfriend?
birthday card and money?
recognised the writing?
I knew what it was going to say?

How did I show this?
heart beat faster?
picked it up quickly?

I felt so excited when I looked at the envelope.

Where was it?
on table?
on doormat?
in mailbox?

What did I do?
tear it open?
pick it up?
look at the postmark?

What did it say?

9 Write your ideas into a story. Remember to
  • set the scene (where and when did it take place?).
  • give any necessary background information (what happened before?).
  • conclude the story (what was in the envelope? a letter? happy news? sad news?).

10 Finally, when you have finished, check your grammar, spelling, and punctuation.

◀ WRITING GUIDE PAGE 172 ▶

1 Read the text below. Use the word given in capitals at the end of each line to form a word that fits in the space in the same line. There is an example at the beginning.

Telepathy

Results of a recent survey show that one third of Americans believe in telepathy –

0 _communication_ , that is, between two people without using any of   COMMUNICATE

the five senses. Twenty-five per cent of Americans claim to have ¹_____   ACTUAL

had a ²_____ experience. Knowing who's on the phone when it rings   TELEPATHY

is probably the most common everyday experience of this kind . Yet ³_____   CORRECT

guessing who is on the phone before you answer it should ⁴_____ be   HARD

a matter of great surprise. Given the ⁵_____ number of people who   LIMIT

call any one of us in a year, and given our ⁶_____ of how long it is   KNOW

since someone last called us, we could make a ⁷_____ guess as to   SENSE

who will ring us next.

Laboratory results are also ⁸_____ with anecdotal accounts.   CONSISTENT

Even professional mind-readers fail to repeat what seem ⁹_____ results   ORDINARY

under ¹⁰_____ conditions. No experiment has shown results higher   SCIENCE

than would be predicted by the laws of probability.

2 Complete these sentences with the correct forms of the verbs in brackets.

a Don't forget _____ (post) this letter, will you? It's very important.

b When you've finished _____ (clear) the table, can you tidy your room?

c Job applicants should be good at _____ (deal) with people and should be prepared _____ (work) at weekends.

d The groom thanked everyone for coming and went on _____ (say) how happy he was.

e Will you stop _____ (use) my pen and buy your own?

f I didn't expect _____ (get) such a good mark in the exam.

g You can't avoid _____ (meet) people you don't like if you live in a village.

h I don't know if I want the job. It will mean _____ (move) to London.

3 Choose the correct alternative in these sentences.

a He was sleeping so *soundly/brilliantly* that he didn't hear the explosion.

b The opposite of *heavy/strong* tea is 'weak' tea, but the opposite of a *strong/severe* wind is a 'light' wind.

c The toothache was so *severe/strong* that I just wanted the tooth taken out.

d I've got a suggestion to *put/make*.

e I have such a *hard/heavy* work schedule at the moment that I don't have much free time.

f After several hours someone *came up with/carried out* a solution to the problem.

g I had a *strong/hard* suspicion that he was lying to me.

7 Free time

Introduction

1 Work in pairs or small groups. Which of the photographs show activities similar to things you do in your free time?

2 What proportion of your time is free time? How could you increase this?

3 How difficult is it for you to balance work, study and family with free time for yourself?

4 Read the statements below and decide which are true for you. Then, compare your answers in pairs.

a I spend more time doing things I have to do than doing things I want to do.
b If I'm not doing something productive, I feel that I'm wasting my time.
c I can't remember the last time I felt completely rested and ready for the next day.
d If I suddenly find I have extra free time, I don't know how to fill it.
e I can't think of the last time I really enjoyed myself.
f At the end of a typical week I'm too tired to go out and have fun.

Reading

Think ahead

1 Imagine you have won a magazine competition. The prize is your ideal weekend away. Answer these questions. Then, compare answers in pairs.

Where would you go? How would you spend your time?
Who would you go with?

2 Read these descriptions of short holiday breaks. Choose the one you would enjoy most and the one you would enjoy least.

holidays with a difference

Fancy a holiday with a difference? Take a look at these seven breaks where you can get away from it all and learn to do something really useful.

A Dublin, Ireland

Have your own image carved in stone. The organisers of this creative course have both trained in stone work and have worked on several major European projects. On their courses near Dublin in Ireland, all the stone and tools are provided and they guarantee that after a bit of hammering you'll be returning home with a finished piece for your home or garden. The courses run once a month from April to October. The price includes lunch and refreshments. Accommodation isn't included, but there is plenty available locally.

B The Welsh mountains

Living with farm animals can be a test of character. This might not quite be co-habiting, but at Caecrwn Farmhouse in Brecon, you can definitely find out how to rear and market them. This introductory course is set on a small farm with views of the Welsh Mountains. Weekends are filled with the fun of the farm, and appetites are satisfied with delicious home-cooked local food. Accommodation is in a converted barn and, for added charm, the farm also has a range of animals including chickens, ducks, geese, sheep and goats to keep kids entertained. Residential weekends, all meals included, are held throughout the year.

C Barcelona, Spain

In the heart of Barcelona's gothic quarter, not far from the famous Ramblas, you can take part in a farmhouse cheesemaking course on the site of one of the city's first butter-making factories. The course runs twice a month and never caters for more than twelve people. You will be instructed on how to produce fresh cheese and analyse what makes a good one. Finish off with a meal of fruit, wine and – of course – cheese.

D Edinburgh, Scotland

A little bit of elbow grease, plenty of oil and a spot of common sense: this cycle maintenance course is the equivalent of getting a degree in bicycle mechanics. The Edinburgh Bicycle Cooperative runs courses most weekends, and you can choose between an intensive course on the complete bike or, if you prefer, learn how to build a wheel, which you can take away at the end. Alternatively, if you want to go it alone, one-on-one tuition is also available.

E Devon, England

If you don't mind the feeling of seaweed between your toes and fingers, a seaside safari in sunny Devon will suit you nicely. It's a bit wet but it's fun. An instructor will show you how to handle all the creatures that live in the sea, from crabs and star fish to lobsters and limpets. And if that's not exciting enough for you, there are over forty other activities, including orienteering and raft-building. All the activities can be pre-booked or chosen on the day, and are included in the price.

F Rural Gloucestershire, England

Take your pup and teach him a new trick or two. Set in rural Gloucestershire, this is a hands-on way to train man's best friend. Before you know it, your dog will be fetching his stick from the water – and shaking his coat all over you. There are courses throughout June and July, and prices include farmhouse accommodation – your dog is welcome to stay in your room – with all meals and tuition.

G Abano Terme, Italy

Ancient emperors loved it, even Mozart took a fancy to it. And what better way to experience the thrill of being caked in mud than when it's helping you to lose weight while detoxifying, toning and revitalising the skin on your face and body? It might look ridiculous, but it's all in a good cause. The Italian resort of Abano Terme, near Mottegrotto, specialises in such delights, and combines it with soothing thermal bathing to wash all the mud away. Many of the mud therapy sessions are held in special rooms where guests must arrive with an empty stomach. The mud therapy cycle lasts an average of one to two weeks, with six to twelve mud packs applied daily.

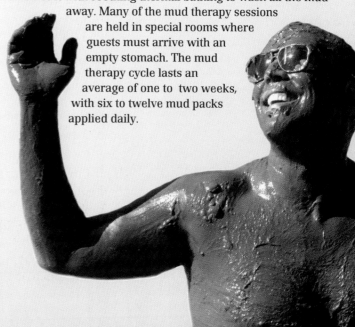

Multiple matching

3 Read the descriptions of the holidays again. For questions 1–14, choose which break (A–G) is referred to. Each one may be chosen more than once. When more than one answer is required, these may be given in any order. There is an example at the beginning.

Which holiday(s)

lasts longer than a weekend?	0	G			
provides activities to occupy children?	1				
allow participants to take something home with them?	2		3		
takes place on a historic site?	4				
involve participants living on a farm?	5		6		
involve participants getting wet?	7		8		9
involves working with young animals?	10				
aims to improve your appearance?	11				
teaches participants how to make a particular kind of food?	12				
provides private lessons?	13				
teaches participants something about sculpture?	14				

 over to you What skills have you got that might enable you to organise activities like these for people of your own age?

Prefixes

4 What do the words in italic mean in these extracts from the text? What are the meanings of the prefixes in these words?

a Living with farm animals can be a test of character. This might not quite be *co-habiting*, …
b All activities can be *pre-booked* or chosen on the day.
c Lose weight while *detoxifying*, toning and *revitalising* the skin.

5 Match the prefixes in a–f with their meanings 1–6.

a *anti*clockwise   1 after
b *ex*-husband   2 in the middle of
c *mid*week   3 half/partly
d *post*-war   4 against/opposite
e *semi*precious   5 below/insufficient
f *under*age   6 former

6 Form words with the meanings below using an appropriate prefix from 5.

a a university graduate who is studying for a higher qualification
b someone who was once the president of their country
c liquid to put into a car in winter to stop the water from freezing
d train system which is below street level
e twelve o'clock at night
f a house joined to another house on one side

Grammar and practice

Passive verbs

1 Underline the verbs in these sentences from the text. Which are passive and which are active? Name the tenses.

  a Weekends are filled with the fun of the farm, and appetites are satisfied with delicious home-cooked local food.

  b Residential weekends are held throughout the year.

  c You will be instructed on how to produce fresh cheese.

  d Learn how to build a wheel, which you can take away at the end.

  e All the activities can be pre-booked or chosen on the day.

2 How is the passive formed?

3 Rewrite sentences 1a–e, changing passive into active verbs and active into passive verbs. How do the changes you have made affect the meaning?

4 Who performs the action in these passive sentences?

  a You will be taught by experts how to make traditional Spanish cheese.

  b Courses are run most weekends by unpaid volunteers.

5 In sentences 1a–e, who performs the action in each case? Why is this information not included in the sentences?

    ◀ GRAMMAR REFERENCE PAGE 183 ▶

6 Complete the text with the passive forms of verbs from this list.

    book   equip   furnish   guarantee   include   locate   make   reserve   serve

Hotel Donatella

A friendly atmosphere 1_____ at the Donatella, a small family hotel, which 2_____ in the ancient centre of the city. All fifteen bedrooms 3_____ to a high standard and have en suite facilities. Rooms 4_____ with satellite TV, a mini-bar and direct-dial telephones. Some rooms 5_____ for non-smokers. Breakfast 6_____ in the price and 7_____ between 7 a.m. and 10 a.m. in the Breakfast Room. Dinner is available between 7 p.m. and 10 p.m. and can 8_____ at Reception. A small charge 9_____ for use of the hotel's private car park.

7 Rewrite this text, changing the verbs in italic into the passive and making any other necessary changes. Do not include the person who performs the action unless it is important.

Congratulations!

You have won an all-expenses paid weekend for two in London.

One of our chauffeurs *will meet you* at Heathrow Airport and *drive you* into central London. We *will put you up* in a five-star hotel close to Harrods, the world's most famous department store. We *have reserved* a luxury suite for you on the tenth floor. In addition to this, the competition organisers *will be giving you* £1000 'pocket money'. You *can spend* this money as you like.

Have/get something done

8 What is the difference in meaning between these sentences? Who took the photographs in each case?
   a I took photographs of my birthday party.
   b Photographs of my birthday party were taken.
   c I had photographs taken of my birthday party.

9 What are the different meanings of *have something done* in these two sentences?
   a I had my tooth filled.
   b They had their car stolen.

   ◀ GRAMMAR REFERENCE PAGE 184 ▶

10 Rewrite these sentences using *have* or *get*. The first one has been done as an example.
   a The mechanic changed the oil in my car.
      I had the oil in my car changed.
   b The hairdresser cut my hair in a completely different style.
   c A decorator has repainted our apartment.
   d An electrician is going to repair my video next week.
   e My jacket is being cleaned at a specialist cleaner's.
   f The town hall has just been rebuilt for the council.

11 Think of as many answers to these questions as you can.
   a What can you have done at the dentist's?
   b Why do people go to the hairdresser's?
   c Why do people take their cars to a garage?
   d If you didn't want people to recognise you, which features of your appearance would you have changed?

12 What do you have done for you, rather than doing for yourself? Make a list and compare your answers with other students.

Cloze

13 Read the text below, and think of the word which best fits each space. Use only one word in each space.

HASSLE-FREE TRAVEL

If you have four weeks to spare, there's no better way of seeing Europe than going by train. Across most of Europe the railways are fantastic. Trains run frequently and ¹_____ clean and punctual. But the best ²_____ about it is that you can travel the length and breadth of the continent because the network ³_____ so extensive. InterRail is what happened when the national rail networks got together and decided ⁴_____ offer people under twenty-six the chance to travel across Europe with just one ticket, which ⁵_____ bought for a fixed price. Since then it has ⁶_____ extended to cover travellers ⁷_____ twenty-six. You can just get on and ⁸_____ most services, although you ⁹_____ to pay a little extra for some trains. These are usually high speed services, ¹⁰_____ as the TGV in France. You can pay the supplement ¹¹_____ you want to, or you can find an alternative route. You can select one particular zone, ¹²_____ you can go for the all-zone option. Your plans may change once you are travelling, ¹³_____, for complete flexibility, it is best to choose the all-zone ticket. The fantastic thing about InterRailing is that you get on a train in the middle of one city, and you get off in the middle of another. There are ¹⁴_____ problems with getting from an airport terminal or collecting ¹⁵_____ baggage.

Vocabulary

1 Read these newspaper headlines. Match each headline to one of the sports symbols and name each sport.

KEEPER GETS RED CARD
3 MINUTES AFTER KICK-OFF

DISASTER AFTER PIT STOP FOR WHEEL CHANGE

Vital seconds lost in handlebar mix-up

Finalist let down by unreliable serve

GOLD FOR BRITISH SPRINTER

Fans riot after heavyweight knocked out in first round

Three holes to win The US Open

Slam-dunk wins game

Sports vocabulary

2 What is the name for the person who does each of the sports you have listed?

EXAMPLE   *Someone who does* athletics *is an* athlete.

3 What equipment is associated with these sports? Think of two or three essential items for each sport.

EXAMPLE   *tennis: racket, ball, net*

4 Which sporting activities take place … ?

on: a pitch   a course   a court   a circuit   a (race)track
in: a pool   a gym   a ring   a rink

5 Read this text and choose the best option (a, b, c or d) to fill each gap.

> To be good at whatever sport you 1_____, you need to 2_____ a lot of time and energy on it.
> Professional footballers, for example, need to develop particular 3_____, like passing the ball and
> tackling, but they also need to improve their stamina and general 4_____. They 5_____ most
> days. This usually involves running round the 6_____ and doing lots of exercises.

1	a	do	b	make	c	practise	d	take
2	a	dedicate	b	devote	c	give	d	spend
3	a	talents	b	qualities	c	skills	d	gifts
4	a	state	b	fitness	c	shape	d	form
5	a	prepare	b	train	c	perform	d	rehearse
6	a	pitch	b	grass	c	circuit	d	course

over to you

Which sports and activities have you actually taken part in yourself? Which are your favourite and least favourite?

Which sports and activities do you enjoy watching live or on TV?

dos and don'ts

- Read the sentences or notes you have to complete. Decide what kind of information you need to listen for.
- Listen to the recording and complete any sentences you can. Don't worry if you can't complete many at this stage.
- Listen again to complete the rest of the sentences. Check the sentences you have already completed.
- Check all your answers are grammatically correct and make sense. Don't write more than three words in any space.
- Don't leave any sentences unfinished.

1 🎧 You will hear someone being interviewed about an unusual hobby. For questions 1–10, complete the sentences. Use the *Dos and Don'ts*.

1 Jaine works as a _____ executive.

2 In international competitions, Jaine has

   _____ .

3 Jaine started body-building as a way of getting

   _____ .

4 Before she goes to work in the morning she spends a couple of hours in _____ .

5 At lunchtime, Jaine normally does exercise instead of having lunch and a _____ her colleagues.

6 It doesn't matter to Jaine if she misses

   _____ .

7 These days Jaine eats good food such as turkey,

   _____ .

8 She doesn't feel _____ if she has a cream cake or a bar of chocolate.

9 Much to her surprise, Jaine _____ the first time she competed.

10 The World Championship competition Jaine entered took place in _____ .

over to you

What kind of person do you think Jaine is? Would you be able to diet and train regularly like she does?

How much time and energy do you spend on your hobbies?

Speaking

Lead in

1 Imagine you are planning to go on a two-week camping holiday. What essential items would you need to take?

Two-way task

2 You also have room to take two non-essential items with you. Here are some of the non-essential items you could take. Talk to your partner about how useful each of these items would be. Then, say which two things you would choose to take with you.

radio

kite

computer

ball

coffee-maker

chess set

book

Discussion

3 🎧 You will hear Part 4 of an FCE Speaking test. Listen to two candidates, Megumi and Fabienne, talking about camping, and answer these questions, making a note of any reasons they give.

a What does Megumi enjoy about camping?
b What does Megumi miss from her normal life?
c What is Fabienne's idea of a perfect campsite?

4 One of the candidates you heard uses the word 'maybe' in most of her answers. Why does she do this? What other phrases with the same meaning could she have used?

tip!

In Part 4 of the Speaking paper, give reasons and explanations for your opinions. Don't forget this is your last chance to impress the examiner! Your answers should be as full and as natural as possible.

5 Work in pairs. Ask each other these question about camping.

a What is the most exciting thing for you about camping?
b What annoys you most about camping?
c What's the first thing you do when you return home after camping?
d What type of holiday do people of your age in your country prefer?
e Where do most people from your country spend their holidays?
f If they go to other countries, which are the most popular destinations?

dos and don'ts

- Read the whole text for general understanding. Don't look at the four choices yet.
- Read the text again and try to fill each space as you come to it. Study the four choices, A, B, C and D and the words on either side of the space.
- Try to eliminate three of the four choices. There may be a grammatical reason why choices are impossible.
- If you are not sure, make a sensible guess. Don't leave any spaces empty.

1 For questions 1–15, read the text below and decide which answer (A, B, C or D) best fits each space. There is an example at the beginning. Use the *Dos and Don'ts* above to help you.

recharge your batteries

Working all year without a holiday is like 0 __C__ a car for twelve months without changing the oil. You might 1_____ going, but you are probably heading for a breakdown. Holidays are an easy 2_____ to recharge your batteries and prepare for the 3_____ challenge. But a recent study came up with an interesting 4_____ – less than a third of Americans are planning to 5_____ a holiday at all this year. Maybe those people who aren't taking a 6_____ work for firms that are not holiday-friendly.

It's certainly 7_____ considering holiday time when you go looking for work, even if it may not be at the 8_____ of your list of items to ask about. While many job-seekers may feel very reluctant to 9_____ holidays at interviews or during salary negotiations, some younger workers don't 10_____ to negotiate extra free time. In fact, many of them negotiate 11_____ weeks of holiday for a slightly 12_____ salary. 13_____ off is very important to them. They have come to 14_____ it, they'll certainly take it, and they don't really 15_____ whether it offends their boss or not.

0	A	riding	B	travelling	C	driving	D	going
1	A	persevere	B	continue	C	carry	D	keep
2	A	method	B	way	C	possibility	D	choice
3	A	second	B	next	C	close	D	near
4	A	response	B	information	C	consequence	D	finding
5	A	go	B	take	C	make	D	get
6	A	pause	B	stop	C	break	D	rest
7	A	fine	B	good	C	useful	D	worth
8	A	top	B	first	C	peak	D	height
9	A	talk	B	comment	C	remark	D	mention
10	A	hesitate	B	mind	C	wait	D	worry
11	A	surplus	B	excess	C	spare	D	additional
12	A	less	B	lower	C	fewer	D	minor
13	A	Relaxation	B	Break	C	Time	D	Leisure
14	A	expect	B	hope	C	count	D	wait
15	A	think	B	bother	C	care	D	fear

Vocabulary

Phrasal verbs with
come

1   Replace the phrases in italic in sentences a–h with a phrasal verb with *come* and a word from this list.

across   along   apart   forward   round (x2)   up   up with

a   The music of the seventies was not very interesting until punk *arrived*.
b   When I picked up your CD case, it just *fell to pieces* in my hands.
c   Let me know if you *find by chance* any old family photos while you're tidying the cellar.
d   When Nick *recovered consciousness* after the operation, he didn't know where he was.
e   It was obvious that I couldn't carry the box myself, but nobody *offered* to help me.
f   'I'm sorry, but I won't be able to see you this evening,' said Jenny. 'Something *unexpected has just happened*.'
g   'Why don't you *call at my flat* for a drink on Thursday,' Karen suggested.
h   Jeremy often *thinks of* ideas for solving problems at work.

2   Discuss these questions in pairs.

What would you do if you came across a secret diary belonging to one of your friends?

How do people feel when they come round after being unconscious?

What is the most original idea you have ever come up with?

Which word?

3   Choose the correct words in each set to complete the sentences which follow.

method   possibility   choice

a   I considered the _____ of starting my own business.
b   There is no single correct _____ of teaching a language.
c   If you are rich enough, there is a huge _____ of luxury holidays.

pause   stop   rest

d   The minister spoke for two hours without a _____.
e   After a good night's _____ they continued their journey.
f   The train slowed down and gradually came to a _____.

less   fewer   minor

g   These days, _____ young people smoke than twenty years ago.
h   Don't worry – it's a _____ problem.
i   We'd better hurry – we've got _____ time than I thought.

height   peak   top

j   There's a fantastic view from the _____ of the building.
k   She reached the _____ of her career iin her mid-thirties.
l   For most of the flight the plane was at a _____ of 20,000 feet.

excess   spare   surplus

m   Butter, cheese and yoghurt are produced from _____ milk.
n   If your suitcases are too heavy, you will have to pay _____ baggage.
o   We've got a _____ room, so you can stay the night if you like.

Listening

Lead in

1 Discuss these questions in groups.

   a   What different kinds of music can you think of, e.g. classical, jazz?

   b   In what situations do people listen to or hear music?

   c   Other than enjoyment, what reasons do people have for listening to music?

Multiple choice

2 🎧 You will hear people talking in eight different situations. For questions 1–8, choose the best answer, A, B or C.

1 You will hear someone being interviewed. What question are they answering?
A What different kinds of music do you enjoy?
B Where do you go to listen to music?
C What is your favourite type of music?

2 You will hear someone describing an event she went to. What kind of event was it?
A an opera
B the film version of a musical
C a rock concert

3 You hear someone describing something she finds annoying. What is she describing?
A the use of personal stereos in public
B a particularly noisy type of music
C increasing levels of noise pollution

4 You will hear the presenter of a radio programme talking. What kind of programme does he present?
A a phone-in programme
B a request programme
C a top-twenty hits programme

5 You will hear someone talking about their favourite situation for listening to music. What situation is this?
A when he's on a long train journey.
B when he's on a long walk
C when he's driving his car

6 You will hear someone talking about a common human experience. What is this experience?
A trying hard to remember a past event
B remembering a past event without trying
C remembering the first time you heard a song

7 You will hear a man talking about somewhere he has just been. Where was this?
A the doctor's
B the dentist's
C a concert

8 You will hear someone talking about the beneficial effects of music. Who is the speaker?
A a teacher
B a musician
C a doctor

 over to you

One of the speakers talks about memories associated with a particular song. Are there any songs that have special associations for you? Can you remember the situation you were in when you first heard the song?

Where and when do you listen to music? How important is music to you?

Writing

Formal letter

1 Read this example of a Part 1 task and answer the questions.
 a What is the main purpose of the letter?
 b What key facts should be included?
 c How formal or informal should the style be?

> You have recently joined a leisure centre which has not lived up to your expectations. You decide to complain to the management, pointing out the differences between their publicity and what you have found. Read the leaflet and the notes you have made. Using this information, write a suitable letter to the leisure centre. Write between 120 and 180 words in an appropriate style.

centre2K

Open 8–midnight, 7 days a week

'State-of-the art' gym — *two machines out of order*

Classes in all sports

Heated swimming pool — *water freezing cold*

Friendly, experienced staff — *unable to help*

Disco on Fridays and Saturdays – dance music with top DJs

Snacks and drinks available at all times — *café closed early! - 10.45*

Insist on written (!) explanation - otherwise demand refund of membership fee!!

Check out our website www.centre2K.com

2 Read this letter written in answer to the task. Is the relevant information included, and is the style appropriate?

3 Underline and correct any errors in spelling, grammar and punctuation. Then rewrite any parts that are in an inappropriate style.

Dear Sir,

I am writing to complain about Centre 2K, which I visited yesterday evening. This was only my second visit. I became a member since two weeks having seen your publicity leaflet which was pretty impressive.

First of all, I went for a workout in a gym and found that two of your 'state-of-the-art' machines was out of order. I thought one of the staff might be able to help, but it took me ten minutes to find someone. Although he was very freindly, he didn't have a clue about the machines.

Next, I went for a swim. Unfortunately, the water in the pool wasn't heated, despite the fact that it was a cold evening.

Finally, I decided to go to the café for a hot drink. However, when I got there it was closed, even though it was only 10.45.

I am furious. Unless I receive a full explanation in writing from you within seven days I'll cancel my membership and request my membership fee back.

Yours

4 Find and underline five phrases in the letter which express a contrast. There are two each in paragraphs 2 and 4, and one in paragraph 3. The first has been underlined in the letter.

5 Which of the five words or phrases cannot be used to join contrasting ideas within one sentence?

6 Complete these sentences with appropriate contrasting phrases. More than one answer may be possible.

   a _____ it was raining, I went for a run.
   b Jon usually beats me at tennis. _____, yesterday I beat him easily.
   c I enjoy playing golf, _____ I'm not very good at it.
   d I tried to ring you yesterday, _____ I couldn't get a reply.
   e He went to work by car, _____ he knew the traffic would be very heavy.
   f _____ the fact that I felt terrible, I got up and went to work as usual.

7 Complete these sentences with your own ideas.

   a Even though I take regular exercise, …
   b I enjoy watching sport on TV, but …
   c Despite the fact that she couldn't drive, …
   d I've never been to Australia. However, …
   e Although I learnt to swim when I was quite young, …

8 You are going to write a formal transactional letter. First, read the task and the other information provided. What key points should be included?

> You have enrolled on a weekly swimming class at your local leisure centre. Read the leaflet giving details of your class, and the notes you have made about some recent problems. Then write a letter of complaint to the manager of the leisure centre, explaining why you are dissatisfied and demanding an improvement in the situation. Write a letter of 120–180 words in an appropriate style.

NEW CLASS FOR ADVANCED SWIMMERS

- **Classes every Monday and Thursday – 6–8 p.m.**
- **Experienced instructors**
- **Options include: diving and life-saving**
- **Have the pool to yourself**

Check out our website
www.centre2K.com

started late 6.20 twice!

couldn't answer my questions

life-saving option not available because group of twenty noisy school children there last week!

9 Before you write, remember to make a paragraph plan. Use the sample answer opposite as a model. Also, decide on an appropriate style.

10 When you write, use contrasting language to highlight good and bad points or to point out the difference between your expectations and your actual experience.

11 When you have finished writing, read through your letter, checking grammar, spelling and punctuation, and style.

◀ WRITING GUIDE PAGE 162 ▶

Overview

1 Read the text below and look carefully at each line. Some of the lines are correct, and some have a word which should not be there. If a line is correct, put a tick (✓) in the space. If a line has a word that should not be there, write the word in the space. There are two examples.

Camping – dos and don'ts

0	You've finally arrived at your destination place and you're	_place_
00	looking for somewhere to set up your tent. So what should	✓
1	you be looking for? You need to look for a relatively high level	_____
2	ground, and, whatever you must do, never pitch your tent on	_____
3	a slope or you will find yourself rolling around out of your	_____
4	sleeping bag all night. Don't forget to check it that there is a	_____
5	water source nearby. Water is essential for camping: you'll	_____
6	need it for the drinking and cooking. You don't want to have	_____
7	to walk far with a twenty-litre container, do you? Find out	_____
8	a suitable area for cooking. Don't cook never in your tent.	_____
9	Locate a flat area away from some leaves, grass or twigs,	_____
10	which may catch fire. And never leave an unattended campfire	_____
11	burning. Another thing you must do is keep the campsite clean.	_____
12	After meals, wash the whole dishes, and put the rubbish	_____
13	in an appropriate place. Remember to follow the campsite	_____
14	rules, which they were made so that everyone can	_____
15	be enjoy the site. Leave it as you would like to find it yourself.	_____

2 Complete the sentences using a word from list A and a suitable prefix from list B. You may need to change the form of the words.

A charge   circle   date   day   freeze   wife

B anti   ex   mid   post   semi   under

a My brother is divorced, but he still gets on well with his _____.

b Can I give you a _____ cheque? There's no money in my bank account at the moment.

c The little children sat in a _____ while their teacher read them a story.

d The sun's at its hottest at _____.

e Winter's coming. I hope you've remembered to put _____ in your car.

f The waiter has _____ me. I only paid £10, but it should have been £15.

8 Media

Introduction

1 Work in pairs or small groups. Look at the photographs which show different modern media. Discuss these questions.

a How effective is each medium in communicating information and ideas?
b Do you use all these media?
c Which newspapers do you read?
d What are your favourite radio and TV programmes?

2 Read this extract from the novel *1984* by George Orwell. How does the author regard the media?

> The invention of print, however, made it easier to manipulate public opinion, and the film and the radio carried the process further. With the development of television, and the technical advance which made it possible to receive and transmit simultaneously on the same instrument, private life came to an end. Every citizen … could be kept for twenty-four hours a day under the eyes of the police … The possibility of enforcing not only complete obedience to the will of the State, but complete uniformity of opinion on all subjects, now existed for the first time.

3 Discuss these questions.

a Who controls the different media in your country?
b Do you think the media has the kind of influence or power that Orwell predicted when he wrote *1984*?

Listening

Lead in

1 Do you use the Internet? Make a list of things you can do on the Internet. You may be able to make use of some of these words and phrases.

chat room
to download
MP3
online
search engine
to surf
website

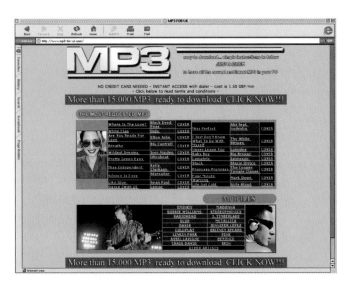

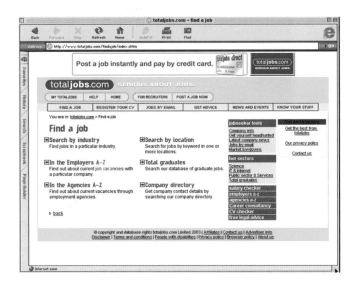

Multiple matching

2 🎧 You will hear five people talking about how they use the Internet. For questions 1–5, choose which main use A–F each speaker describes. Use the letters only once. There is one extra letter you do not need to use.

A as a way of contacting old friends

B as a source of up-to-date information

C as a way of making new friends

D as a source of free entertainment

E for keeping in touch with people

F for buying things unavailable from other places

Speaker 1	1
Speaker 2	2
Speaker 3	3
Speaker 4	4
Speaker 5	5

over to you

How do you think the Internet will develop during the next fifty years in relation to these areas?

• entertainment • work • money • politics • personal communications

What dangers or problems could be associated with these future developments?

Grammar and practice

Reporting statements

1 Read these reported statements. What words did the speakers actually use in each case?

  a My friends all said it was really easy to use.
  b Most of the music shops in town said they'd never even heard of the band.
  c I said I'd go and visit her next year if I could.
  d They say they're losing sales because people like me aren't buying as many CDs.

2 Answer these questions.

  a What usually happens to verb tenses in reported speech?
  b How is sentence 1d grammatically different from the other three sentences? How does this difference affect the meaning?

3 Report these statements made by some other people on the programme.

  a 'I've stopped getting a daily paper.'
  b 'I'm having regular chats with my older brother who's in Thailand.'
  c 'I've even met one of them who still lives quite near here.'

◄ GRAMMAR REFERENCE PAGE 184 ►

Reporting questions

4 Read these examples of reported questions. What other changes, in addition to verb tense changes, do we need to make when we report questions?

  a 'Have you got the CD in stock?'
    Mick asked if they had the CD in stock.
  b 'When did you order the new CD?'
    My friend asked me when I had ordered the CD.

5 When do we use *if* in reported questions? What other word could we use instead of *if* in 4a above?

6 Report these questions.

  a 'Are you on email?' the girl asked him.
  b 'Do you use the Internet?' Val asked Rob.
  c 'How long have you been interested in jazz?' Nick asked me.

  d 'Which of your old school friends did you contact, Sharon?' Rachel asked.
  e 'Would you like to contact people you were at school with?' Julie asked Tim.

◄ GRAMMAR REFERENCE PAGE 185 ►

Time references

7 The sentence below can be reported in two ways. What is the difference in meaning between sentence a and sentence b?

'I'll see you tomorrow,' Lizzie told Graham.

  a Lizzie told Graham she would see him *the next day*.
  b Lizzie told Graham she would see him *tomorrow*.

8 How could we change the following time references in reported speech?

last week   next month   next week
three days ago   today   tomorrow   yesterday

◄ GRAMMAR REFERENCE PAGE 185 ►

Other references

9 What other references may change when we report speech? Look at these examples.

  a 'Do you think this meat is all right?' Terry asked his wife.
    Terry asked his wife if she thought the meat was all right.
  b 'Shall we eat here?' Carol asked Denise.
    Carol asked Denise if they should eat there.

10 Report these sentences, making all necessary changes.

  a 'Does this work have to be finished today, Mr Hunt?' Marsha asked.
  b 'Were there any phone calls for me yesterday?' asked Mr Gilbert.
  c 'This car was stolen two weeks ago,' the police officer informed Ian.
  d 'I wrote to her last week, and I phoned this morning,' Dorothy said.
  e 'I've arranged to meet them after lunch tomorrow,' Matthew said.

11 Read sentences a–h and answer questions 1–4.

a She *told* Bob she was leaving the next day.
b She *told* Bob to leave her alone.
c She *asked* Bob why he had done it.
d She *asked* Bob to leave his keys.
e She *warned* Bob not to try and get in touch.
f Alan *advised* Bob to try and forget her.
g She *suggested* talking it over.
h They *suggested* that we should leave.

1 How is the structure after *tell* different in sentences a and b? What is the difference in meaning?
2 How is the structure after *ask* different in sentences c and d? What is the difference in meaning?
3 What structure is used after *warn* and *advise* in sentences e and f.
4 What structures can be used after *suggest*?

◄ GRAMMAR REFERENCE PAGE 186 ►

12 Rewrite sentences a–h above in direct speech.

Key word
transformations

13 Complete the second sentence so that it has a similar meaning to the first sentence, using the word given. Do not change the word given. You must use between two and five words, including the word given.

1 'You'd better not swim there. It's dangerous!' the man told us.
   warned
   The man _____ there because it was dangerous.

2 'I wouldn't buy Dave a book if I were you, Pete,' said Laura.
   advised
   Laura _____ Dave a book.

3 'Take that chewing gum out, Claire!' the teacher said.
   told
   The teacher _____ the chewing gum out of her mouth.

4 'Can you speak Spanish, John?' asked Marie.
   asked
   Marie _____ speak Spanish.

5 'I'll pick you up from work if you like, Tracy,' said Jason.
   offered
   Jason _____ from work.

6 'See you after class, Angie!' said Mike.
   said
   Mike _____ Angie after class.

Speaking

Lead in

1 How do you react to advertisements on television? Do you enjoy watching them? Do you change channel? Do you do something else while the adverts are on?

2 Can you think of a current TV advertisement which has particularly impressed you, perhaps because it is funny or shocking in some way?

Long turn

3 Work in pairs.

Student A   Compare and contrast advertisements 1 and 2 and say which of the two will attract more attention. Remember you have to speak for about one minute.

Student B   When your partner has finished speaking, answer this question: What do you think of large advertisements in the street?

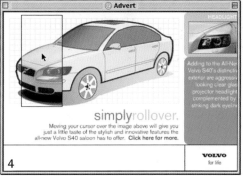

tip!

In Part 2 of the Speaking paper, when you are not talking, it is important to listen to what your partner is saying. You will be asked to make your own comment when your partner has finished speaking.

4 Work in pairs.

Student B   Compare and contrast advertisements 3 and 4 and say what you think the main purpose of advertisements is. Remember you have to speak for about one minute.

Student A   When your partner has finished speaking, answer this question: Have you ever been persuaded to buy anything by an advertisement?

over to you

Look at the four advertisements again.

What kind of person do you think each advertisement is appealing to?

What technique does each advertisement use to sell its product?

Vocabulary

Compound nouns

1 Many compound nouns are formed from these combinations:

two or more nouns
verb + preposition
preposition + verb

How are these compound nouns formed?

bookcase   breakdown   checkout   credit card   input   lunch-time   music shop

2 Underline six compound nouns in this text. How many of each type are there?

No news is good news

An American news editor once said, 'If news is not really news unless it is bad news, it may be difficult to claim we are an informed nation.' The stories below are from The Good News Network, which does not publish bad news.

- Miami's crime rate has fallen dramatically. In the past eight years, homicides, break-ins and assaults have been cut in half. Robberies of tourists have dropped 95%.

- 13.3 million teenage Americans donate time and effort to community service each week – a participation rate of almost 60%.

- Lake Tahoe is the clearest it's been in five years thanks to a $900 million clean-up organised by developers and environmentalists.

3 Use a noun from each list to make compound nouns which describe jobs.

computer	assistant
news	lecturer
shop	programmer
television	reader
university	reporter

4 Use a noun from each list to make compound nouns which are related to computers and the Internet.

disk	board
key	drive
mouse	engine
search	mat
web	site

5 Use a word from each list to make compound nouns with meanings a–e.

break	break	a	lipstick is an example of this
by	down	b	the sudden start of a disease or a war
make	off	c	when a plane leaves the ground
out	pass	d	a road which takes traffic round a town or city
take	up	e	failure of a marriage

6 Use a noun from each list to make compound nouns which are related to mobile phones.

key   book
mail   pad
phone   tone
ring   saver
screen   message
text   box

Word formation

7 Read the text below. Use the word given in capitals at the end of each line to form a word that fits in the space in the same line. There is an example at the beginning.

John Simpson – Still doing crazy things

Why should I, at an age when ⁰ _sensible_ people are starting to think   SENSE

about their ¹_____, want to go on doing crazy things? Why am I   . RETIRE

still standing on foreign pavements, arguing with gunmen and ²_____? RIOT

³_____ not because I have to. As the head of the BBC's foreign   CERTAIN

reporting, I can do what I want. I have a ⁴_____ office at Television   PLEASE

Centre, filled with producers and correspondents who are ⁵_____   PERSON

friends.

I could exist perfectly well on a diet of international summit ⁶_____,   MEET

conferences and ⁷_____. I could stay at decent hotels, eat at   ELECT

reasonable hours, plan my social life ⁸_____ and never again set   PROPER

foot in ⁹_____ parts of the world. I could also go mad. That kind   DANGER

of life – safe, ¹⁰_____ and easy – would bore me to death.   PREDICT

Exam techniques • READING PART 3

dos and don'ts

- Read the gapped text quickly. Think about what information might be missing and make a brief note in each space.
- Read all the missing paragraphs or sentences. Underline any reference words, such as names, pronouns or times.
- Match each paragraph or sentence with a space. Check your notes to identify topic links.
- Check that any reference words and other language connections fit in the context.
- Read the whole text to check that it makes sense.
- If you are not sure, make a sensible guess. Don't leave any spaces empty.

1   You are going to read a magazine article about people's TV viewing habits. Seven sentences have been removed from the article. Choose from the sentences A–H the one which fits each gap. There is one extra sentence which you do not need to use. There is an example at the beginning. Use the *Dos and Don'ts* above to help you.

A   They can be very stubborn, and they soon realise that the more stubborn they are, the more quickly they get their own way.

B   Women, on the other hand, are not as interested in physical control as in emotional control.

C   This television conflict is part of a bigger power game which goes on in homes, even though most of the players are unaware that they are playing a game at all.

D   In the end, maybe it doesn't matter who is the controller.

E   This is a video machine which watches you as you watch TV.

F   She quickly agrees before he realises that the only brochures she gave him were those for the South of France.

G   The big decisions, like where to live and which school to send the children to, are usually joint decisions.

H   Or, perhaps more importantly, who decides what you are going to watch next?

over to you

Who decides which TV programmes you and your family watch?

What are the advantages and disadvantages of having a large number of TV channels to choose from?

Do you think that television programmes can influence the way you behave or think?

So and such

2   What do these extracts from the article show about the use of *so* and *such*?

a   Many of them are *so* sensitive to non-verbal communication that they can pick up atmospheres.

b   It's *such* a subtle game, that many people don't even know they're playing it.

Imagine the scene. You and your family are relaxing after a hard day's work. You've just watched the news on TV. What are you going to watch next? | 0 | H | Whose finger is on the button? Deciding what to watch on TV is a battle of wills that is fought in homes all over the world. According to psychologists, it is much more serious than simply deciding between a soap opera and a sports programme, or between pop music and politics. | 1 | The game is called 'Who's Boss?'

'It's such a subtle game,' says psychologist Dr David Lewis, 'that many people don't even know they're playing it. It's all about the balance of power in the home and who's in control. Unconsciously, people begin to play the game as soon as they meet their future husband or wife. By the time the couple get married, the rules of the game are already well-established. | 2 | When it comes to less important things, like deciding

WHOSE FINGER IS ON THE BUTTON?

where to go on holiday or what sort of car to buy, it's a different matter. Here's just one example of this process at work. He looks through a pile of holiday brochures and announces his preference: 'The South of France'. | 3 | Similarly, she may decide what time the children should go to bed and on how the home should be decorated, but he chooses the new car and decides what the family does at weekends.

'Family power struggles are fascinating,' says Dr Lewis. 'Of course, some people are naturally more dominant than others, and the most dominant personality in a family tries to lead. These days, even though so many couples make a conscious effort to have a true and equal partnership, men generally have a greater need to appear to be in physical control. | 4 | On the whole, they're more manipulative and can make the man think something was his idea in the first place.'

The tussle over what to watch on TV is a good example of this fight for control. Recently, research psychologists persuaded 400 families to have a 'C-Box' installed in their living rooms. | 5 | They found that 80% of the time it was the man in the house who had his finger first on the button, followed by the eldest child, then the youngest child and only then the woman of the house. 'A child with a strong personality can totally dominate a family,' says Dr Lewis. 'Most kids are far less innocent, far more knowing than their parents realise. Many of them are so sensitive to non-verbal communication that they can pick up atmospheres and sense the strengths and weaknesses of the adults around them. | 6 | When the 'C-Box' was used to study groups of children on their own watching television, the researchers found that the children who had the remote control liked to show off their power by irritating everyone and changing channels every two or three minutes.'

So, next time you've got your finger on the button ready to zap the rest of the family with your assertiveness, think about the power game you're playing.

3 Which of these words and phrases can follow *so* and which can follow *such*?

a lot of people   few cars   hot weather   little insects
little time   many people   much money   tall trees

4 Complete these sentences with *so* or *such*.
   a That programme was _____ exciting that I couldn't get to sleep afterwards.
   b I'd no idea that it was _____ an interesting film.
   c I've never seen _____ few people in town.
   d Why are you behaving _____ aggressively?
   e _____ a lot of daytime TV programmes are cheap and badly made.

Writing

Discursive composition

1 Read this Part 2 composition task and answer the questions.

a How should a composition like this start and finish?

b What do you think is the best way of answering this kind of question – by agreeing, by disagreeing or by giving both sides of the argument?

c What is an appropriate style for this composition?

> Your teacher has asked you to write a composition giving your opinion on the following statement.
>
> *Newspapers should be allowed to reveal secrets about the private lives of famous people.*
>
> Write your composition in 120–180 words.

2 Read this discursive composition, ignoring the gaps. Then, answer these questions.

a What is the purpose of each of the four paragraphs?

b What are the main points made in the second and third paragraphs?

c Where are the writer's opinions expressed?

d Is the style appropriate?

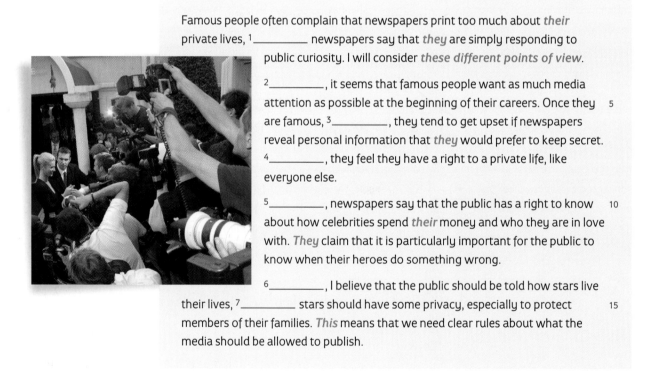

Famous people often complain that newspapers print too much about *their* private lives, ¹_____ newspapers say that *they* are simply responding to public curiosity. I will consider *these different points of view*.

²_____, it seems that famous people want as much media attention as possible at the beginning of their careers. Once they 5 are famous, ³_____, they tend to get upset if newspapers reveal personal information that *they* would prefer to keep secret. ⁴_____, they feel they have a right to a private life, like everyone else.

⁵_____, newspapers say that the public has a right to know 10 about how celebrities spend *their* money and who they are in love with. *They* claim that it is particularly important for the public to know when their heroes do something wrong.

⁶_____, I believe that the public should be told how stars live their lives, ⁷_____ stars should have some privacy, especially to protect 15 members of their families. *This* means that we need clear rules about what the media should be allowed to publish.

Connecting ideas

3 Complete the composition using appropriate words and phrases from this list. More than one answer may be possible.

although   however   in fact   on balance
on the one hand   on the other hand   whereas

4　Match each phrase in the list below with its purpose a, b or c.

a　to introduce additional information
b　to introduce information which contrasts with what has gone before
c　to summarise or conclude an argument

apart from that　　as well as (that)　　besides (this)　　in conclusion
by contrast　　furthermore　　in short　　nevertheless　　on the contrary
on the whole　　to conclude　　to summarise　　to sum up　　what is more

5　What do the phrases in italic in the discursive composition refer to?

EXAMPLE　*their* refers to famous people (line 1)

Think, plan, write

6　You are going to write a composition. First, read the task.

a　What is your first reaction to the statement about advertising?
b　Would you prefer to write only your own opinions on the subject or both sides of the argument?

> Your teacher has asked you to write a composition discussing the following statement:
> *There should be a complete ban on the advertising of dangerous products like cigarettes and alcohol.*
> Write your composition in 120–180 words.

7　Before you write, think about the topic. Discuss some of these questions in pairs.

Do you agree that cigarettes and alcohol are 'dangerous products'?
Where are cigarettes and alcohol currently advertised? Who is influenced by these adverts?
Why do some people want a 'complete ban'? Would such a ban be effective? Would it discourage people from smoking or drinking?

8　Make a list of two or three points on each side of the argument:

In favour of a ban	Against a ban
_____	_____
_____	_____
_____	_____

9　Plan the content of each paragraph, using the sample answer opposite as a model. Use connecting words and expressions to link ideas between sentences and paragraphs.

10　When you write, don't forget to check that you have answered the question in full. Make sure the style is appropriate.

11　Finally, when you have finished, check your grammar, spelling and punctuation.

◀ WRITING GUIDE PAGE 167 ▶

1 Read the text below. Use the word given in capitals at the end of each line to form a word that fits in the space in the same line. There is an example at the beginning.

Cybercafé dangers

In a typical week, teenagers, 0 _travelling_ professionals and tourists TRAVEL

are in 1_____ for one of the computer terminals at a twenty-four-hour COMPETE

cybercafé in New York's Times Square. The café is 2_____ booked FULL

every evening.

Cybercafés like this are a 3_____ to many people because they CONVENIENT

provide food and drink as well as Net access. But in 4_____ to ADD

people without home computers, cybercafés could be 5_____ to ATTRACT

all sorts of 6_____. Like public telephones, cybercafés are CRIME

open to anyone, without the need for any kind of 7_____. REGISTER

With thousands of customers 8_____ cafés like this every day, VISIT

law-breakers could 9_____ go unnoticed. Although some cafés ask EASY

for photo 10_____ before customers can log on, others don't. IDENTIFY

2 Rewrite this conversation in reported speech. Use the reporting verbs in brackets.

Jayne   I'm going on holiday tomorrow. (say)
Ben   Are you going anywhere special? (ask)
Jayne   Yes, Australia. We'll be staying in Perth for a week and then going on to Sydney. (reply)
Ben   Who are you going with? (ask)
Jayne   With two of my friends from work. (reply)

3 Rewrite these sentences in direct speech.

a Ben said he'd always wanted to go to Australia.
b Jayne asked him if he'd like to go with them.
c Ben replied that he certainly would.
d Jayne said she'd see if there were any places left on the flight.
e Ben said he wasn't sure if he could afford it.
f Jayne offered to lend him the money.

4 Complete these sentences with *so* or *such*.

a There's _____ little time left – we'll really have to hurry.
b I don't know how people can drive _____ fast in the rain.
c I can't remember when we last had _____ cold weather
d That was _____ a difficult exam. I'm sure I haven't passed.
e But you've worked _____ hard – I'm sure you'll be OK.

9 Around us

Introduction

1 Work in pairs or small groups. Discuss these questions. Photographs 1 and 2 show two kinds of extreme weather – extreme cold and extreme heat.

   a   How can extreme weather like this affect people's lives?

   b   What kind of weather do you most dislike and why?

2 Photographs 3 and 4 show two types of natural disaster – flooding and a forest fire.

   a   Which of the two do you think would affect more people? Why?

   b   What safety measures can people take to avoid natural disasters like these?

Reading

Think ahead

1 Answer these questions about volcanoes. Guess if you don't know.

a Approximately how many active volcanoes are there in the world?
   1 150   2 550   3 1,350

b How many people live in the vicinity of an active volcano?
   1 1 million   2 10 million   3 1 billion

c Where is the world's largest active volcano?
   1 Italy   2 Hawaii   3 Mexico

2 Read the text quickly to check your ideas.

They died where they stood. Violently, with almost no warning. Wealthy women in their jewels. Armed soldiers. Babies. Almost 2,000 years ago a seaside town in southern Italy had the misfortune to be in the shadow of Mount Vesuvius – one of Europe's active volcanoes – at the wrong time.
5 The 16,000 inhabitants of the Roman towns of Herculaneum and neighbouring Pompeii who were buried beneath 30 metres of dust on an August night in AD 79 bear silent witness to the destructive force of volcanoes.

Objects of terror and fascination since the beginning of human time,
10 volcanoes take their name from Vulcan, the Roman god of fire. Today there are some 1,350 active volcanoes in the world. At any given moment, somewhere between one dozen and two dozen are throwing out ash and molten rock from the earth's core.

Approximately one billion people live in their dangerous shadows.
15 Experts expect the number to rise. The rapid growth of population, greater competition for land and an increase in urban migration are driving more and more people to settle around volcanoes, significantly increasing the potential loss of life and property in the event of eruptions.

20 Despite major advances in technology, the ability to predict when a volcano might erupt remains imprecise. But meeting the challenge is vital because volcanoes are 'people magnets.' A recent study identified 457 volcanoes where there are one million or more people living within 100 kilometres. Many of these volcanoes – several in Indonesia
25 and Japan, for instance – have surrounding populations greatly exceeding one million. Today, 3.75 million people live within 30 kilometres of the summit of Mount Vesuvius in the southern Italian city of Naples. 'What do they do if it starts erupting? No one can imagine evacuating a city the size of Naples,' said
30 C Dan Miller, chief of the US Geological Survey's Volcano Disaster Assistance Program.

'Persuading people to move permanently out of hazard zones is not usually an
35 option. Many of the land-use patterns are long established, and people just won't do it,' Miller went on. 'The only thing you can do is have systematic volcano monitoring to detect the earliest departure from normal activity.'

Nowadays it is easier to predict volcanic activity, 40 but evaluating the threat of eruption is frequently still difficult. Mexico City knows the problem well. The city, which has a population of more than twenty million, lies within 60 kilometres of the summit of Popocatepetl, a volcano which has 45 erupted at least fifteen times in the last 400 years. The flanks and valleys surrounding 'Popo' have been evacuated several times since 1994 in response to earthquakes and eruptions of volcanic ash and plumes of steam. Each time the mountain 50 has settled down without a major eruption, although some activity has continued. Yet when, or if, a major eruption will occur next remains unknown.

'There could be weeks, months, or years between the time a volcano shows some activity and the time of 55 its eruption,' said Miller. 'It may never erupt. Most people are willing to be evacuated once. But if nothing happens, the loss of credibility could cause people to ignore future warnings.'

Volcanic eruptions, when they do come, are 60 sometimes relatively slow and quiet. There was no loss of life when the world's largest active volcano erupted in 1984. The people who lived in the proximity of Hawaii's Mauna Loa volcano had plenty of time to get out of the way when it erupted in 65 1984. Its lava crept down the slope at about the speed of honey. At other times the eruption is sudden and violent, and evacuation unfortunately comes too late.

Multiple choice

3 Read questions 1–7 below. Then, read the article again and choose the correct answers.

1 What happened when Mount Vesuvius erupted in AD 79?
   A The rich managed to escape.
   B It covered many towns with dust.
   C A few people were killed.
   D People were unprepared.

2 What do experts think will happen in the future?
   A More volcanoes will become active.
   B People will move away from volcanic areas.
   C More people will set up home near volcanoes.
   D Around one billion people will die in volcanic eruptions.

3 According to the article, what is the present situation regarding volcanic eruptions?
   A Eruptions are most likely to happen in Indonesia and Japan.
   B Experts can predict when there will be a volcanic eruption.
   C Most large cities have no appropriate evacuation plans in place.
   D People will be less affected than before.

4 What does 'do it' in line 37 refer to?
   A go and live somewhere else
   B build farms on the land
   C force people to leave the area
   D leave the area until the danger has passed

5 What does the article say about Popocatepetl?
   A There was a major eruption in 1994.
   B Experts expect a major eruption within a few years.
   C Nobody knows whether it will erupt again.
   D People who live nearby are fed up with being evacuated.

6 Why was the eruption of Mauna Loa less dangerous?
   A People had been evacuated from the area beforehand.
   B People were able to keep ahead of the lava.
   C Scientists had warned people well in advance.
   D It was not a major eruption.

7 What would be the most appropriate title for this article?
   A Volcanoes: Sleeping threat for millions.
   B Volcanic eruptions and other natural disasters.
   C Volcanic activity in Italy.
   D Volcanic eruption: A study of volcanic behaviour.

over to you
Why do people choose to live near volcanoes? Would you?

Why would it be so difficult to evacuate a large city? Can you think of any solutions to the problems?

Word-building

4 Underline all the nouns in the text related to these root verbs. What do they have in common?

compete   erupt   evacuate
fascinate   populate   migrate

5 Underline all the adjectives in the text related to these root verbs and nouns.

act danger destroy system volcano

6 Complete these sentences with an appropriate word made from the root word in brackets.

a A great deal of _____ research is being carried out on volcanoes. (science)
b It is _____ to play golf during a thunderstorm. (danger)
c The early nineteenth century was a period of mass _____ from Ireland. (migrate)
d The police made a _____ search of the area where the crime was committed. (system)
e I have never really understood the _____ some people have for tornadoes. (fascinate)
f The _____ of Western European countries is ageing. (populate)
g Despite the fact that he is in his eighties, he still leads an _____ life. (act)
h There was fierce _____ between the companies for the government contract. (compete)

Grammar and practice

Relative clauses

1 Complete these sentences from the article with the relative pronouns *who*, *which*, *that*, or *whose*. Give as many alternatives for each answer as you can. Then, check your ideas with the article.

a The city, _____ has a population of more than twenty million, lies within 60 kilometres of the summit of Popocatepetl, a volcano _____ has erupted at least fifteen times in the last 400 years.

b The people _____ lived in the proximity of Hawaii's Mauna Loa volcano had plenty of time to get out of the way when it erupted in 1984.

2 Look at these two sentences. In which sentence does the speaker have one sister? In which sentence does the speaker have more than one sister?

a My sister who lives in Mexico has two children.
b My sister, who lives in Mexico, has two children.

In which sentence is the information in the relative clause essential?

3 Decide whether the relative clauses in the following sentences are defining (they contain essential information) or non-defining (they contain non-essential information). If the clause is non-defining, add commas.

a Scientists who study volcanic activity are known as vulcanologists.
b Vulcanologists who study volcanic activity are often able to warn of possible volcanic eruption.
c Lava which is the hot molten rock emitted from a volcano when it erupts is not necessarily the most dangerous thing associated with a volcano.
d One of the worst things is volcanic ash which can be carried on the wind for thousands of kilometres.
e Dozens of planes which have flown through clouds of ash have crashed or suffered serious damage.
f Not all countries whose inhabitants are at risk from volcanic eruption are able to carry out large-scale evacuation.

4 Which of the relative pronouns in 3 can be replaced by other relative pronouns?

◀ GRAMMAR REFERENCE PAGE 186 ▶

5 Relative clauses can also be introduced by *why*, *where*, and *when*. Complete these sentences with one of these words, adding commas where necessary.

a Bushfires are natural phenomena particularly common in Australia, but which also occur in many places around the world _____ there are plenty of forests that can burn.

b The Northern Territory is most at risk of bushfires at the end of the dry season in September and October _____ temperatures have risen but monsoon rains have not yet arrived.

c The reason _____ most bushfires start is because people are negligent or start them deliberately.

Can the relative pronoun be left out in any of these sentences?

6 Look at the following pairs of sentences. What are the differences between the two sentences in each pair? What rules can you work out?

a That's the man to whom I spoke.
That's the man who I spoke to.

b The speaker, about whom I'd heard so much, gave an extremely interesting talk.
The speaker, who I'd heard so much about, gave an extremely interesting talk.

◄ GRAMMAR REFERENCE PAGE 187 ►

7 Complete the following sentences with relative pronouns. Indicate where there is more than one possibility and add commas if necessary.

a I don't like people _____ are big-headed.
b Have you seen the awful jacket _____ Sophie's bought?
c She wanted to know the reason _____ I had turned down her invitation.
d We were unable to get tickets for the group's Wembley concert _____ was a sell-out.
e They have designed a microwave _____ can defrost a frozen chicken in just ten seconds.
f We went back to look at the house _____ we used to live.
g Nicole Kidman _____ latest film was shot in LA has said she'd like to work in the theatre again.
h The book was returned to the person _____ name was inside.
i The number _____ you are dialling is out of order.
j I prefer to go to Greece in winter _____ there are fewer tourists about.

Cloze

8 Read the text below and think of the word which best fits each space. Use only one word in each space.

THE GREAT PLAINS BLEW AWAY

For many centuries, the Great Plains of the American West, [1]_____ the buffalo roamed, sustained the way of life of native American hunters. In the late nineteenth century, both buffaloes and Indians were driven out [2]_____ white settlers. At first they grazed cattle on the land, which did not have a negative effect [3]_____ the ecology of the region. But at the beginning of the twentieth century, crop-growing farmers moved in. The grass [4]_____ dug up, and wheat and [5]_____ crops were planted. In the 1930s there was a succession of droughts in the region. Crops were ruined and the soil, [6]_____ longer anchored by the root system of the original grass and baked by temperatures [7]_____ often rose above 38°C, simply blew away. Many thousands of farmers lost [8]_____ farms, and with their families went west in search [9]_____ work. Many headed to California, only to find that they were [10]_____ welcome there. The government of the time [11]_____ nothing to help the migrants. [12]_____, it agreed to pay a subsidy to the farmers [13]_____ had remained to plant trees and grass to anchor the soil. In [14]_____ of these measures, another severe drought in the 1950s caused huge dust storms once again. This time the government was persuaded to pay out even more in subsidies [15]_____ that millions of acres could be converted back into grassland.

Speaking

Lead in

1 Name five activities people do which harm the environment.

2 Compare your answers with a partner. Then, put the activities in order from the most harmful to the least harmful.

Two-way task

3 Work in pairs. Imagine that you have been asked to organise a project in your school about how people can improve the environment. Talk to each other about how each of the activities in the photos affects the environment, and say which two activities would be the easiest to avoid doing.

Discussion

4 Discuss these questions.
   a Which environmental issue do you think is the most important? Why?
   b Which environmental issue concerns people most where you live?
   c What has the government of your country or your local council done to improve the environment? What should they do?
   d Noise pollution is an issue that affects many people today. What are the main causes, and what can be done about it?

Vocabulary

Lead in

1 What is the weather like in different regions of your country at different times of the year?

2 Has the climate of your country changed in the last five to ten years?

3 What does this extract say is to blame for climatic changes?

In recent years the greenhouse effect has become the focus of large-scale scientific investigation. There is growing evidence that past emissions of greenhouse gases (carbon dioxide, chlorofluorocarbons and nitrous oxide) could already be altering the earth's weather patterns and temperatures. Average global temperatures are steadily increasing, and if this trend continues the consequences for our planet could be disastrous. Carbon dioxide is believed to be responsible for approximately half of global warming. Tropical deforestation also leads to global warming by destroying one of the earth's only ways of absorbing excess atmospheric carbon.

Dependent prepositions

4 Certain nouns, adjectives and verbs are followed by particular prepositions. Look back at the extract above and find out which preposition follows *consequences*, *responsible* and *leads*.

5 Match these nouns with the correct prepositions. Then, complete the sentences with a noun and a preposition.

noun			preposition	
agreement	cure	respect	at	on
anger	damage	tax	for	to
ban	effect	threat		

a Many of our medicines come from plants that grow in rainforests. Perhaps someday the _____ cancer will be found in a tropical rainforest.

b Deforestation poses a serious _____ indigenous peoples, as well as to the climate.

c Environmentalists warn that unless people show more _____ the environment, humankind will pay a heavy price.

d In many countries the government _____ leaded fuel is higher than that on unleaded fuel.

6 Choose the correct preposition which follows these adjectives.

a Environmentalist groups in Britain are opposed *against/to* new road-building projects. They argue that they are harmful *for/to* the environment, often destroying plant and animal habitats.

b Environmentalists warn that unless governments become more aware *of/to* the effects of their actions, the world we leave our children will be very different *to/with* the world we know today.

c Everyone is capable *of/to* making lifestyle changes which would be beneficial *to/in* the environment. Walking or cycling to work is much better *for/to* you than taking the car.

d Although only comprising 7% of the global population, the USA is responsible *for/to* 22% of all greenhouse gas emissions.

7 Match these verbs with the correct prepositions.

verb			preposition	
appeal	contribute	invest	in	on
believe	depend	sympathise	to	with
complain	insist	result	about	

8 Match these sentence beginnings a–e with their endings 1–5, adding the correct appropriate preposition.

a In all of nature, but particularly in rainforests, plants and animals depend

b Logging for tropical timber and gold mining have contributed

c Local councils need to invest more money

d It's no good complaining

e I sympathise

1 _____ recycling schemes.

2 _____ pollution. You have to be prepared to do something about it.

3 _____ each other for survival.

4 _____ people who live near big airports.

5 _____ the destruction of the tropical rainforest, though they are not the only factors involved.

dos and don'ts

- For each sentence you have to rewrite, read the first sentence and the gapped sentence.
- Think carefully about how the key word can be used grammatically in the gapped sentence. Consider, for example, whether it needs a dependent preposition, whether you need to change the form of another word, or whether the second sentence should be active or passive.
- Complete each sentence using between two and five words. Don't change the key word.

1 Complete the second sentence so that it has a similar meaning to the first sentence, using the word given. You must use between **two** and **five** words, including the word given. You must not change the word given. Use the *Dos and Don'ts* above to help you.

EXAMPLE   *0 Many plant species will probably become extinct in the coming years.*
   likely
   Many plant species <u>are likely to</u> become extinct in the coming years.

1   Cars are banned from the city centre.
   ban
   There _____ in the city centre.

2   A holiday in Florida is cheaper than one in California.
   as
   A holiday in Florida is _____ one in California.

3   The last time I saw Alex was at Jade's party.
   since
   I _____ Jade's party.

4   My brother was always on time until he got friendly with Jack.
   used
   My brother never _____ until he got friendly with Jack.

5   Many people are sorry that they ever started to smoke.
   up
   Many people regret _____ .

6   The film was so boring that I fell asleep half way through it.
   such
   It was _____ that I fell asleep half way through it.

7   That athlete is good enough to win the gold medal.
   capable
   That athlete _____ the gold medal.

8   They've postponed the wedding until the spring.
   put
   The wedding _____ until the spring.

9   Not understanding what they were talking about, he said nothing.
   understand
   He said nothing _____ what they were talking about.

10 His mother suggested he got his hair cut before he went for the interview.
   advised
   His mother _____ his hair cut before he went for the interview.

Listening

Think ahead

1 Discuss these questions in pairs.

What are holiday resorts in your country like?
Do you prefer going on package holidays or travelling independently?

2 What positive and negative effects can tourism have on a country?

Multiple choice

3 🎧 You will hear part of a radio programme about tourism. Are any of your ideas about the positive and negative effects of tourism mentioned?

4 🎧 Listen again. For questions 1–7, choose the best answer A, B or C.

1 By the year 2015, it is estimated that the number of people working in the tourist industry will be
   A four times the present number.
   B twice as many as now.
   C similar to today's numbers.

2 Jeremy Allen is interested in the effects of tourism on
   A all countries.
   B western countries.
   C developing countries.

3 What do hotel restaurants often do?
   A buy their food from abroad
   B pay local farmers less than they should
   C employ foreign waiters

4 Hotel gift shops often sell items
   A made from local materials.
   B made in other countries.
   C produced by local people.

5 People are often moved out of their homes so that
   A more tourist accommodation can be provided.
   B native tribespeople can be given homes.
   C more safari parks can be opened.

6 Jeremy Allen says that in order to improve the situation people should
   A go on package holidays.
   B go on organised tours.
   C go to less well-known places.

7 According to Jeremy Allen, if you see a wild animal you shouldn't
   A photograph it.   B run after it.   C feed it.

over to you

Do you think visitors to your country have a positive or negative effect on the economy, culture and environment?

What changes would you make to the tourist industry in your country?

Writing

Informal letter

1 Read this Part 1 task and answer the questions.
  a How should the letter to your friend begin and end?
  b Should the letter be written in a formal or informal style?

> A British friend has sent you a letter asking you to go on holiday with them. They have also included a newspaper cutting about the holiday. Read the letter, the newspaper cutting and the notes you have made. Then, using the information in your notes, write a suitable reply to your friend in 120–180 words.

Would you like to come with me? **Yes!**
I don't really fancy going on my own! We could go this summer **When?**
instead of having a beach holiday. Anyway, I'm sending a copy of the cutting so you can read all about it.

How long for?

What other projects? Can you choose?

How basic? Toilet?

How much?

NEPAL

Location: Kankali Village, Nepal

Project: NKV 502 Rural Community Development programme.

Dates: various

Duration: 14 or 21 days

Work: At Kankali you will have the unique opportunity to assist the local community in developing various projects to help tourism in the area, such as making a trekking trail and building picnic areas.

Accommodation: This will be with local families, who will provide traditional Nepalese food. Facilities are very basic.

Leisure: At the end of the holiday, volunteers can spend some time trekking on the Annapurna trail. All activities are included in the holiday price, but you will need to cover the costs of food and drink on your days off.

Asking for information

2 Read the handwritten notes and write out the direct questions in full. For example: *When do you want to go?*

3 Write the questions in an indirect form, starting with an appropriate phrase given below.
  a You didn't say … *when you wanted to go.*
  b Can/Could you find out …
  c I'd like to know/Do you know …
  d Can/Could you tell me…

Dear Sam,

Thanks for your letter. It was really great to hear from you. I'm glad everyone is well.

In answer to your question, I'd love to go. The holiday sounds very interesting and would certainly be a change from the beach! I've heard Nepal is a fascinating place! 1_____. I assume it'd be July or August. August would suit me better, but I could go in July. I notice you can go for two weeks or three weeks. 2_____. I don't mind if it's the same price. Which brings me to the most important question – MONEY– 3_____.

One or two other things. 4_____ and whether you can choose what you do. I'm not very good at building things! 5_____. (Is there a toilet?)

Anyway, write back when you've got more information.

Best wishes,
George

4 Read this letter, which is a good answer to the question, and complete the text with a mixture of appropriate direct and indirect questions.

5 Use these prompts to make direct questions. Then put them into an indirect form.
a Where exactly / Kankali village?
b How far / from airport?
c Holidays like this all year round?
d What sort / clothes should / bring?
e How long can you stay / Nepal / end of the holiday?

Think, plan, write

6 You are going to write a letter. First read the task and underline all the key information or questions you must include in your answer.

> You have received a letter from your friend, Sam. Read the letter and your notes. Then, write to Maria, asking for information about the holiday in Nepal. Write 120–180 words.

Dear George,

After I got your letter, I remembered that Maria went to Nepal last year – in fact, to the same village – Kankali. You remember Maria, don't you? ———— Of course!

I was thinking that we would get much more useful information from her than from the people that organise the holidays. Could you drop her a line? You always got on with her much better than me. What I'd like to know is:

How old are the other volunteers?
Is it hard work?
Do you need to be a good walker to do the Annapurna trail?

Send her my best wishes, and obviously ask any questions of your own. ———— I want to know about the food, what clothes to take, if it's worth going.

Sam

7 Plan the content of your letter. Here is a possible paragraph plan.
Paragraph 1   Remind Maria who you are, tell her some news about yourself and ask how she is.
Paragraph 2   Tell Maria why you are writing.
Paragraph 3   Ask her what you want to know. Remember to use a mixture of direct and indirect questions.

8 Finally, when you have finished, check your grammar, spelling and punctuation. Make sure that you haven't missed anything out and that your letter sounds friendly.

◄ WRITING GUIDE PAGE 164 ►

Overview

1 Complete these paragraphs with the appropriate relative pronouns, adding any necessary commas.

Mount Vesuvius ¹_____ is situated near the Bay of Naples is one of the world's most famous active volcanoes. The Romans ²_____ believed it to be extinct built the city of Pompeii in its shadow. The violent eruption ³_____ took place in AD 79 proved them wrong.

The eruption ⁴_____ happened when no one was expecting it has gone down as one of the worst in recorded history. It happened during the daytime ⁵_____ people were going about their daily lives.

The remains of the 2,000 inhabitants of Pompeii ⁶_____ did not escape lay forgotten for centuries. When excavation began in the eighteenth century, the remains were found of a much-loved family dog ⁷_____ collar bore an inscription saying that he twice saved his owner's life.

2 Complete the second sentence so that it has a similar meaning to the first sentence, using the word given. Do not change the word given. You must use between two and five words, including the word given.

1 Swimming in that river is dangerous.
   safe
   It _____ in that river.
2 The police searched for clues.
   search
   A _____ by the police.
3 Although he's ninety, he still drives.
   despite
   He still drives _____ .
4 I can't understand why he is fascinated by snakes.
   fascination
   I can't understand _____ snakes.
5 They have spent a lot of time and money on the project.
   deal
   A _____ time and money has been spent on the project.

3 Complete these sentences with an appropriate preposition.

a Do you believe _____ ghosts?
b Are you any good _____ maths? Could you help me with these problems?
c His flat is similar _____ mine.
d Some people are afraid _____ heights. Personally, I'm scared _____ the dark.
e That singer appeals _____ teenagers and over-fifties alike.
f Jamie insisted _____ helping me clear up after the party.

Innovation

Introduction

1 Work in pairs or small groups. Look at these photographs of everyday objects. What are they being used for? What was their original use?

2 Are there any objects that you use for something other than the original use?

3 How many different uses can you think of for each of these objects?

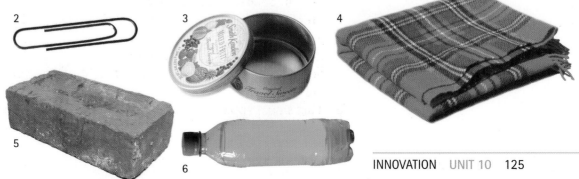

Reading

Lead in

1 You are going to read an article about people's attitudes to inventions. Look at the list of inventions below. Do you think people will put them in their favourite or their least favourite lists?

the motor car   the radio   nuclear power   the bicycle   the mobile phone
the printing press   the television   the plastic bag   the landmine

2 Read the text and check your ideas. Which invention is not mentioned?

3 _____
Another survey carried out by the Fuji Research Institute in
20 Japan, in which 2,000 adults in the Tokyo region were asked
to rate the ten greatest inventions of the twentieth century,
placed instant noodles, an 'invention' from 1958, at the top
of their list. Instant noodles have been commercially
produced since 1971 with almost fifty billion cups now
25 consumed worldwide each year.

4 _____
Nonetheless, it seems astounding that in the country which
is a world leader in technology a food product should be
voted ahead of personal stereos, video games, CDs and
cameras, which came third, fourth, fifth and sixth. Also
30 interesting is the fact that the motor car was not ranked at
all, possibly because it was invented overseas. Incidentally,
karaoke was in second place.

INVENTIONS: THE TOP TEN?

0 _H_
Inventions have been around for as long as we have. Some
have had a dramatic impact on the world we live in and on
our way of life; others have simply made life that little bit
easier. Most have influenced our lives in a positive way, but
5 some, it has to be said, have been anything but beneficial.

1 _____
According to a recent survey carried out by a British radio
station into what their listeners' ten favourite and ten least
favourite inventions were, the bicycle came top of the
favourites list, though it was felt that voting had been
10 unfairly influenced by members of a cycling organisation.
Radio, perhaps not surprisingly, came out second top of the
list of favourite inventions, followed closely by the computer.

2 _____
Heading the list of least favourite inventions were atomic and
nuclear weapons, with landmines coming in at second place
15 and the humble plastic bag coming third. Other inventions
which featured in this dislike list were mobile phones, car
alarms and speed cameras. The internal combustion engine
entered both lists but was more disliked than liked.

5 _____
The question 'What's the most important invention in the
past 2,000 years?' was also presented to a gathering of
35 Nobel prize winners and other serious thinkers recently.
Although there was some disagreement as to what
constituted an invention, there were a couple of clear
winners. The printing press was chosen above any other
invention. Johannes Gutenberg's invention of movable type
40 in the fifteenth century had a huge impact on the spread of
information, with his amazing invention allowing every
family to afford books and learn to read.

6 _____
Disagreement over what is the most important or the best or
worst invention only goes to prove that it is a matter of
45 personal choice and perspective. One man's meat is another
man's poison. The classic example is nuclear power. A cheap
and 'clean' source of power in the conventional sense, it also
has drawbacks: in the wrong hands it could be responsible
for wiping out the world as we know it. The combustion
50 engine is the same. Environmentalists would say that it is
responsible for more deaths and pollution than any other
invention in the last 1,000 years and wish that it had never
been invented. But many of us would overlook this for the
simple fact that we wouldn't want to live without our cars.

126 UNIT 10 INNOVATION

3 The headings A–H below have been removed from the article you have just read. Read the article again more carefully and put the headings back in the correct place. There is an example and an extra sentence.

A Unpopular choices
B No one likes this
C Surprisingly not so popular
D Accurate results?
E Advantages and disadvantages
F A tasty choice
G The expert's opinion
H Large and small breakthroughs

over to you What are your top three favourite inventions?

What do you think is the worst invention ever?

Phrasal verbs with *carry* 4 Match these beginnings a–e with their endings 1–5.

a A British radio station carried
b The sound of the sea always carries me
c When she goes to the sales, she gets so carried
d Don't stop for my sake. Just carry
e Her courage carried her

1 on with what you were doing.
2 out a survey into their listeners' favourite and least favourite inventions.
3 through a difficult time.
4 back to when I was a child and spent summer holidays at the seaside.
5 away that she buys more than she needs.

5 Complete these sentences with the correct form of *carry* and a word from this list.

away   back   on   out   through

a The police are going to _____ an investigation into the incident.
b When the teacher asked the students to pay attention, some of them _____ talking.
c Some people get _____ at Christmas and spend more than they can afford.
d The money she lent me will _____ me _____ to the end of the month when I get paid.
e That song _____ me _____ to when I was a teenager and had my first real date.

Grammar and practice

Wishes and regrets

1 We use *wish* to talk about situations we would like to change but can't. Decide whether the following sentences refer to a present or future situation, or a past situation. What do you notice about the verb tenses after *wish*?

   a Environmentalists wish that the car had never been invented.

   b I wish I could fly.

   c I wish I was/were more imaginative.

2 We also use *wish* to refer to someone else's habits or intentions which we would like to change. These wishes can express impatience and irritation, or simply regret. What do you notice about the verb tenses after *wish* in these sentences?

   a I wish someone would invent something for opening champagne bottles more easily.

   b I wish you wouldn't keep interrupting me.

3 Which of these sentences expresses the stronger regret?

   a I wish I had patented my idea.

   b If only I had patented my idea.

4 Answer these questions using *wish*.

   a What things would you like to change about your appearance, your job, your home, etc.?

   b What things would you like to be able to change about something in the past?

   c What things would you like to change about someone else's behaviour?

◀ GRAMMAR REFERENCE PAGE 188 ▶

5 Complete each of these sentences so that it has a similar meaning to the first sentence. Use up to five words including the word you are given. Do not change this word.

   1 Unfortunately, I haven't got enough money to go on holiday this year.
      afford
      I wish _____ on holiday this year.

   2 You never clean the bath when you've finished!
      wish
      I _____ the bath when you've finished!

   3 Pete regrets forgetting to send Sally a Valentine card.
      remembered
      Pete wishes _____ Sally a Valentine card.

   4 'It wasn't a good idea to go to bed so late,' said Justin, yawning.
      earlier
      'I wish I _____,' said Justin, yawning.

   5 'I'd love to be the same height as my sister,' said Jodie enviously.
      tall
      Jodie wishes _____ her sister.

   6 I regret telling John.
      only
      If _____ John.

I'd rather and It's time ...

6 In these sentences, how is the verb tense different when the speaker is expressing a preference about their own action and when they are expressing a preference about somebody else's action?

   a I'd rather walk home.

   b I'd rather you walked home.

7 Which of these sentences suggests more urgency? Which form of the verb is used in each case?

a It's time the children went to bed.   b It's time for the children to go to bed.

◀ GRAMMAR REFERENCE PAGE 188 ▶

8 Complete these sentences with a verb in an appropriate form.

a It's 5.25. It's almost time _____ home.

b I'd rather we _____ inside the cinema than outside, in case it's raining.

c 'It's high time you _____ a haircut, Corporal,' the sergeant yelled.

d 'Would you rather I _____ you what I've bought you for your birthday, or would you rather not _____?'
'I'd rather you (not) _____ me. I like surprises.'

e Isn't it about time you _____ that suit to the dry-cleaner's? When was the last time you had it cleaned?

f 'Have you done the washing up yet?'
'I'd rather _____ it tomorrow.'
'Sorry, but I'd rather you _____ it now.'

g It's time you _____ your room. It's a terrible mess.

Error correction

9 Read the text below and look carefully at each line. Some of the lines are correct, and some have a word which should not be there. If a line is correct, put a tick (✔) in the space. If a line has a word that should not be there, write the word in the space. There are two examples.

An accidental invention: Post-it® notes

0	I had not realised quite how many of inventions and discoveries had	*of*
00	come about by accident until fairly recently when I was given a book	✓
1	on the subject. I came across some very interesting facts indeed.	____
2	Did you know, for example, that the Post-it notes, those small, yellow	____
3	sticky pieces of paper which we all use were not planned but	____
4	were the result of a failed experiment? It seems that a man who named	____
5	Spencer Silver had been working in the 3M research laboratories in 1970	____
6	trying to find out a strong adhesive. He developed a new adhesive but it	____
7	was even weaker than what 3M were already manufactured. It stuck	____
8	but could easily be lifted off. It was so super weak instead of super	____
9	strong! No one else knew what to do with it, but Silver did not throw	____
10	it away – he had kept it. Then one Sunday four years later, another	____
11	one 3M scientist called Arthur Fry was singing in the church choir. He	____
12	used pieces of paper to keep on his place in the hymn book, but they	____
13	kept falling out of. Remembering Silver's adhesive, Fry put some on the	____
14	paper. With the weak adhesive, the paper stayed in place but came off	____
15	without damaging to the paper. In 1980, 3M began selling Post-it notes	____
	world-wide. Today they are one of the most popular office products available.	

Speaking

1 How were people's lives different before the breakthroughs illustrated below were made? What other technologies did people use?

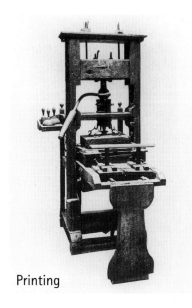

Printing

Photography

Telecommunication

Electricity

Air travel

Two-way task

2 Work in pairs. You have been asked to write an article about important historical breakthroughs. The pictures show some suggestions. Talk to each other about how these breakthroughs have affected the way we live. Then say which two you would include in your article.

Discussion

Which of these historical breakthroughs has most affected your life?
What inventions or discoveries would you like to see in the future?
Why are some inventions more successful than others?

Vocabulary

The name's the thing

How do inventions get their names? Sometimes they are named after their inventor, like the jacuzzi, named after Roy Jacuzzi. Sometimes the names are purely *descriptive*. They say what the invention does or how it does it, like the can opener, the automatic washing machine, or the *mechanical* digger. Some inventions are named by combining clever words or sounds together, like the mint sweet 'tic-tacs' or the chocolate bar 'Kit Kat'. Others are named by using initials or acronyms, like SCUBA® (Self-contained Underwater Breathing Apparatus). Nowadays, especially, a great deal of *careful* thought goes into naming any invention or new product as a catchy name can guarantee the first few sales. Giving a product the wrong name can have a *disastrous* effect on sales. The Vauxhall Nova's name had to be changed for the Spanish car market. In Spanish 'no va' makes the car sound anything but *speedy* and *reliable*. It means 'it doesn't go'.

Lead in

1 According to the text, how are new products and inventions named? Can you think of any other examples?

2 What are your favourite product names?

Adjective suffixes

3 Look at the adjectives in italic in the text. What nouns or verbs are they related to? What suffix has been added to the root word?

4 Complete these sentences with an adjective related to the word in brackets.
   a Post-Its® are small yellow pieces of _____ (stick) paper.
   b Some gadgets are more _____ (use) than others, but some are completely _____ (use).
   c For financial reasons, many inventions are never made. It doesn't always make _____ (economy) sense to follow through ideas.
   d It is always _____ (advise) to patent new ideas.
   e The skirt is made from a _____ (fashion) _____ (stretch) material.
   f When the new product was launched it got a _____ (favour) response from the public.
   g People who work in advertising need to be _____ (create) and come up with _____ (origin) ideas.
   h You should wear _____ (protect) clothing when you do _____ (science) experiments which involve handling _____ (danger) chemicals.

5 Complete these questions with an adjective related to the word in brackets. Then, discuss the questions in pairs.
   a Is the town or city where you were born situated in an _____ (agriculture) area or in an _____ (industry) area? Which products or foodstuffs are produced there?
   b What are your _____ (politics) views?
   c Do you find swearing _____ (offend)?
   d What is done for _____ (home) people by the government of your country? What should be done, in your opinion?
   e Would you wear fashionable clothes even if they were not _____ (comfort)?

Listening

Think ahead

1 Look at these gadgets. What do you think they are for? How useful are they?

2 Why do people buy gadgets?

Sentence completion

3 🎧 You will hear an interview with Paul Turner, a self-confessed gadget enthusiast. As you listen, tick any gadgets in the pictures that he mentions.

4 🎧 Listen again and complete these sentences.
   a   Paul is _____ by gadgets.
   b   The main difference between Paul's generation and his fathers' generation is their attitude to _____.
   c   Paul's father thinks gadgets are not _____.
   d   Paul has thirty-eight _____.
   e   Paul's wife thinks her husband is _____ with gadgets.
   f   Paul would buy anything that made his life easier or _____.
   g   Paul sometimes gives up on gadgets if the instructions are _____.
   h   When Paul's sister gets a new gadget, she gets _____ after a few weeks.
   i   Many people buy gadgets because _____ have them.
   j   His current favourite gadget catches _____.

over to you

What gadgets and appliances do you have at home or at work, which you couldn't do without?

What was the last appliance or gadget you bought? Why did you buy it? Has it lived up to your expectations?

Do you agree that people's attitudes to gadgets depend on their age and on their gender?

Vocabulary

Lead in

1 The following new words were included in the latest edition of the Oxford English Dictionary. What nouns were combined to make the new words? What do you think the new words mean?

screenager   japanimation   skorts   frankenfood   adultescents

2 Read this short text to check your ideas.

Innovation in language

The English language is constantly changing. New words are being invented all the time though not all of them are long-lasting. Lexicographers who work on revised editions of the world-famous Oxford English Dictionary have to decide which new words to include and which not to include. In other words they have to decide which words will stand the test of time. To be included in the dictionary, words must have been used five times in five different sources over five years. Here are some of the words which were included in the 2002 revised edition.

screenager	a teenager who is addicted to the computer or internet.
japanimation	type of animated cartoon which originated in Japan. The characters have a distinctive appearance - big-eyed and round-faced, with a lock of hair hanging in front of an eye.
frankenfood	GM food (derived from 'Frankenstein' and 'food')
skorts	an item of clothing worn by female tennis players (derived from 'skirt' and 'shorts')
adultescents	people of middle age whose clothes and activities are typically associated with youth culture.

Compound adjectives

3 Find examples of compound adjectives in the text and add them to the correct category below.

a Some compound adjectives end with a present participle, e.g. hard-*working*, _____.

b Some compound adjectives end with a past participle, e.g. long-*haired*, _____, _____.

c Some compound adjectives end with an adjective, e.g. oven-*ready*, _____.

4 What could be described using these compound adjectives?

fat-free   mass-produced   home-made   king-sized   cold-blooded   hard-wearing

5 Which compound adjectives could be used to describe the following

a a river which flows fast
b chewing gum which contains no sugar
c a business which is growing fast
d someone who has grey hair
e someone who looks good

6 Compound adjectives are often used to describe people's appearance and character. How could people with these features or characteristics be described?

a someone with dark skin
b someone with long legs
c someone with brown eyes
d someone who has a very high opinion of themselves
e someone who is unaffected by criticism
f someone who is very kind

7 Write a short description of another student in the class. Include two or three compound adjectives.

Writing

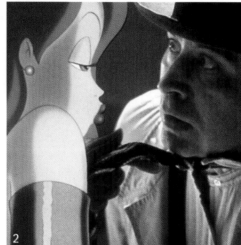

Article

1   Look at these stills from innovative films in the history of cinema. What innovation does each film illustrate? What other innovations have there been?

2   Read this Part 2 task. What information would you include in your answer?

> Your English class has decided to write a monthly magazine for other students of English in your school. One of the features will be 'The top 100 films ever'.
>
> Choose your favourite film and write an article of 120–180 words saying why you think it should be included in the list.

3   Read this article and answer the questions.
   a Is the information you expected included?
   b What style is the article written in?
   c Can you think of an appropriate title?

GLADIATOR

Which films would you include in your 'Top 100 films ever'? My guess is that Gladiator would be on that list. If it is not, then let me try to convince you why it should be.

Set in Rome in the third century AD, Gladiator tells the story of the Roman general Maximus, played by Russell Crowe, who goes from being the most favoured general in the Roman army to becoming a slave. The film takes us back to the cruelty and violence of Ancient Rome as we follow the events which eventually lead to Maximus' triumph.

What is most remarkable about the film is not the acting, which is excellent, nor the story, which is absorbing. It is the special effects, which recreate Rome and its amphitheatres so vividly. Computer graphics were used to amazing effect in the film – 98% of the spectators in the amphitheatre were computer generated – and you really feel you were there.

So Gladiator gets my vote. In my opinion, and hopefully in yours too, it is a landmark in the history of cinema.

4 These common techniques are often used at the beginning of an article. Which one is used in the answer above?

    a describing an unusual or dramatic scene
    b addressing the reader directly, possibly asking a personal question
    c surprising the reader with a strong opinion
    d describing a puzzle or problem which needs an answer

5 Match each of these opening paragraphs with a technique in 4.

a This just has to be the best thriller I've ever seen in my entire life, and I've seen a lot. *The Shining* starring Jack Nicholson is the scariest movie ever.

b You don't know which comedy to vote for because there are so many good ones, isn't that right? Well, read on and your problem will be solved.

c It's night, you're in a log cabin in the middle of nowhere, and the man you thought you knew is starting to behave very strangely indeed. This is the situation faced by Emily Jacobs, played by Kate Angeles, in the suspense movie *The Long Night*.

6 What is the main purpose of the final paragraph of the article about *Gladiator*?

    a to summarise the main points of the article
    b to leave the reader with a question to think about
    c to express a personal opinion or recommendation

7 Match each opening paragraph in 5 with these final paragraphs. What is the main purpose of each final paragraph?

a Once you've seen the film, and obviously I'm not going to spoil it by telling you how it ends, ask yourself this question: Would you have done the same as Emily did?

b So if, like me, you enjoy being scared, you really must see this film. I guarantee you won't be disappointed.

c All of these features – the intelligent script, the superb acting, and the excellent camerawork – combine to make this one of the funniest films ever made.

8 You are going to write an article in 120–180 words saying which film you think should be included in the list of 100 best films, and why.

9 Remember to include these features.

    Write in an appropriate style – neutral or informal.

    Write an appropriate title, opening paragraph and final paragraph – remember what their functions are.

    Give the reader as much information as they need but don't include too much of the story.

    Say why you think the film is so good.

10 Finally, when you have finished, check your grammar, spelling, and punctuation.

◀ WRITING GUIDE PAGE 166 ▶

Overview

1 Read the text below. Use the word given in capitals at the end of each line to form a word that fits in the space in the same line. There is an example at the beginning.

The Turner Prize

The Turner Prize, 0 _undoubtedly_ Britain's most well-known art award, is also   DOUBT

its most 1_____. The £20,000 prize is awarded annually to the British   CONTROVERSY

artist who has, in the opinion of a jury, made the greatest 2_____ to art in   CONTRIBUTE

the previous twelve months.

The four short-listed candidates exhibit a work of their 3_____ at the 'Turner   CHOOSE

Prize 4_____' at Tate Britain, one of London's main galleries. The award   EXHIBIT

ceremony, which is televised live, takes place in December, when the 5_____   WIN

is announced by a well-known celebrity.

The prize, which is a showcase for the 6_____ in contemporary British art, has   LATE

its critics. One of the main 7_____ directed against it is that it appears   CRITIC

to ignore more 8_____ forms of art like painting. In recent years the prize   TRADITION

has gone to a video artist, a sculptor and a 9_____, which seems to   PHOTOGRAPH

support the critics' 10_____.   ARGUE

---

2 Complete these sentences with the correct form of a verb.

a John regrets losing his temper.
 John wishes he _____ his temper.

b You are interrupting me. It's so annoying!
 I wish you _____ me. It's so annoying.

c Unfortunately I can't go to the party.
 I wish I _____ to the party.

d It's a pity I didn't meet her when I was single.
 I wish I _____ her when I was single.

e I'd love to have green eyes instead of brown eyes.
 I wish I _____ brown eyes. I wish I _____ green eyes.

f I really regret not applying for that job.
 I wish I _____ for that job.

g I really think we should leave now.
 It's time we _____ .

h He's thirty-six. He should get a job.
 It's time he _____ a job.

i I'd prefer you not to bring Andrew.
 I'd rather you _____ Andrew.

j I'd like you to tell me your answer now, not later.
 I'd rather you _____ me your answer now, not later.

3 Complete these sentences with the correct form of *carry* and another word.

a The smell of freshly baked bread _____ me _____ to when I was a child.

b Emily _____ working after the birth of her baby.

c They had just enough coal to _____ them _____ the winter months.

d We thought we'd go to Greece for our holiday, but, when we went to the travel agents, we got a bit _____ and booked a world cruise.

e The food company is going to _____ a survey into people's eating habits.

11 Communication

Introduction

1 Which of these methods of communication do you use most frequently? Put them in order, starting with the most frequent.

letters   telephone   email   text messaging   faxes   face-to-face communication

2 For people in your country, how important are the non-verbal means of communication shown in these photographs?

body language

eye contact

facial expressions

gestures

3 Discuss these questions in pairs.

How do you use *gestures* to express emotions?
When you are talking to someone, is it normal or acceptable to *touch* them or to *stand very close* to them?
How much can you tell about a person's character from the *expression on their face*?
Is it polite or impolite to maintain *eye contact* when you are talking to someone?

Reading

Lead in

1 Look at the expressions on these faces and choose the word which best describes the emotion being expressed. Discuss your answers in pairs.

anger   fear   sadness
disgust   surprise   enjoyment

2 Try to copy each expression in the photographs. How easy do you find this? Are any expressions difficult to make?

Gapped text

3 You are going to read an article about a project to classify human facial expressions. Seven paragraphs have been removed from the article. Choose from paragraphs A–H the one which fits each gap 1–6. There is one extra paragraph which you do not need to use. There is an example at the beginning.

I know just how you feel

Do you feel sad? Happy? Angry? You may think that the way you show these emotions is unique. Well, think again. Even the expression of the most personal feelings can be classified, according to Mind Reading, a DVD displaying every possible human emotion. It demonstrates 412 distinct ways in which we feel: the first visual dictionary of the human heart.

0 H

Every other feeling was thought to derive from Darwin's small group. More complex expressions of emotion were probably learned and therefore more specific to each culture.

1

The project was conceived by a Cambridge professor as an aid for people with autism, who have difficulty both reading and expressing emotions. But it quickly became apparent that it had broader uses. Actors and teachers, for example, need to understand a wide range of expressions.

2

Once these emotions were defined and classified, a DVD seemed the clearest and most efficient way to display them. In Mind Reading, each expression is acted out by six different actors in three seconds. Any other method of showing all 412 emotions, such as words, would have been far less effective.

3

'Although they were given some direction,' says Ms Collis, 'the actors were not told which facial muscles they should move. We did think of trying to describe each emotion, but it would have been almost impossible to make clear rules for this. When someone feels contempt, for example, do their eyebrows always go down?'

4

Ekman has written out a pattern of facial muscular movements to represent each emotion. Fear, for example, uses six simultaneous 'action units' including stretching the lips and dropping the jaw.

5

Apparently, the most difficult expression to reproduce is the smile. Ekman says a smile isn't only about stretching the lips, but tightening the tiny muscles around the eyes. These are difficult to control, and few people can do it.

6

In fact, this finding is of interest to police authorities, who are seeking Ekman's help in interpreting even the tiniest 'micro-expressions' – lasting only one twenty-fifth of a second – to detect whether someone is lying.

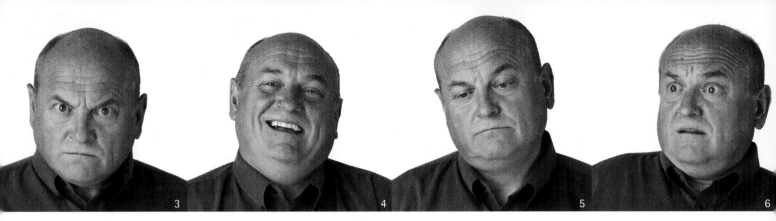

A Someone who has tried to establish such rules is the American, Professor Paul Ekman who has built a database of how the face moves for every emotion. The face can make forty-three distinct muscle movements called 'action units'. These can be combined into more than 10,000 visible facial shapes.

B But now it is believed that many more facial expressions are shared worldwide. They seem to be programmed into the human brain. The *Mind Reading* DVD is a systematic visual record of these expressions.

C The explanation for this is simple: we may find it difficult to describe emotions using words, but we instantly recognise one when we see it on someone's face. 'It was really clear when the actors had got it right,' says Cathy Collis, who directed the DVD.

D Ekman has also found that although it is possible to classify and describe the natural expression of emotions, it may not be possible for people to reproduce them artificially. According to Ekman, we can't decide to be happy or sad; it simply happens to us.

E Research has also been done to find out which areas of the brain read emotional expression. Chris Ashwin, at the Cambridge autism research centre, has taken magnetic resonance imaging of the brain to track how it perceives fear.

F The professor and his research team first had to define an 'emotion'. They decided that it was a mental state that could be preceded by 'I feel' or 'he looks' or 'she sounds'. Using this definition, 1,512 emotion terms were identified and discussed. This list was eventually reduced to 412, ranging from 'afraid' to 'wanting'.

G If we learnt to recognise whether someone was using their eye muscles when they smiled, we would be able to distinguish true enjoyment from false. Such an ability would provide useful information in a range of different situations.

H Attempts to classify expressions began in the mid-1800s, when Darwin divided the emotions into six types – anger, fear, sadness, disgust, surprise and enjoyment. He said that the expression of these feelings was universal and recognisable by anyone, from any culture.

over to you   With a partner describe in detail how one of the expressions shown in the photographs is being made.

Grammar and practice

1   These three conditional sentences are grammatically different. Which verb tenses are used in the two parts of each sentence?
Type 0   If you *smile* genuinely, the muscles around your eyes *move*.
Type 1   If you *communicate* effectively in the interview, you *will* probably *get* the job.
Type 2   Even if I *told* you the truth, you *wouldn't believe* me.

2   The three sentences above are also different in meaning. Which sentences refer to
a   an unlikely event or situation?
b   something that actually happens?
c   a likely event or situation?

3   Which of these two conditional sentences refers to a future possibility? Which refers to something imaginary or impossible?
a   If he applied for that job, I'm sure he'd get it.
b   If he was a few years younger, I'm sure he'd get the job.

4   What is the difference in meaning between each of these pairs of sentences?
a   If I get the chance, I'll work abroad.
    If I get the chance, I may work abroad.
b   If I got the chance, I'd work abroad.
    If I got the chance, I might work abroad.

◀ GRAMMAR REFERENCE PAGE 189 ▶

5   Complete these sentences with your own ideas to form type 0 conditional sentences. There is an example at the beginning.
a   If I have bad news to pass on, I usually *send an email or a text message*.
b   If I have good news to pass on, I _____.
c   If someone has upset me, I _____.
d   If I need a friend's advice, I _____.
e   If I want to apologise for something I've done, I _____.

6   Conditional sentences are often used to persuade, to warn, to threaten and to promise. Complete these sentences with your own ideas.
a   If you watch too much television, _____.
b   If you don't go to bed earlier, _____.
c   I'll do the washing up if _____.
d   If you lend me your car for the evening, _____.
e   If you don't work harder, _____.
f   I'd spend more time at home if _____.

7   Which verb tenses are used in this type 3 conditional sentence?

If you *had given* me your number, I *would have sent* you a text message.

8   What is the main difference in meaning between this type 3 conditional sentence and the type 0, 1 and 2 sentences above?

Key word transformations

9 Type 3 conditional sentences are often used for making excuses. Complete the second sentence so that it has a similar meaning to the first sentence. Use up to five words including the word given. Do not change this word.

1 I didn't answer the phone because I didn't know it was you.
   had
   If I _____, I would have answered the phone.

2 I didn't know you were back from your holiday, so I didn't phone you.
   if
   I would have phoned you _____ you were back from your holiday.

3 If she'd had my address with her, she'd have sent me a postcard.
   because
   She didn't send me a postcard _____ my address with her.

4 He forgot to put his watch on – that's why he was late.
   been
   He wouldn't _____ he hadn't forgotten to put his watch on.

5 I'd have bought you a present, but I forgot when your birthday was.
   if
   I'd have bought you a present _____ when your birthday was.

6 We got in from work really late – that's why we didn't come to your party.
   would
   If we hadn't got in from work so late, _____ to your party.

10 What would you have done if you had been in this situation?

MOTORWAY NIGHTMARE
When Jill Frame broke down on the motorway at 9 p.m. last Tuesday night, she got out of her car and went to find a telephone. The nearest one was on the opposite side of the six-lane motorway.

◀ GRAMMAR REFERENCE PAGE 189 ▶

Mixed conditionals

11 What is the difference in meaning between these two sentences?
   a If I hadn't broken my leg, I would have gone on holiday with you.
   b If I hadn't broken my leg, I would go on holiday with you.

12 Complete these sentences with present or future results.
   a If I hadn't learned to read, _____.
   b If I'd won the lottery at the weekend, _____.
   c If I'd saved all my money for the last year, _____.
   d If I hadn't had a good education, _____.
   e If I'd been born into a very rich family, _____.
   f If my mother hadn't met my father, _____.

◀ GRAMMAR REFERENCE PAGE 190 ▶

Unless, as long as, provided that

13 Rewrite these sentences replacing *if* with the words in brackets.
   a If you don't work harder, you'll fail your exams. (unless)
   b You'll pass your driving test if you practise enough. (as long as)
   c You can borrow my car if you buy your own petrol. (provided that)
   d You can only telephone me if you have some important news. (unless)

◀ GRAMMAR REFERENCE PAGE 190 ▶

14 Now finish these sentences in several different ways. Two possible answers are given for the first one.
   a I'll come on holiday with you provided that ...
      ... you don't smoke in the car. / ... you do your share of the cooking.
   b I'll never speak to you again unless _____.
   c I'll lend you the money you need as long as _____.

Listening

Think ahead

1 A friend gives you an expensive present. Unfortunately, you have recently bought the same thing for yourself. Your friend asks you if you like their present. What do you say?

2 Think of an occasion when you told a deliberate lie. Discuss these questions.

a Was it a serious lie, or just a bit of fun?
b Did you lie for your own benefit or for someone else's?
c Did anyone find out about the lie?

Multiple choice

3 🎧 You will hear people talking in eight different situations. For questions 1–8, choose the best answer, A, B or C.

1 The first speaker was at her boyfriend's house. What was her excuse for not staying for lunch?
A She said she had arranged to eat at home.
B She said she had already had lunch.
C She said she didn't like his mother's cooking.

2 You will hear someone being interviewed about his job. What is the job?
A an economist   B a TV interviewer   C a politician

3 You hear someone talking about meeting a neighbour in town. Why didn't the speaker say anything about her sister?
A The rumour was not true.
B The neighbour might tell other people.
C She didn't know anything.

4 You hear someone talking about a party she went to. Why did the speaker say that her cousin was a famous footballer?
A to see the man's reaction
B to impress the man
C to continue talking to the man

5 You hear someone talking about an accident he was involved in. What was the cause of the accident?
A The speaker had fallen asleep while driving.
B There had been a lot of traffic on the road.
C Something had gone wrong with the car.

6 You hear someone describing an occasion when she answered the phone. Why was her brother angry?
A He had wanted to speak to Annie.
B He had wanted to answer the phone himself.
C He had wanted to speak to Barbara.

7 You hear a conversation about something which someone bought. What was wrong with this thing?
   A It was broken.　　　B It was not genuine.　　C It wasn't very good.

8 You hear someone talking about doing something for her sister. Why didn't the speaker tell her sister her exam results?
   A She shouldn't have opened the letter.
   B It would have spoiled her sister's holiday.
   C She couldn't contact her sister.

over to you Have you ever known a compulsive liar or someone, like the third speaker, who lies for fun? How do you react to people like this?

Collocations with *say, speak, talk* and *tell*

4 *Say, speak, talk* and *tell* have similar meanings, but are used in different ways. For example, we *tell* a lie, not *talk* a lie. Complete these sentences with the correct form of the appropriate verb.
   a Can you _____ a second language?
   b Sorry, I can't _____ you the time – I haven't got my watch on.
   c If you've got such strong opinions, you should _____ your mind.
   d Some people _____ a short prayer before a meal.
   e Have I _____ you the joke about the rabbit who went to the butchers?
   f I swear to _____ the truth, the whole truth and nothing but the truth.
   g You know nothing about the subject. You're _____ rubbish.
   h My mother used to _____ me stories about when she was a child.

Confusing verbs: *hope, wait, expect, look forward to*

5 Match the verbs in italic in sentences a–d with their meanings in sentences 1–4.

   a I *hope* you feel better soon.
   b I'm *looking forward to* seeing you again.
   c He got off the train and *waited for* a taxi.
   d I *expect* it'll rain tomorrow.

   1 to believe that something will happen
   2 to stay somewhere until something happens
   3 to want something to happen or be true
   4 to want something to happen because you know you will enjoy it

6 Choose the correct verb in these sentences.

   a We've been *looking forward to / waiting for* the bus for half an hour.
   b We're *expecting / waiting for* good weather on our holidays.
   c I'm really *looking forward to getting / waiting to get* his letter.
   d I've bought you a little present. I *hope you like / expect you'll like* it.
   e A Has the postman been yet?
      B Why? Are you *expecting / looking forward to* a letter?
   f I've worked hard this week. I'm really *looking forward to / hoping for* the weekend.

Speaking

1 What are your strengths and weaknesses as a language learner? What do you find easy and difficult? What are your favourite and least favourite classroom activities?

2 Work in pairs.

Student A Compare and contrast photos 1 and 2 and say in which situation you think the more effective learning is taking place. Remember you have to speak for about one minute.

Student B When your partner has finished speaking, answer this question: Which of the two classrooms would you prefer to learn in?

3 Work in pairs.

Student B Compare and contrast photos 3 and 4 and say which situation you think is more enjoyable for the student involved. Remember you have to speak for about one minute.

Student A When your partner has finished speaking, answer this question: If you wanted to improve your spoken English, which of the two situations would you prefer?

over to you

How do you prepare for language exams? Do you have any special ways of revising or learning vocabulary and grammar?

What do you do outside the classroom – and in addition to homework – to improve your English?

Vocabulary

Lead in

1 Read this extract from an email. Why do you think the writer objected to the word his friend used to describe him?

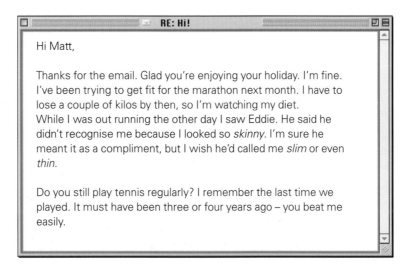

> **RE: Hi!**
>
> Hi Matt,
>
> Thanks for the email. Glad you're enjoying your holiday. I'm fine. I've been trying to get fit for the marathon next month. I have to lose a couple of kilos by then, so I'm watching my diet. While I was out running the other day I saw Eddie. He said he didn't recognise me because I looked so *skinny*. I'm sure he meant it as a compliment, but I wish he'd called me *slim* or even *thin*.
>
> Do you still play tennis regularly? I remember the last time we played. It must have been three or four years ago – you beat me easily.

Positive or negative?

2 The story in the email shows that the words people choose can communicate positive or negative ideas. The two words in italic in these sentences have related meanings. Which of the words conveys a more negative idea?

a I've just bought a(n) *cheap / inexpensive* second car.
b To succeed in business you have to be *determined / ruthless*.
c My brother's a *well-built / fat* man in his mid-thirties.
d Is your coat made of *fake / imitation* leather?
e My neighbour spends all her time *chatting / gossiping* to friends.
f The football fans were *excited / hysterical* when their team scored.
g We had dinner at a(n) *expensive / pricey* restaurant last night.
h John *smiles / sneers* whenever he sees me.
i The *old / elderly* man next door takes his dog for a walk every day.

3 Which of these words would you prefer people used to describe you, for example in a reference for a job?

a cold / reserved
b self-satisfied / self-confident
c easy-going / lazy
d serious / dull
e curious / nosey
f arrogant / outgoing
g cowardly / shy
h intelligent / smart

over to you There is a well-known English saying: 'Sticks and stones may break my bones, but words can never hurt me.' Can you remember an occasion when you have been hurt by words or when you have used words to hurt another person?

Writing

Formal letter

1 Read this example of a Part 1 task and answer the questions.

a What is the main purpose of replying to the letter?
b What information should be included in the reply?
c How formal or informal should the style be?

> You have applied to join a four-week summer course at a language school in an English-speaking country. You have now received this letter from the school. Read the letter on which you have made some notes, then, using the information, write a suitable reply in 120 to 180 words.

We are writing to confirm your place on our four–week summer course. Please tell us on which date you will be arriving. You will be collected from the airport by taxi. We also now need the following additional information:

Saturday June 30th - Heathrow

English friend meeting me

What kind of accommodation do you require?

* With a family?
* Self-catering apartment?
* Shared room in college with a student of another nationality?

Yes, but not sharing with another student

Would you be interested in the following trips?

* London – an overnight stay, including a theatre visit
* Stratford – a theatre visit and a picnic by the river
* Brighton – a day at one of Britain's coolest seaside resorts!

Yes

Yes

No, did course there last year

Please let us know if you require any further information from us.

When to pay fees. Now or July?

2 Read this letter written in answer to the question.

a Underline any phrases which are written in an inappropriate style.
b Compare ideas in pairs. Then, rewrite these parts in the correct style.

Dear Ms Simpson,

Thanks for your letter which I got this morning. It's brilliant that I'm coming to your school.

In answer to your question about my arrival, I will be getting to Heathrow Airport the day before the course starts, which is July 1. However, an English friend is meeting me, so there is no need for you to send a taxi. Thanks all the same – it was a nice thought.

Secondly, as regards accommodation, I would prefer to stay with a family and I would like to be alone. It isn't that I'm antisocial – it is just that I wish to practise my English conversation.

Finally, as far as trips are concerned, I would like to go to London and Stratford, but not Brighton. I know the town very well as I studied there last year.

My only question to you is, when do I have to pay the course fees? Can I pay in July, or do you want the money now?

Can't wait to meet you all.

Love,

Maria

3 Underline the phrases the writer uses to focus attention on the subject of each paragraph.

4 Rephrase the sentences containing focusing expressions using other phrases from the list below.

EXAMPLE   *In answer to your first question, I will be arriving at Heathrow Airport …*

As regards … , …   Regarding …
As far as … is concerned …   Moving on to your next point / question …
As for … , …   With regard to …

5 You are going to write a formal transactional letter. First, read the task and the letter to which you are going to reply.

You have enrolled on an intensive English language course in order to improve your chances of passing an important exam. The school has sent you a letter asking about your particular language needs and about what you hope to gain from the course.

Read the letter on which you have made some notes, then, using all the information, write a suitable reply. Write your letter in 120–180 words in an appropriate style. Do not include any postal addresses.

… which begins on October 4. We now require the following information from you to assist us in providing you with a course to suit your particular language needs.

Definitely grammar
Terrible!

In which aspect of language do you feel most confident?
Grammar   Vocabulary   Conversation

very slowly - loads of mistakes. Strong accent!

Which of the 'four skills' do you need most extra practice in?
Listening   Speaking   Reading   Writing

Why is it important for you to pass this exam?
* I need to pass for the job I want to do.
* I want to study this language at university.

Australia

* I am going to live in an English-speaking country

Pairs or groups - need speaking practice!

Do you prefer to work individually, with one other student, or in small groups?

We look forward to receiving your reply.
Yours sincerely,

6 Before you write, remember to make a paragraph plan – use the sample answer opposite as a model. Also, decide on an appropriate style.

7 When you write, think about the topic of each paragraph you have planned, and decide on appropriate phrases (focusing expressions) to introduce these topics at the beginning of each paragraph.

8 When you have finished writing, read through your letter, checking grammar, spelling, punctuation and style.

◀ WRITING GUIDE PAGE 162 ▶

Overview

1 Read the text below and think of the word which best fits each space. Use only one word in each space. There is an example at the beginning.

Do they know what they're saying?

Parrots have been imitating human speech 0 _*for*_ thousands of years. We all love them for it. There are more 1_____ 300 species altogether in the parrot family, including lovebirds, cockatoos, macaws and budgerigars. 2_____ all of them can mimic human speech, but all can 3_____ a lot of noise. It seems 4_____ the ancient Persians were taken in by the charm of parrots more than 2,500 years 5_____, with writers at the time describing how these birds 6_____ speak several languages. Perhaps 7_____ most fascinating thing about talking birds, however, is 8_____ or not they actually have any idea of what they 9_____ saying. It is a difficult subject 10_____ investigate, but the results of a research project in the US with a grey parrot called Alex suggests that 11_____ least some parrots use language effectively to communicate. Under the guidance of Professor Pepperberg, Alex has 12_____ taught to ask for a variety of objects. The study 13_____ found that Alex can tell the difference 14_____ them; he refuses when a wrong item is offered to him 15_____ shows an ability to select and decide, linked directly to the use of language.

2 Choose the correct verbs in these conditional sentences.
a If I have a headache, *I take / I'd take* some tablets and go to bed.
b If the classroom caught fire, *we'll go / we'd go* down the fire escape.
c We'd have won the match if our goalkeeper *hasn't / hadn't* been injured.
d You can come to the party, as long as *you bring / you'll bring* something to eat and drink.
e If I see Nick, *I tell / I'll tell* him you'd like to speak to him.
f I'd be a lot richer now, if I *accepted / had accepted* that job in America last year.
g I can't help you unless *you tell / you'll tell* me what the problem is.
h If I were you, *I'll phone / I'd phone* him back straightaway.

3 Complete these sentences with the correct form of one of the verbs in brackets.
a The trouble with you is that you never _____ what you think. (say / speak)
b You've got to learn to _____ your mind. (say / speak)
c I'm OK at writing in Russian, but I'm not very good at _____ it. (speak / tell)
d He hardly ever _____ the truth. In fact I'd say he was a born liar. (say / tell)
e Good luck in the competition tomorrow. I really _____ you win. (expect / hope)
f Are you _____ starting your new job? (expect / look forward to)
g What a surprise! I didn't _____ to see you here this evening. (expect / hope)

12 Society

Introduction

1 Work in pairs or small groups. What positive or negative aspect of society does each photo illustrate?

2 Choose two of the photos and discuss these questions.

Are the photos representative of the situation in your country? What similarities and differences are there?
What is being done to solve these problems in your country? What would you do?

Reading

Think ahead

1 Discuss these questions in pairs.

Are people born bad?

Is it possible for people to change their character? How?

2 You are going to read a text about five people who got into serious trouble with the police when they were young but went on to become respectable members of society. Read the text quickly and answer these questions.

a What crimes did each of them commit?

b What event or person caused each of them to change?

c What jobs did they go on to do?

A MICHAEL MADSEN

Hollywood actor Michael Madsen had a long history of delinquency before he decided to leave his life of crime behind. When he was twenty-one, Madsen and his friend, Mark, were caught robbing a sports goods store in Arizona. Madsen recalls seeing a police officer pointing a gun at his head, ready to shoot. 'I think at that moment it could have been over for me,' he says. As a juvenile, he had been arrested for various things including car theft, drink-driving and burglary, but it wasn't until this arrest that he realised that the criminal life wasn't for him. After his release, he went to see a theatre production of *Of Mice and Men*, which inspired him to become an actor, and, as his acting career took off, Madsen's life began to straighten out. 'I am a good role model to my kids,' says the father of five, who often plays a criminal on screen.

B ALAN SIMPSON

Former US Senator, Alan Simpson, served two years probation when he was seventeen for vandalising property. Simpson, whose father had also been a US senator, grew up in a loving, stable home. His mother once told Time magazine that 'Alan did have a temper', and she recalls punishing him for throwing rocks at other children. Simpson remembers the look his parents gave each other when the judge passed sentence. 'They must have thought: "Where have we failed?"' Simpson thanked his probation officer publicly during his first election campaign, saying he had been a great influence on his life and had helped him make it to that moment. He strongly believes in giving kids a second chance and believes that most children will and do turn out all right in the end.

C TERRY K RAY

Terry K Ray got into trouble from an early age. When he was ten, he threw a bottle top at his best friend during a fight. Unknown to him, the bottle top had a piece of glass in it, cutting his friend above the eye. The friend's father called the police and filed a complaint, and Ray was put in a juvenile detention centre for six months. During the next few years Ray constantly got into fights. His mother punished him by beating him, but when, aged fourteen, he refused to let his mother hit him any longer, she kicked him out. Reflecting on this period of his life, Ray remarked, 'I had so much anger, so little respect for authority and such a short fuse that I could easily have killed someone.' Today Ray is a successful criminal defence lawyer and family man. He says he owes this to several individuals - teachers and counsellors - who helped him.

D LAWRENCE WU

Son of Chinese immigrants who both had university degrees, Lawrence Wu was an extremely bright child. Wu's problems didn't start until his early teens when his father left home, leaving his mother to raise him and his brothers. When the family was forced to move to a poorer neighbourhood, Wu joined a local gang. It was an instant jump to 'coolness'. But, when he started coming home with low grades, his mother kicked him out. Wu gradually dropped out of school. He was constantly in trouble for fighting rival gangs, but when he was arrested along with a friend for attempted murder he decided he had to leave the gang. Wu moved back in with his mother, who helped him make the transition from gang life back to school. He eventually made up his lost years of education, and graduated in law. Wu now works as a corporate tax lawyer, but still thinks about the damage and pain he caused his family.

E BOB BEAMON

Former long-jump Olympic athlete, Bob Beamon, was already getting into trouble by the time he was nine. Beamon's mother had died when he was an infant and his step-father had done little in the way of parenting, ending up in prison himself. At fourteen, Beamon ran away from home, joined a gang and regularly got into fights. He vividly recalls the day when he stood in front of the judge accused of assaulting a teacher. 'The judge was obviously interested in helping kids. He must have seen something in me,' Beamon reflects. 'He said he was going to take a chance. Instead of sending me to jail, he sent me to an alternative school along with other juvenile delinquents.' It was a place where he had time to learn that there was more to life than trouble.

3 Read the text again. For questions 1–14, choose from the people A–E. Each person may be chosen more than once. When more than one answer is required, these may be given in any order. There is an example at the beginning.

Which of the people

went back to school?	0	D	
were forced to leave home?	1		2
did the same job as his father?	3		
have children?	4		5
belonged to a gang?	6		7
are grateful to somebody?	8		9
was good at sport?	10		
had a supportive parent or parents?	11		12
injured a friend?	13		
was arrested for stealing?	14		

over to you

At what age do you think children should be held legally responsible for their actions?

Should parents be held responsible for their children's actions?

Should society punish criminals or try to re-educate them?

Crime vocabulary

4 Complete these sentences with the correct word from this list.

burglary   drink-driving   hooligans   mugger   shoplifting   vandalism

a The youth admitted smashing up the telephone box. Such acts of _____ are commonplace nowadays.

b The man lost his licence for _____. He was well over the limit when the police stopped him.

c The _____ assaulted me and stole my wallet and mobile phone.

d The store detective stopped the couple at the exit and accused them of _____.

e Football _____ are not real fans. They're only interested in fighting rival supporters.

f The _____ took place in the five minutes I was out of the house. They took my video.

5 Complete these sentences with the correct form of *rob* or *steal*.

a That bank _____ twice this year. Each time over £500,000 _____.

b More and more people are fitting their cars with anti-theft alarms in an attempt to stop them from _____.

c 'Oh, no! I _____! They've taken everything. My credit cards, cash, the lot!'

d The thieves were accused of _____ jewellery worth over £250,000.

e The shoplifter _____ £500 worth of goods from the store.

f Several of The Aden Gallery's best paintings _____ last night.

Grammar and practice

Probability and possibility

1 Underline the modal verbs in these sentences.

   a It might have been Madsen, not his friend Mark, who had the idea of robbing the store.
   b Lawrence Wu's mother can't have been pleased when her son joined a gang.
   c 'They must have thought: "Where have we failed?"'

2 Match the meaning of each modal verb in 1 with these explanations.

   a The speaker is almost certain that something is the case.
   b The speaker is almost certain that something is not the case.
   c The speaker is not certain that something is the case but thinks it is possible.

3 Read the following dialogues and decide whether the second speaker is talking about a past, present or future situation.

   a 'Is that Pete driving that BMW?'
      'Yes. He must have sold his sports car.'
   b 'I haven't seen Jennifer for ages!'
      'She might be studying. She's got exams soon.'
   c 'Isn't Daniel coming?'
      'He might come later.'
   d 'I'm starving!'
      'So am I. It must be almost lunchtime'

4 Which structure follows the modal verbs in each dialogue in 3? What other structures or words do you know with similar meanings, for example, *maybe*?

◀ GRAMMAR REFERENCE PAGE 190 ▶

5 Complete these sentences using an appropriate modal verb and the correct form of the verb in brackets.

   a Joan loves chocolate cake, but she didn't want any when I offered her some. She _____ (be) on a diet, or she _____ (be) hungry.
   b Susan seems to be angry with me, but I don't know why. I _____ (say) anything to annoy her because I haven't seen her for ages.

   c James didn't answer the door when I rang his doorbell last night. The doorbell has a very quiet ring, so he _____ (hear) me.
   d I think Nicole _____ (be) married don't you? She wears a wedding ring, though to be honest I've never heard her mention her husband, so I suppose she _____ (be) divorced.
   e Have you seen Peter anywhere? He _____ (leave) the building because his jacket's right there. He never goes out without it.
   f Julie _____ (get) a shock when she received her exam results. She was expecting an A but she only got a C.
   g The missing teenager _____ (wear) jeans and a white T-shirt – no one's quite sure.
   h I can't find my keys anywhere. I _____ (leave) them at home. I'm always doing that.
   i I don't know where Darren is. He _____ (forget). He never does. Something _____ (happen) to him. He's always so punctual. I suppose his car _____ (break down).
   j If it wasn't you, then Kathy _____ (take) the last chocolate. No one else could have.

6 Read the newspaper report and answer the questions.

MILLIONAIRE MURDERED IN HIS HOME

Millionaire Raymond Miller was murdered in his own home late on Friday evening. He was shot once in the head. Police believe the crime was motivated by money. Miller's personal safe was discovered to be empty. It is believed that the millionaire usually kept at least twenty thousand pounds in cash in the house. Police are currently interviewing three suspects about the crime.

   a Where was Raymond Miller murdered?
   b When was he murdered?
   c How was he murdered?
   d What do police believe was the motive?
   e How many suspects are they interviewing?

7 🎧 Inspector Hurst is in charge of the murder case. He is reporting his progress to his superior officer. Listen and complete the suspects' profiles at the top of the next page.

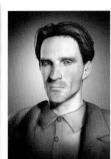

Simon Prince

Relationship to Miller
_____

Marital status
_____

Possible motive
_____

Bad habits
_____

Margaret McKenzie

Relationship to Miller
_____

Marital status
_____

Possible motive
_____

Bad habits
_____

Timothy Carlyle

Relationship to Miller
_____

Marital status
_____

Possible motive
_____

Bad habits
_____

8 Look for clues in this photograph of the crime scene. In pairs, talk about who you think might have murdered the millionaire.

EXAMPLE

The murderer must have known the victim because there are no signs of forced entry.

9 🎧 Listen to the next conversation between Inspector Hurst and his superior officer. Did you guess correctly?

Listening

1 Do you think money is more important or less important to people in today's society than it was in the past?

2 What problems can it cause?

Multiple matching

3 🎧 You are going to hear five people talking about the problems related to money. For questions 1–5, choose which problem A–F each speaker talks about. There is one extra letter you do not need to use.

A getting into debt
B health problems
C compulsive gambling
D family breakdown
E telling lies
F crime

Speaker 1 ☐ 1
Speaker 2 ☐ 2
Speaker 3 ☐ 3
Speaker 4 ☐ 4
Speaker 5 ☐ 5

over to you

What is your attitude to money? Rewrite these sentences so that they are true for you, then compare ideas with a partner.

I never buy anything I don't need.
If I want something, I save up till I can afford it.
I save about 10% of my income
I worry about what I will live on when I am old.
I would only do a job if it was well paid.

Speaking

Lead in

1 What do these comments actually mean? Does the person who made the comments disapprove of the behaviour of the person they are referring to or their appearance?

  a 'What does he look like!'
  b 'What he needs is a kick up the backside!'
  c 'She thinks she's a cut above the rest of us.'
  d 'Act your age!'
  e 'She looks like mutton dressed as lamb.'

2 Why do you think people make disapproving comments like this about other people? Do you do it? Do people do it to you?

3 Why might the people in these photos be treated differently?

Long turn

4 Work in pairs.

Student A Compare and contrast photos 1 and 2 and then say whether you think being rich makes people happy.

Student B Time your partner. Tell them when they have spoken for one minute. When your partner has finished speaking, answer this question: Would you rather be rich or good-looking?

Student B Compare and contrast photos 3 and 4 and then say which of these people you most admire.

Student A Time your partner. Tell them when they have spoken for one minute. When your partner has finished speaking, answer this question: Are old people in your country as active as this?

over to you

How do you react to beggars? Do you ignore them or give them money? Do you think begging in public should be allowed?

What is done for homeless and unemployed people in your country? What do you think should be done?

Do you think people should always be allowed to dress and look however they want?

Grammar and practice

Lead in

1 Look at these birthday cards and match each card with the correct continuation a–c. What do they tell you about some people's attitude to age?

a ... it won't change a thing, you'll still be a year older.
b ... and you can't see it for the candles.
c ... just make up an age and stick to it.

Articles

2 Complete this short text with the articles *a*, *an*, or *the*, or leave the spaces blank where no article is needed.

At sixty-three, I was unexpectedly made redundant from my job of forty years. Not wanting to retire yet, I decided to look for ¹_____ new job to take me up to ²_____ retirement age and to prevent me from just sitting at ³_____ home all day. Finding one, however, turned out to be ⁴_____ most difficult task I've ever faced, since ⁵_____ elderly are often viewed negatively by ⁶_____ employers. After a year and nearly ⁷_____ hundred applications, I was invited to ⁸_____ interview in ⁹_____ Scotland. I was nervous but I needn't have been. ¹⁰_____ interview was very relaxed, and ¹¹_____ interviewer was impressed by my experience and took me on. I couldn't believe my luck. It's ¹²_____ brilliant job. I'm working as ¹³_____ activity organiser on ¹⁴_____ cruise ship for older people in ¹⁵_____ West Indies. Sailing round ¹⁶_____ Caribbean is not my idea of ¹⁷_____ work at all.

◀ GRAMMAR REFERENCE PAGE 191 ▶

3 Discuss these questions in pairs or small groups.

How are old people treated in your country?
Is unemployment a big problem in your country? Does it affect any particular age group?
How can you change negative attitudes towards the elderly?
What, if anything, worries you about getting old?

Vocabulary

Lead in

1 Do you give money to charity? Which charities do you support?

2 What fund-raising events are there in your country? How do they raise money?

Multiple-choice cloze

3 Read this text about a charity event which takes place in Britain, and answer these questions.

  a How often does it happen?
                             c Who takes part in it?
  b How much money been raised so far?

Comic Relief is a charitable organisation ^{0}___*B*___ in London. It was set ^{1}_____ by comedians in 1985 in response to the famine in Ethiopia, and uses comedy and laughter to ^{2}_____ serious messages across. Since then ^{3}_____ two thousand celebrities have given their time and talent to Comic Relief, helping to raise £220 million pounds to date.

Every two years, Comic Relief organises a nationwide fundraising event ^{4}_____ 'Red Nose Day'. It's usually on a Friday in March. On Red Nose Day everyone in the country is ^{5}_____ to put on a red nose and do something silly to raise money ^{6}_____ charity. In an event that ^{7}_____ the country, people from all walks of life do their bit for poor and under-privileged people in the UK and Africa.

In schools, uniforms are replaced by fancy ^{8}_____; in offices across the nation, assistants ^{9}_____ over from their bosses for the day. Every contribution is important, ^{10}_____ it is standing in the street ^{11}_____ money from passers-by, or taking ^{12}_____ in a sponsored event like sitting in a bathtub full of baked beans for twenty-four hours, or not talking for a(n) ^{13}_____ day.

The event is televised in the evening, when the combination of comedy and hard-hitting documentaries persuades ^{14}_____ to make donations on their credit cards – over the phone or ^{15}_____ the Internet – to those less fortunate than themselves.

4 Read the text again and decide which answer A, B, C or D best fits each space. There is an example at the beginning (0).

0	A	established	B	based	C	constructed	D	stationed
1	A	on	B	off	C	out	D	up
2	A	have	B	do	C	get	D	make
3	A	over	B	plus	C	more	D	additional
4	A	known	B	named	C	called	D	described
5	A	stimulated	B	encouraged	C	cheered	D	helped
6	A	to	B	for	C	towards	D	on
7	A	co-operates	B	combines	C	joins	D	unites
8	A	clothes	B	wear	C	dress	D	costume
9	A	take	B	make	C	do	D	get
10	A	if	B	whether	C	while	D	since
11	A	collecting	B	earning	C	asking	D	gathering
12	A	involvement	B	place	C	participation	D	part
13	A	whole	B	all	C	total	D	full
14	A	spectators	B	viewers	C	audience	D	observers
15	A	by	B	across	C	through	D	on

Writing

Lead in

1 How many ways of raising money for a charitable cause can you think of? Use the photos to give you some ideas.

  a Which would raise the most money?
  b Which would be the easiest to organise?

Report

2 Read the Part 2 task and answer the questions.

  a What style would you write the report in?
  b What information would you include in your answer?
  c Would you make a recommendation?

> Your local children's hospital needs some new equipment. They have asked local schools to help them raise money to buy it. The head teacher of your school has asked you to make some suggestions on how the school could do this. Write your report for the head teacher in 120–180 words.

3 Read this report and answer the questions.
  a How many suggestions has Eleni made?
  b Do you agree with her recommendation?

> To: The Head Teacher
>
> From: Eleni Kouros
>
> Subject: Ideas for raising money to help to buy equipment for the local children's hospital.
>
> Fund-raising activities
> One thing we could do is to organise a sponsored race with a prize for the winner.
> This could be a romantic evening meal for two at a local restaurant. I am sure that one of the restaurants in town could be persuaded to give the prize.
>
> *Another thing we could do concerns the end-of-year concert, which is usually free.* At the next concert we could charge people. People who sit at the front could pay more than people who sit at the back. All the proceeds would go to the hospital. I am certain our parents would be happy to contribute.
>
> Recommendation
> *I personally think the concert would be the best idea as it does not need much organisation.* Students who are not actually taking part could help by printing and selling the tickets as well as showing people to their seats on the night. That way everyone would be involved.

Complex sentences

4 You can make your writing more interesting by combining your ideas in more complex sentences like the sentences in italic above. How could the sentences in colour be written as one sentence?

5 Join these sentences together using the word or phrase in brackets.

a You could collect money in the town centre on a Saturday. This is the busiest time. (which)

b We collected a lot of money. The hospital was able to buy the equipment they needed. (so that)

c They were able to buy a kidney dialysis machine. They were also able to buy some toys. (in addition to)

d The weather was very bad. People still collected a lot of money. (Despite)

e The concert was a huge success. We're going to organise another one next year. (as)

f Children donated toys they don't play with any more. They also donated books they don't read any more. (both … and)

g The sponsored bike ride was very enjoyable. It raised a lot of money too. (not only … but also)

h A local restaurant offered a prize of a dinner for two. The restaurant also gave a donation to the hospital. (as well as)

i The school raised £500. It wasn't enough to buy the equipment. (Although)

j The head teacher thanked all the students. They had helped to make the event a success. (who)

Think, plan, write

6 You are going to write a report. First read the task.

> The council of your town or city is concerned that some young people are getting into trouble because they are bored. For this reason, they plan to distribute an information sheet which will give young people who live in the area details of activities which they can do cheaply or for free. The council has asked local people for their ideas. Write your report for the council in 120–180 words telling them what activities young people could do.

7 Before you write, make a list of possible activities you could include. Think of some examples for each of these categories.

social activities   sports activities   voluntary work

8 Choose two or three activities and write some factual information about them. The information does not need to be true.

How much does it cost to do them?
Where and when do they take place?
Who should people contact for more information?

9 When you write, keep in mind these questions.

Who is going to read the report?
What is the report about?
Is the style and layout appropriate?

Use the sample answer opposite as a model, and try to use some complex sentences.

10 Finally, when you have finished, check your grammar, spelling and punctuation.

◀ WRITING GUIDE PAGE 169 ▶

Overview

1 Complete the second sentence so that it has a similar meaning to the first sentence, using the word given. Do not change the word given. You must use between two and five words, including the word given.

1 They arrested Simpson because he had vandalised property.
vandalising
Simpson _____ property.

2 Terry Ray said he was successful because of his teachers.
owed
Terry Ray said _____ his teachers.

3 Ray wouldn't allow his mother to hit him any more.
let
Ray refused _____ him any more.

4 The judge wanted to help kids.
interested
The judge _____ kids.

5 I'm almost positive Susan heard what I said.
have
Susan _____ what I said.

6 Maybe John didn't want to come.
not
John _____ to come.

7 Elderly people need to keep active.
the
It's important _____ active.

8 The concert was very popular so they're going to put on a repeat performance.
such
It _____ that they're going to put on a repeat performance.

2 Complete the spaces with *a / an, the* or no article.

a ¹_____ police arrested Smith for ²_____ attempted theft. He was caught breaking into ³_____ store on ⁴_____ Main Street which sells ⁵_____ electrical appliances. ⁶_____ shop alarm had gone off when ⁷_____ front door was forced open, and ⁸_____ passer-by had telephoned ⁹_____ police station to advise them of ¹⁰_____ incident.

b Promoting ¹_____ good causes can be good for business too. Businesses have been making ²_____ charitable donations for ³_____ long time. The term 'cause-related marketing' was first used by American Express to describe its efforts to raise money to restore ⁴_____ Statue of Liberty. Every time ⁵_____ cardholder used their charge card, American Express donated some money towards refurbishing ⁶_____ monument, eventually raising nearly $2 million. ⁷_____ number of new cardholders went up 45% and card usage increased. This type of marketing suits everyone. The customers feel good when they buy ⁸_____ product concerned, and the companies appear thoughtful and caring.

Extra material

Unit 4 page 56 exercise 4 The feeling that a painting is watching you can be both impressive and worrying. But this illusion is not that hard to explain. Find a photo of someone looking directly into the camera. From any angle, the eyes still look into the camera, and still seem to stare at you. The image is two-dimensional. This means that if it appears to look at you from one angle, it will appear that way from every angle. The effect is achieved in the same way by painters. If an artist chooses to depict a person looking out at viewers, he or she will paint the eyes as if they were 'gazing into the camera'. The success of the illusion depends on the artist's skill in portraying eyes that stare straight out.

Unit 4 page 57 exercise 6

Student A Compare and contrast photos 1 and 2 and say which office you think would be less stressful to work in. Remember you have to speak for about one minute.

Student B When your partner has finished speaking, answer this question: Do you think people work harder in comfortable surroundings?

Student B Compare and contrast photos 3 and 4 and say which shopping area you think is likely to attract more shoppers. Remember you have to speak for about one minute.

Student A When your partner has finished speaking, answer this question: Why do you think some people spend a lot of spare time shopping?

Writing guides

Formal letter (Part 1)

How should I approach the task?

You recently won a competition organised by a satellite TV company. Unfortunately, there are a number of problems with the prize you have received. Read the original advertisement for the competition, on which you have made some notes. Then, using the information in your notes, write to the television company explaining the situation and asking them to resolve the problems.

Write a letter of between 120 and 180 words in an appropriate style.

travel and learn learn and travel

enter
THE GREAT WORLDWIDE TV COMPETITION

You could win a Language-learner's pack containing

poor picture quality —
- a travel video
one cassette broken —
- two audio cassettes
not sent —
- a textbook

All you have to do is finish this sentence in not more than fifteen words:

I enjoy WWTV's Travel and Learn show because ...

If I win a Language-learner's pack, please send me the pack for:
(tick language of your choice)

French	☐	German	☐
English	☑	Japanese	☐
Russian	☐	Spanish	☐

— *Russian pack sent!*

What is the purpose of the letter? The task will tell you exactly what you have to do. This may include: asking for or giving information; initiating action or responding to a request; giving feedback on suggestions; making complaints, suggestions, or corrections.

Who will read it? Probably someone who you do not know well, if at all. This may be a named individual, or an unnamed representative of an organisation, possibly a person in a position of authority or responsibility.

What style should I use? Be polite. Use indirect expressions, formal linking phrases and set phrases wherever appropriate. Avoid being too familiar, or using contractions and colloquial language.

What information should I include? In a transactional letter you will need to read all the information you are given. This will include the task itself, plus one or more additional texts, such as letters, memos, adverts, and hand-written notes. You must respond to all the questions and points in the texts or notes.

How should I structure a formal letter?

Begin a formal letter in one of these ways:

- *Dear Mr/Mrs/Miss/Ms Lodge* – use the person's title and surname if you know it.
- *Dear Sir/Madam* if you don't know the person's name or whether they are a man or a woman. ——————— Dear Sir/Madam,

Say why you are writing. Clearly state the subject ——————— I am writing to complain about the prize I was sent for or context. winning your 'Travel and Learn' competition for language learners. There are four different problems with the pack I received.

Organise all the essential information from the task prompts in a clear and logical way in the main paragraphs of the letter. You may need to add some extra ideas of your own.

Firstly, the language pack you sent was for learners of Russian, not English. I clearly remember ticking the 'English' box. In addition to this, the textbook mentioned in the advert was missing and one of the two audio cassettes was broken and impossible to play.

Furthermore, I watched the Russian video and I am afraid to say that the picture quality was very poor. I hope this is not typical of your videos.

Say how you expect the other person to respond ——————— Naturally, I am still interested in learning English, and I to your letter if this is appropriate. would be grateful if you could send me the correct pack. However, I am not prepared to return the Russian pack until I have received the replacement and checked the contents carefully. I also expect to receive a full refund for the cost of returning the Russian pack to you.

I look forward to hearing from you.

Finish your letter in one of these ways:

Yours sincerely, if you have started your letter with the name of the person you are writing to.

Yours faithfully, if you have started your letter ——————— Yours faithfully,
Dear Sir/Madam.

(Name)

What phrases can I use?

Saying why you are writing	I am writing to complain about / enquire about / tell you about / suggest … I would like to request further information about … I would be most grateful if you could send me details of … In response to your letter of *26 February*, I am writing to …
Organising information	Firstly, … Secondly, … In addition, … Furthermore, … Lastly, …
Asking for action	I would be grateful if you could … It would be helpful if you would … Please could you …
Closing the letter	I look forward to hearing from you.

Informal letter (Part 1)

> You receive a letter from your British penfriend. Read their letter carefully and the notes you have made on it. Then, using the information in your notes, write a suitable reply, making alternative suggestions.
>
> Write a letter of between 120 and 180 words in an appropriate style.

You won't believe this but I won first prize in a competition. I get a free flight to anywhere in Europe and £500 spending money!!! The only condition is that I have to use it in the next six months. I can't believe that my family are pleased about me going! What I'd really like to do is to come and see you. Would it be possible to stay with you? — *No problem.*

Important exams mid June!!

If not, could you book me into a cheap hostel? Can you get time off? – say a fortnight – as I'd really like to spend

Sounds good!

some time travelling around, and it would be much nicer if you could come as well. I thought of coming in June. — *July better for me!*

Anyway write back soon and let me know what you think.

All the best

Nic

What is the purpose of the transactional letter? To respond to a request for action from somebody else, such as to give information or make suggestions. Alternatively, it could be to initiate action, for example, to request information or invite somebody to do something. The task will tell you exactly what you have to do.

Who will read it? The person or people you have been asked to write to.

What style should I use? An informal style. Slang and colloquial expressions are sometimes appropriate, for example, if you are writing to a friend, but not if you don't know the person. Contractions are always appropriate.

What information should I include? In a transactional letter you will need to read information which is included in a variety of texts, for example letters, memos, adverts, and your hand-written notes. You must answer all the questions in the texts or notes and make reference to any other comments.

How should I structure an informal letter?

Begin an informal letter
Dear + the person's first name. ———————

Begin by asking some personal questions ———
or making some personal comments.

Say why you are writing. ———————

If you need to change arrangements or
turn someone down, give reasons. ———————

Give the information that
you have been told to give.
Add some more details of
your own if you like.

End your letter with an appropriate
comment. Don't just stop abruptly.

Finish your letter in an appropriate way:
Best wishes – if you don't know the person
very well.
Love or *All the best* – if you are writing to a
friend

Dear Nic,
It was good to hear from you. Lucky you winning a flight to Europe and £500 spending money! I've never won anything in my life!

About your planned visit, it would be absolutely great to see you again but June wouldn't be the best time. I don't think the Principal of my school would let me have time off for a start, but more importantly I've got an important exam on June 14 and I really need to study hard. What about July? I'm on holiday then. Or even August.

Of course you can stay at my house. My parents would be very upset if you stayed at a hostel. They're always telling me to invite you over for a holiday. You can stay as long as you like.

I'd love to travel round with you. There are loads of places I've never been to, even though it's my country.

Anyway, write back soon and let me know what you think.

Love,
Sam.

What phrases can I use?

Letter openings

How are you? I'm fine.
Thanks for your letter. It was really nice to hear from you.
I'm sorry I haven't written for such a long time but …

Saying why you are writing

You asked me to recommend some (places to stay in my country) ….
I've managed to find out some information about (language schools) for you.
About your planned visit, ….

Letter endings

Write back soon.
Look forward to seeing you soon.
Give my regards to your parents.

Article (Part 2)

How should I approach the task?

You have seen this announcement in an English-language magazine for young people of your age.

You Write – We Print

Family celebrations are often memorable occasions. Write an article describing a family celebration that you remember well. The three most interesting articles will be published in our next issue.

Write your magazine article in 120–180 words.

Who will read the article? Readers choose articles that interest them and ignore those that look dull.

What information should I include? You may have to describe personal experiences or express opinions and ideas which people of your age can identify with. What you write need not be true.

What is the purpose of the article? To inform readers about a particular topic in an entertaining way.

What style should I use? Magazine articles, especially for young adult readers, are often written in a light-hearted style. The title and opening paragraph should try to capture the readers' attention.

How should I structure an article?

A day to remember (1)

(2) Have all the members of your family ever met together in the same place at the same time? It happened to me quite recently and was a remarkable event. (3)

(4) The occasion I have in mind took place last summer. It was my grandparents fiftieth wedding anniversary, and my brother Tim decided to organise a surprise party for them. He phoned everyone in the family and told us his plan. Most importantly, we mustn't say anything to our grandparents.

(5) On the eve of the anniversary, we arrived at Tim's house at midday. By three o'clock, there were over a hundred people there, including cousins, uncles and aunts I hadn't seen for years. Everyone was excited as they waited for the 'happy couple' to arrive.

(5) My grandparents, who thought they were visiting my brother, arrived at four o'clock. you can imagine what happened when they found us all waiting for them. I have never seen anyone look so surprised and so happy.

(5) The celebrations went on until the next morning. (6) Now, we're looking forward to celebrating their sixtieth anniversary.

(1) Think of an interesting title which will make people want to read your article.

(2) Start your article in an interesting way. You could ask the reader a question or make a strong statement.

(3) The first paragraph should involve the reader in some way. Try to end the paragraph in a way which makes the reader want to continue reading.

(4) Build on the interest you have raised in the first paragraph. This may mean answering the question or telling the next part of the story.

(5) Use each paragraph to mark the next stage of your article.

(6) Finish the article in an interesting way. This could be humorous or thought-provoking.

What phrases can I use?

Addressing the reader directly
Have you ever …?
What do you think about …?

Making a strong statement
There's nothing worse than …
You may not agree with me, but I think …

Describing a personal experience
It happened to me when …
This is what happened when …
The occasion I have in mind …
I'll never forget the time …

Conversational expressions
You can imagine …
If you ask me …
Another thing is that …

Discursive composition
(Part 2)

How should I approach the task?

You have had a class discussion about the way animals are treated in modern society. Your teacher has asked you to write a composition giving your opinion on the following question:

Should animals be used in scientific experiments to try out new drugs, medicines or beauty products?

Write your composition in 120–180 words.

What is the purpose of the composition? Compositions are usually set by teachers for students. They give students the opportunity to express their opinions on subjects which may be controversial.

Who will read it? Probably only the teacher, but possibly other students in your class.

What style should I use? Compositions are formal pieces of writing. Your opinions should be expressed in a clear and logical way. Use discourse markers to make clear how your different points are related.

What information should I include? A good discursive composition includes clearly-stated opinions supported by well-chosen examples and convincing reasons.

How should I structure a discursive composition?

(1) In many countries, experiments are carried out on animals to test drugs, medicines and beauty products like shampoo or shower gel. Scientists say they need to use animals, but many ordinary people believe these experiments are cruel. I will discuss both points of view and express my own opinion. (2)

(3) Scientists argue that cures for human diseases would not be found if animal experiments were banned. They claim that it is safer to test new medicines on animals before giving them to humans. They say that the animals they use do not suffer.

(4) On the other side of the argument, many people believe that animals feel pain as much as humans, and the mistreatment of innocent creatures, like monkeys or mice, for scientific research is cruel and immoral. They think human volunteers should be used instead.

(5) In my opinion, there is no justification for using animals to test beauty products. However, I believe that it may be necessary to use animals for testing drugs which may save human lives.

(1) The first paragraph of your composition should introduce the subject and outline the main arguments related to it.

(2) State what you intend to do in your composition.

(3) The second paragraph should provide more detail in support of one side of the argument.

(4) The third paragraph should present the other side of the argument.

(5) The concluding paragraph should clearly express your own opinion.

What phrases can I use?

Stating an aim
I will discuss both points of view and express my own opinion.

Expressing personal opinions
In my opinion, …
I (do) believe that …
On balance, it seems to me that …

Reporting other people's opinions
Scientists argue/claim/say that …
Many people believe that …

Expressions which introduce a contrast
On the other side of the argument, …
However, … , but …

Letter of application
(Part 2)

How should I approach the task?

> A language school in Britain is offering twenty-five students the chance to study English for one month this summer absolutely free. Scholarships will cover fees, accommodation with a British family and travel costs.
>
> Write a letter of application giving your reasons for applying for the scholarship and saying how the course would benefit you.

Who will read the letter? Letters of application are usually read by the personnel manager of a company or other organisation, or the director of a school or college.

What is the purpose of the letter? It may be to apply for a job, scholarship, or a place on a course of study.

What style should I use? Write in a formal style. Avoid being too familiar, contractions and colloquial language. Be clear and don't repeat yourself. Use set phrases and formal linking phrases where appropriate.

What information should I include? Give essential and relevant personal information. Make a number of points in support of your application. The task may tell you what kind of information to include.

How should I structure a letter of application?

(1) Dear Sir/Madam,

(2) I saw your advertisement in the Daily News on Friday 23 March, and I would like to apply for a scholarship to study in Britain for one month this summer.

I am seventeen years old and have been studying English for five years (3). I am taking the First Certificate examination in June next year, and, if I was awarded a scholarship to study at a language school in Britain, it would really help me to improve my spoken English and my listening (3). I have never been abroad before because I cannot afford it and both my parents are unemployed. This would be a wonderful opportunity for me to visit an English-speaking country and learn about the British way of life at the same time (3).

I hope you will consider my application. I look forward to hearing from you soon.

(4) Yours faithfully,
Federico Accinni

(1) Begin a formal letter in one of these ways.
Dear Mr/Mrs/Miss/Ms Lodge – use the person's title and name if you know it.
Dear Sir/Madam if you don't know the person's name or whether they are a man or a woman.

(2) Say why you are writing and where (and when) you saw the advertisement.

(3) Give relevant personal information about yourself, which might include age, education, work experience, interests etc. and give reasons in support of your application.

(4) Finish your letter in one of these ways. *Yours sincerely*, if you have started your letter with the name of the person you are writing to. *Yours faithfully*, if you begin *Dear Sir/Madam*.

What phrases can I use?

Reasons for writing
I would like to apply for the job of ... which was advertised in the *Daily News* on Friday 21 February.
I am writing to apply for ...
I am writing with regard to ...

Giving personal information
I am a twenty-two-year-old Chinese student.
I have just completed a three-year course in ...
I have been studying English for six years.
My interests are ...

Concluding
I am available for interview at any time.
I hope you will consider my application.
I look forward to hearing from you soon.

Report (Part 2)

How should I approach the task?

> A group of students from Australia is coming to stay in your town as part of an exchange programme. The director has asked you to write a brief report suggesting places the group should visit and activities they could take part in during their stay.
>
> Write a report of between 120 and 180 words.

What's the purpose of the report? You may be asked to give information, evaluate something, or make suggestions and recommendations.

Who will read it? Usually the people who are asking for the report. This may be an official group or somebody in authority, like a boss or a college principal.

What style should I use? Be clear and avoid unnecessary detail. Give essential information and recommendations. An impersonal style is often appropriate, avoiding overuse of the pronoun 'I'.

What information should I include? Make a number of points in answer to the question. Give some description and explanation. Conclude with a personal recommendation.

How should I structure a report?

Introduction (1)

This report will consider what a group of exchange students from Australia could do while they are staying in our town. Several visits and other activities will be suggested.

Places to visit (2)

Since our town is well-known as a cultural centre, many foreign visitors find the following particularly interesting places to visit:

- the cathedral   • the palace
- our market, which is famous as a place where local craftsmen sell traditional products.

Activities (2)

In the past students from abroad have said they would like to meet and do things with students here. For this reason, joint activities between our visitors and our college students should be considered. The following could be organised:

- a sports competition
- an arts or music event

Recommendations (2)

As our Australian visitors will be staying for some time, I suggest a variety of visits and activities are planned. (3)

During their first week, they could visit historical sites and go to the market. Later, a tennis competition involving local students could be held.

Finally, during their last week, our visitors could be invited to take part in a musical evening at our college.

(1) Use clear headings to help the reader see how the report is organised. *Introduction* and *Recommendations* or *Conclusion* are often appropriate.

(2) Give each section in the report its own paragraph. Use numbers or bullets to make them stand out.
Where appropriate, divide sections into paragraphs.

(3) Use your conclusion to summarise briefly. Make sure that you express your personal recommendation if this is asked for in the question. Make points clearly and directly.

What phrases can I use?

Stating aims
The aim of this report is to …
This report will consider / examine / compare …
This report is intended to …

Giving reasons
Since / As (our town is well-known), …
For this reason / these reasons …

Making suggestions or recommendations
In view of this, I (would) recommend / suggest (that)…
We / I suggest (that) …
They / We could …

Set Book (Part 2)

How should I prepare to write about the set book?

Get to know the book
- Read it several times.
- Watch a film version. Make notes about the differences.

The story
- Write a short summary of each chapter.
- Make a list of the main events.

The characters
- Make a list of the main characters. Make notes about their appearance and personality. What adjectives could you use to describe them?
- Make notes about the most important relationships in the book.

The time and place
- Make notes on where and when the story is set.
- If it is set in the past, think about any differences there are with the modern world.

Your opinion
- Write notes about why you like the book. Think of adjectives to describe the story, e.g. exciting, unusual, etc.
- Write about your favourite part. What happens? Why do you like it?
- Write about anything you don't like about the book.

How should I approach the task?

Here are examples of each possible task type.

5a	What did you enjoy about the book or one of the short stories you have read? Write a **letter** to a friend, explaining what you liked and describing your favourite part.

5b	'The most interesting characters aren't perfect. They make mistakes and learn from them.' Is this true of one of the characters from the book, or one of the short stories you have read? Write your **composition**, explaining your views.

5c	Your teacher would like to know your opinion of the book or one of the short stories you have read. Write a **report** explaining what is or isn't interesting about the book and giving reasons why you would or wouldn't recommend it for other students to study.

5d	'People behave in similar ways and have similar relationships in every society.' Do you think this statement is true about the characters in the book or one of the short stories you have read? Write an **article** for your college magazine explaining your views.

What is the purpose of the task? You may need to give your opinion of the book, as in a report or an informal letter. Otherwise, you may be required to express an argument about a particular aspect of the book, as in a composition or an article.

Who will read it? A report would be written for an official group or somebody in a position of authority. An article would be read by the readers of the magazine. An informal letter is likely to be to a friend. A composition would normally be written for your teacher.

What style should I use? Follow the notes given on these writing styles in the relevant Writing Guides for a report, a composition, a letter or an article.

What information should I include? In each case only include information about the book that is relevant to the question. Don't be tempted to retell the story or to give unnecessary details.

How should I structure my answer?

5a Animal Farm

Dear Ben

Thanks for your last letter. It's always great to hear from you! (1)

(2) I want to tell you about a really good book I've read. It's called *Animal Farm* (3). I like it because it's so unusual. (4) It's about a group of animals that are fed up with being treated badly by the farmer. One of the pigs dreams about a world where animals live together equally. After that, the animals chase the farmer away and start running the farm together. (5) All the animals are very different characters and they each represent a different idea. (4) This makes the story really interesting.

(2) My favourite part of the book is the ending. The pigs are behaving more and more like humans while the rest of the animals are hungry and overworked. The pigs give a dinner party for some humans. When the other animals look through the window, they can't tell the difference between the pigs and the humans. (5) I think this ending is brilliant because the animals are back where they started.

Read the book! It's fantastic!

See you soon (1)

Simon

(1) Begin and end with suitable expressions.
(2) Give each part of the question its own paragraph.
(3) Refer to the book you want to talk about early on.
(4) Give reasons for your opinions.
(5) Give limited information about the plot for the purpose of context and background.

5b Pride and Prejudice

Elizabeth Bennet (1) is the most important character in *Pride and Prejudice* and at first she seems the most sensible. However, it soon becomes obvious that she is far from perfect (2).

Elizabeth is the second of the five daughters of Mr and Mrs Bennet. Her mother is silly. Her youngest sisters are badly behaved. Her father takes little interest in his family. In comparison, Elizabeth is the most reasonable (3). She is intelligent, she is embarrassed by her mother's behaviour, and she is loyal to her older sister, Anne.

(4) Mr Darcy is attracted to Elizabeth's good qualities, but Elizabeth forms an opinion of him which is completely wrong. She cannot see that, although he's proud, he's a good man. On the other hand, she likes the worthless soldier, Wickham.

It is only after Elizabeth learns that Wickham has lied and that Darcy has been responsible for making sure Lydia and Wickham are married, that Elizabeth realises her mistakes (2). She understands her judgement has been wrong and, at last, she and Darcy can find happiness.

(1) Introduce the subject of your composition in your first paragraph.
(2) Refer back to the question in your introductory and concluding paragraphs.
(3) Make a number of points for one side of the argument.
(4) Make a number of points for the other side of the argument.

What words and phrases can I use?

Look at the vocabulary lists. Combine words to make sentences about the book or short story you have studied.

EXAMPLE

The main character is very sensitive.
The opening is exciting.

Nouns used in books

main character	villain	opening
minor characters	setting	ending
hero / heroine	plot	main event(s)

Adjectives to describe the characters

Positive	Negative
kind	unkind / cruel
generous	mean
clever	stupid
sensitive	insensitive
brave	cowardly

Adjectives to describe the story

Positive	Negative
mysterious	ordinary
exciting	unexciting / dull
original	unoriginal
interesting	uninteresting / boring

Story (Part 2)

How should I approach the task?

An English language magazine is running a short story competition for its readers. The story must begin with the following words:

It was the worst holiday I had ever had

Write your story for the competition in 120–180 words.

What is the purpose of the story? To entertain and interest the reader.

Who will read it? Your story may be for a competition or a magazine. The task may say who will read it, for example, your teacher or other foreign language students.

What style should I use? Use a neutral style – not formal but not too informal either. Use descriptive language: adjectives and adverbs make a story more dramatic.

What information should I include? A good story has an interesting beginning, a middle which maintains our interest and a definite end. You need to set the scene and choose two or three events to describe in detail.

How should I structure a story?

(1) It was the worst holiday I had ever had. (2) I had never been to a holiday camp before, but thought that it would be a good place to meet lots of people my own age. I was so wrong.

(3) The holiday was a total disaster from the start. The first thing that went wrong was that I had to share a room with a bad-tempered (4) seventy-five-year-old woman who went to bed early, snored loudly (4) all night and then complained unreasonably that I woke her up when I came back from the disco at 3 a.m.

(3) The next problem was that I was woken up four hours later by a cheerful (4) voice over an intercom saying, 'Good morning everybody! Time to get up and start the day!' It was impossible to go back to sleep as the announcement was followed by loud music and repeated every five minutes.

(5) At the end of the fortnight I was absolutely exhausted (4) and had not had much fun either. That was the last time I would go to a holiday camp.

(1) Begin or end your story with the words given, if this is asked for in the task.

(2) Include an introductory paragraph. Unless you are writing in the first person, introduce the main characters. Say where and when the events took place, and give any other important background information. Make your beginning interesting so that people will want to read on.

(3) Write one or two middle paragraphs, where you develop the story. Use a new paragraph for a different event.

(4) Add descriptive detail to make it more real.

(5) Include a concluding paragraph, where you bring the story to an end.

What phrases can I use?

Ordering words and phrases

At first, ...

The first thing that happened was ...

Next, ...

After a while, ...

Then, ...

Eventually, ...

In the end, ...

Suddenly, ...

Meanwhile, ...

Grammar reference

Terminology

Jimmy McGregor was the first man to swim from New Zealand to Australia. When he arrived in Australia, he was met by a TV interviewer. 'Strewth, mate,' said the Australian unbelievingly. 'How did you get to be such a good swimmer? That's an impossible distance you've just swum!'

'As you may know,' replied Jimmy, 'there are lots of lakes in Scotland and, from the age of two, my father used to take me to Loch Lomond, which is one of the biggest. He would row me into the middle, help me over the side, and leave me to swim the twenty kilometres back to the shore.'

'That must have been rather hard for a two-year-old,' said the Australian admiringly.

'Yes,' agreed Jimmy. 'However, the hardest part was fighting my way out of the sack!'

Subordinate clause

Sentence

Main clause

Modifier/intensifier: used to strengthen or weaken the meaning of adjectives and adverbs. Also: *so, very.*

Ungradable adjective: can only be used with 'extreme' modifiers like *absolutely*. Also: *huge, freezing, furious, terrified.*

Connective: relative pronoun

Connective: conjunction. Also: *but, so, if*, etc.

Speech marks: used to indicate the actual words that someone says.

NOTE Other punctuation marks come inside the speech marks.

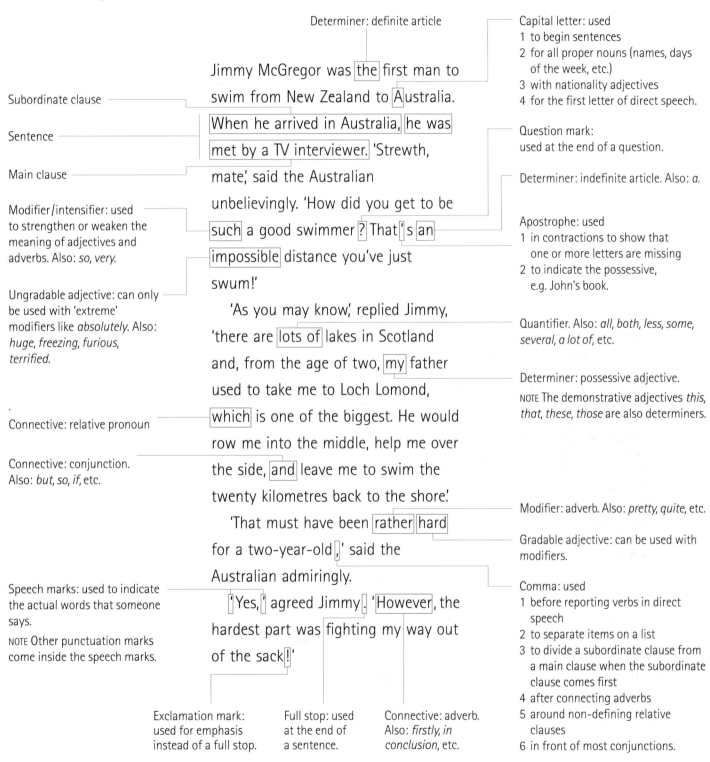

Determiner: definite article

Capital letter: used
1 to begin sentences
2 for all proper nouns (names, days of the week, etc.)
3 with nationality adjectives
4 for the first letter of direct speech.

Question mark: used at the end of a question.

Determiner: indefinite article. Also: *a*.

Apostrophe: used
1 in contractions to show that one or more letters are missing
2 to indicate the possessive, e.g. John's book.

Quantifier. Also: *all, both, less, some, several, a lot of*, etc.

Determiner: possessive adjective.

NOTE The demonstrative adjectives *this, that, these, those* are also determiners.

Modifier: adverb. Also: *pretty, quite*, etc.

Gradable adjective: can be used with modifiers.

Comma: used
1 before reporting verbs in direct speech
2 to separate items on a list
3 to divide a subordinate clause from a main clause when the subordinate clause comes first
4 after connecting adverbs
5 around non-defining relative clauses
6 in front of most conjunctions.

Exclamation mark: used for emphasis instead of a full stop.

Full stop: used at the end of a sentence.

Connective: adverb. Also: *firstly, in conclusion*, etc.

Unit 1

The future

There are many ways of talking about future time in English. This is a summary of the most common forms and their uses.

1 Present continuous

The present continuous is used to refer to future actions or events which have already been arranged.

Are you doing anything interesting at the weekend?
We're spending the summer with our friends in Greece.

2 *Will* future

A Future simple (*will* + infinitive)

The *will* future is used to talk about

1 future facts.
   The *sun will rise* at 6.30 tomorrow morning.
2 predictions or expectations.
   I expect *Helen and John will be* late again.
3 strong intentions.
   When Loretta retires, *I'll definitely apply* for her job.
4 instant decisions about the immediate future.
   The phone's ringing. *I'll answer* it.
5 offers
   I'll take you to the airport if you like.

B Future continuous (*will* + *be* + *-ing*)

This form is used to talk about

1 events or actions that will be in progress at a specific time in the future.
   This time tomorrow, *I'll be travelling* through France.
2 predicted or expected trends.
   In the twenty-second century, *people will be living* to the age of 130.

C Future perfect simple (*will* + *have* + past participle) and Future perfect continuous (*will* + *have* + *been* + *-ing*)

These two forms are used to talk about

1 actions or events that will already be completed by a particular time in the future.
   By the year 2012, *I'll have left* school and started work.
2 the continuous nature of actions and events in the future.
   On Saturday *we'll have been living* here for three years.

NOTES

1 *Shall* is sometimes used instead of *will* after *I* and *we*.
   In a few days *we shall have forgotten* about the accident.
2 *Shall* must be used to start questions which are suggestions and offers.
   Shall we phone to see what time the film starts?
   Shall I carry that heavy case for you?

3 *Going to* + infinitive

This is used to talk about

a intentions or plans.
   After Christmas, *I'm going to get* a job and save up.
   What *are you going to do* when you leave school?
b predictions based on present evidence or knowledge.
   My nose is tickling. I think *I'm going to sneeze.*
   My sister's going to have a baby.

4 Present simple

This tense is used to talk about scheduled, timetabled or fixed events.

   The match starts at 7.30 tomorrow evening.

5 Other ways of referring to the future

a *To be (just) about to* + infinitive
   This is used to talk about actions or events which we expect to happen in the immediate future.
   I must hurry – *the train's just about to leave.*
b *To be on the point of* + *-ing*
   This expression also refers to the immediate future.
   The train is on the point of leaving. Close the doors!

Unit 2

Describing habitual actions

1 Habitual actions in the present

A Present simple

This is the usual way of expressing present habitual actions.

> Whenever *I go* to town, *I spend* too much money.

The present simple is also used for permanent situations.

> *My uncle lives* in Bristol, but *he works* in London.

B *tend to*

The verb *tend to* + infinitive can be used to refer to usual or generally occurring actions.

> *She tends to get up* late at weekends.

C Other ways of expressing habitual actions in the present

1 Present continuous + *always*

This is used mainly to refer to actions which are very frequent.

> *He's always giving* me presents.

It is also used when you are annoyed with yourself or someone else.

> *You're always complaining* about my cooking.

> *I'm always losing* my keys.

2 *will* + infinitive

This is sometimes used instead of the present simple to refer to behaviour which is predictable or typical.

> *I'll sit* for hours watching TV.

3 *keep* + -ing

This is used for habitual actions which are accidental or annoying.

> *I keep bumping* my head on that tree.

2 Habitual actions in the past

A Past simple

When a past simple verb refers to habitual or repeated actions it can be accompanied by a frequency expression.

> When I worked in London, *I usually got* home at six o'clock.

B *used to* + infinitive

This refers to habitual past actions which no longer happen.

> Before I had a car, *I used to cycle* to work.

It can also be used for actions that did not happen before, but happen now.

> *I didn't use to have* foreign holidays. Now I go abroad every year.

> *We never used to watch* TV at breakfast time.

NOTES

1 Remember the question form of *used to*.
  Where *did you use to go* for your holidays?

2 Sentences with *used to* do not need frequency adverbs, but they are sometimes included for emphasis.
  I always *used to be* late for school.

C *would* + infinitive

This refers to habitual past actions.

> Every summer *our parents would take us* to the seaside.

Avoid using *would* in questions and negative sentences, as its meaning can be completely different.

NOTES

There is a difference in meaning between *used to* and *would*.

1 *Used to* can refer to permanent situations as well as habitual actions.
  I *used to be able to see* the church from my bedroom window.

2 *Would* can only refer to actions, not situations. You can say
  He'd catch the 7.30 train.
  but you **cannot** say
  He'd work in London.

3 *Used to*, *be used to*, and *get used to*

Used to has three forms with different meanings.

A *used to* + infinitive

This refers to habitual past actions (see note 2B above).

> My father *used to smoke* 40 cigarettes a day.

B *to be used to* + -*ing*

This means to be accustomed to.

> I must go to bed early. *I'm used to having* ten hours sleep a night.

C to get used to + -ing

This means to become accustomed to, often to something unusual or strange.

> If you come to England, you'll have to *get used to driving* on the left-hand side of the road.

NOTE

Other common verbs which follow the same pattern are *look forward to* and *object to*.

Comparative and superlative adjectives and adverbs

1 Adjectives

A Regular adjectives with one syllable

Adjective	Comparative	Superlative
tall	taller	the tallest
large	larger	the largest
big	bigger	the biggest

NOTES

1 Adjectives ending in two consonants or two vowels and a consonant add *-er/-est*: long, short, bright, smooth, cool, clean, great
2 Adjectives ending in *-e* add *-r/-st*: nice, late, safe, strange, rude, wide
3 Many adjectives ending in a single vowel + single consonant double the consonant and add *-er/-est*: fat, thin, flat, sad, wet

B Regular adjectives with two or more syllables

Adjective	Comparative	Superlative
heavy	heavier	the heaviest
modern	more modern	the most modern
important	more important	the most important
common	more common/ commoner	the most common/ the commonest

NOTES

1 Adjectives ending in *-y* change *y* to *i* and add *-er/-est*: happy, dirty, funny, tidy, busy, early, empty, dry
2 Most longer adjectives use *more* and *the most*: comfortable, independent, insignificant, uninteresting
3 Some two-syllable adjectives can form their comparatives and superlatives in two ways: by adding *-er/-est* or with *more* and *most*: clever, pleasant, gentle, narrow, shallow, simple, tired

C Irregular adjectives

Adjective	Comparative	Superlative
good	better	the best
bad	worse	the worst
old	elder/ older	the eldest/ the oldest
far	further/ farther	the furthest/ the farthest

D Comparative and superlative adjectives in context

1 *more/-er + than*
> I'm *taller than* my brother.
> My brother's *more serious than* me.
> I'm *more intelligent than* he is/him.

NOTES

If the pronoun after *than* is not followed by a verb, use the object pronoun form – *me, him, us, them*, etc.

If the pronoun after *than* is followed by a verb, use the subject pronoun form – *I, he, we, they*, etc.

2 *the most/-est*
> I'm *the tallest* student in the class.
> My sister's *the most intelligent* student in her school.
3 *less + than/the least*
> That film was *less interesting than* the last one I saw.
> It was *the least interesting* film I've seen all year.

E Qualifying comparative adjectives

1 Use these words and phrases to refer to big differences: *far, a lot, much*.
> Cars are *a lot faster* and *much more comfortable* than bicycles.
2 Use these words and phrases to refer to small differences: *a bit, a little, slightly*.
> The weather's *a bit hotter* than it was yesterday.

2 Adverbs

A Regular adverbs

The majority of comparative and superlative adverbs are formed like this:

Adjective	Comparative	Superlative
slowly	more slowly	the most slowly

B Irregular adverbs

Adjective	Comparative	Superlative
well	better	the best
badly	worse	the worst
little	less	the least
much	more	the most

C Adverbs which are the same as adjectives

Adjective	Comparative	Superlative
fast	faster	the fastest
hard	harder	the hardest

Other adverbs of this kind are: *far, long, loud, straight*.

3 *The* + comparative + *the*

This construction links two actions or situations - when one thing happens, another thing follows. A comparative expression in the first clause is balanced by a comparative expression in the second clause. Several grammatical patterns are possible here:

A adjective ... adjective.

The harder a job is, *the more rewarding* I find it.

B adverb ... adverb.

The sooner we start, *the quicker* we'll finish.

C adjective ... adverb, or adverb ... adjective.

The easier a job is, *the more quickly* I do it.

D more (+ noun) ... more (+ noun).

The more money Jack earned, *the more clothes* he bought.

E less (+ clause) ... less (+ uncountable noun), fewer (+ plural countable noun).

The less Bob earned, *the less food/ the fewer holidays* he could afford.

F more (+ clause) ... less (+ clause).

The more you sleep, *the less* you do.

G Other combinations of these patterns are possible. Examples.

The harder Joe worked, *the more* he earned.
The more he ate, *the fatter* he got.

NOTES

1 Neither of the two clauses in *the* + comparative + *the* sentences makes sense without the other.
2 In writing, a comma is used to separate the two clauses.
3 Both clauses need a verb.
4 In some expressions with *better*, no verbs are needed.

Jim   When shall I come round to see you?
Tim   *The sooner, the better.*

4 Other comparative constructions

A *as ... as*

This construction can be used with adjectives or adverbs to make comparisons between two things or people.

I'm *as tall as* my brother.
Trains don't travel *as fast as* planes.

In negative sentences *so* can be used instead of the first *as*.

Cats aren't *so friendly as* dogs.

B Comparative + *and* + comparative

This construction can be used with adjectives or adverbs to refer to a trend.

Towards the end of the film, I became *more and more frightened.*
As the exams approached, I worked *harder and harder.*
Over the last twenty years, televisions have become *less and less expensive.*

Unit 3

Talking about ability

1 Can, be able to

Can and *be able to* are the verbs most commonly used to talk about ability. Sometimes it is possible to use either verb without changing the meaning of the sentence. Sometimes, we have to use *be able to* as there is no appropriate form of *can*.

infinitive	____	*to be able to*
present	*can*	*am/are/is able to*
future	____	*will be able to*
past	*could*	*was/were able to*
present perfect	____	*have/has been able to*
past perfect	____	*had been able to*

2 Present ability

A To talk about a general ability in the present, both forms are possible, but *can* is more usual.
   Gareth *can* run very fast.
   (Gareth *is able to* run very fast.)

B To talk about a learned ability in the present, *can* is more usual. *Know how to* can be used as an alternative to *can*.
   Can you play chess?
   Do you know how to play chess?

3 Future ability

To talk about an ability in the future, we use the future form of *be able to*.
   Will I be able to play better after I've had some lessons?

4 Past ability

A To talk about a general ability in the past, both forms are possible
   Before his accident, Ben *could* jump really high.
   Before his accident, Ben *was able to* jump really high.

B To talk about an ability to do something in the past on one particular occasion, it is not possible to use *could*. We must use the past tense of *be able to* or *manage* (+ infinitive) or *succeed* (+ in + -ing)
   Although she had lost a lot of blood, the doctors *were able to* save the girl's life.

Despite the difficult conditions, the surgeons *managed* to perform the operation successfully and *succeeded* in saving the man's leg.

NOTE
If the event was unsuccessful, it is possible to use *couldn't* as well as the past forms of *be able to*, *manage* and *succeed*.
   Although he did his best, he *couldn't* finish it in time.

5 'Conditional' ability

A To talk about a hypothetical ability in the present or future, we can use *could* or *would be able to*.
   I *could* probably jump further if I had longer legs.
   I *would* probably *be able to* play better if I practised more.

B To talk about a hypothetical ability in the past, we usually use *could + have + past participle* although we can also use *would have been able to*.
   Even if he'd been taller he *couldn't have* reached it.
   Even if he'd been taller, *he wouldn't have been able to* reach it.

6 Other structures used to talk about ability

A To talk about aptitude and capacity for doing something, we can use *be capable of + -ing*.
   He is certainly *capable of breaking* the world record.

B To talk about how well we do something, we can use the structure *be good (brilliant, etc.)/bad (terrible, etc.) at + noun or gerund*.
   I have never been *good at sports*.
   I am particularly *bad at running*.

Unit 4

Modal verbs

1 Obligation

A *must*

Must + infinitive is used for strong obligations which express the authority of the speaker or writer. It is used:

1 for formal rules or laws.
   Passengers *must* fasten their seat belts for take-off.
2 for suggestions, advice or recommendations that the speaker or writer feels strongly about.
   You *must* come to my party. Everyone's going to be there.

B *have to*

Have to + infinitive is used for strong obligations which express the authority of a third person, rather than the speaker or writer. It is used:

1 when the speaker wants to show they are not responsible for imposing the obligation, or do not agree with it.
   I'll be late home tonight. *I have to* work late. My boss said so.
2 when the speaker or writer is reminding someone about a rule or law.
   I'm sorry, but you *have to* wear a seat belt in the back of cars now.

C *have got to*

Have got to is more informal than *have to*. It is often used:

1 for direct commands.
   You've got to stop wasting your money.
2 for emphasis.
   I don't care how hard I have to work, *I've just got to* pass the exam this time.

D *need to*

Need to is used to express needs or necessities, rather than strict obligations.
   If we're going to work together, *I need to* know about your background and experience.

E Negatives

1 *Mustn't* expresses prohibition (negative rules and laws or strong advice).
   Drivers *must not* exceed the speed limit.
   You *mustn't* blame yourself. It's not your fault.

2 *Do not have to/have not got to* express lack of obligation or necessity.
   You *don't have to* wear a uniform, but you can if you like.
3 *Do not need to/needn't* + infinitive are used to express lack of obligation or necessity and are similar in meaning to *do not have to*.
   There are no lessons tomorrow, so *I don't need to* get up early.
   You *needn't* tell me your phone number if you don't want to.
4 *Did not need to* + infinitive means 'It was not necessary, so we didn't do it'.
   The train was delayed so we *didn't need to* hurry.
5 *Needn't have* + past participle means 'It was not necessary, but we did it in spite of this'.
   We had to wait for half an hour on the platform because the train was delayed. We *needn't have hurried* after all.

2 Permission and prohibition

A *can/can't*

This is one of the commonest ways of expressing permission and prohibition.
   Can I use the phone, please?
   In Spain *you can't* leave school until the age of 16.

NOTE
May I … ? means the same as *Can I … ?*, but is more formal and more polite.

B Other expressions of permission
   You're allowed to buy cigarettes when you're 18.
   We were only permitted to take photographs in certain places.
   My parents let me stay out late at weekends.

C Other expressions of prohibition
   You aren't allowed to go abroad without a passport.
   Smoking is not permitted in most cinemas.
   You are not permitted to smoke in this theatre.
   People are forbidden to smoke on the Underground.
   The workers have been prohibited from striking.
   Nigel has been banned from driving for six months.

Unit 5

Past Time

1 Past simple

We use the past simple tense when we want to refer to an action or event which is finished and:

a took place at a specific time and place in the past.
Judy *went* to Spain in 1999.

b took place over a specific period in the past.
She *lived* in Spain between 1999 and 2002.

c was habitual during a specific period in the past.
When Judy lived in Spain, she *ate* dinner at about 10 p.m.

NOTE
A past time reference must either be given or understood from the context.

2 Past continuous

We use the past continuous to indicate:

a a continuous event in the past (which may or may not be unfinished).
Dick *was working* for his uncle when I knew him.

b a temporary event in the past which was in progress before another event took place.
I'll always remember what I *was doing* when I heard the dreadful news.

c an event which started before another event in the past and continued.
When Neil and Cathy eventually turned up, all the other guests *were* already *eating* their dessert.

d simultaneous, continuous actions in the past.
While I *was trying* to phone her, *she was trying* to phone me!

e repeated actions occurring over a period of time in the past.
Before I got my own flat, I *was* always *arguing* with my parents.

3 Past perfect

We use the past perfect to indicate a past event or situation which occurred before another past event or situation.

I*'d been* awake for quite a while before the alarm rang.
Although I arrived on time, Mike *had* already *left*.

NOTE
A time conjunction sometimes replaces the past perfect to show which of the two past events occurred first. In this case both events can be in the simple past tense.

Alex *phoned* me before he *left*.

4 Past perfect continuous

We use the continuous form when we want to emphasise the continuity and duration of an event.

Brian *had been trying* to get a job for over a year before he was offered his present one.

5 Present perfect

We use the present perfect tense when we want to talk about:

a an event which started in the past, continues in the present and may continue into the future.
My parents *have been married* for twenty years.

b a recent event in the past which has relevance to the present.
A man *has appeared* in court charged with the murder of the missing person.

c an event which happened in the past without saying when it happened (because we do not consider this is important).
Have you *seen* Jill?
I*'ve read* Hamlet but I*'ve* never *seen* it performed.

d an event which happened in the past but in unfinished time (with expressions like *today*, *this month*, *this year*, etc.).
I didn't see Tim last week but I*'ve been* out with him twice already this week.

6 Present perfect continuous

We use the continuous form

a to emphasise the continuity and duration of the event.
The Smiths *have been living* in the same house ever since they got married.

b to indicate that a continuous activity in the recent past is responsible for a present situation. This activity may or may not be unfinished.
I'm not crying – I*'ve been peeling* onions.

NOTE
The following verbs can be in the present perfect or the present perfect continuous tense with no real change of meaning, although the continuous form is

often preferred: *live, wait, drive, smoke, work, stay, study, rain*.

> I've *driven* since I was eighteen.
> I've *been driving* since I was eighteen.

Participle clauses

A participle clause contains a present participle, e.g. *seeing*, a past participle, e.g. *seen*, or a perfect participle, e.g. *having seen*. It can be used

a to indicate two events happening at the same time. It can replace a time clause.
> *Walking* down the High Street on Saturday, I saw Paul. (replaces As/When/While I was walking ...)

b to indicate a sequence of events.
> *Raising* their glasses, they wished Darren a happy birthday.

c to indicate a reason. It can replace a reason clause.
> *Not understanding* Albert's question, I was unable to give him an answer. (replaces Because/Since I didn't understand ...)
> *Having spent* my money on a car, I couldn't afford a holiday. (replaces Because/Since I had spent ...)

NOTE

The subject of the participle must also be the subject of the other verb. It is not possible to say *Having a bath, the phone rang*.

Extreme adjectives

1 Most adjectives can be used with *very* or *really* and in the comparative form with *even* for emphasis.
> Yesterday was *very/really* cold, but today is *even* colder.

NOTE
Really is more informal than *very*.

2 Extreme adjectives cannot be preceded by *very* or in the comparative by *even*. If you want to emphasise them, you must use *absolutely* or *really*.
> I was *absolutely/really* furious.

NOTE
You cannot use absolutely with ordinary adjectives.
> ~~Today is *absolutely* cold.~~
> Today is *absolutely* freezing.

Unit 6

Gerunds and infinitives

Certain verbs, adjectives and prepositions must always be followed by the gerund; others must always be followed by the infinitive. Some verbs, however, can be followed by either the infinitive or the gerund.

1 Gerunds
Gerunds are verbs that are like nouns. They are formed by adding *-ing* to the verb and can be used in four ways.

A As the subject of a clause or sentence
> *Eating* out can be expensive.

B As the object of a clause or sentence
> One of my interests is *collecting* antiques.

C After verbs
1 After verbs expressing likes and dislikes (but see 3B2 below).
> I don't enjoy *seeing* you like this.
2 After other verbs such as: *admit, appreciate, avoid, can't help, consider, delay, deny, finish, forgive, give up, imagine, involve, keep, mind, miss, postpone, put off, prevent, report, resist, risk, suggest*.
> Have you considered *buying* a new one?

D After prepositions
1 After all prepositions.
> It's for *opening* bottles.
2 After adjective + preposition combinations such as:
> *nervous/worried   about*
> *bad/good/clever/skilled   at*
> *sorry/responsible   for*
> *interested   in*
> *capable/afraid/frightened/terrified   of*
> *bored   with*
> I'm interested in *applying* for the job.
3 After verb + preposition combinations such as:
> *apologize for, arrest someone for, be/get used to, congratulate someone on, insist on, look forward to, object to, succeed in, warn someone about*.
> My little brother insisted on *coming* with me.

2 The infinitive

A The infinitive is always used after certain verbs:
*afford, agree, arrange, ask, appear, attempt, choose,
decide, expect, help, hope, intend, learn, manage,
offer, pretend, promise, refuse, seem.*
I can't afford *to go* on holiday this year.

B The infinitive is always used after certain adjectives:
*amazed, certain, difficult, disappointed, easy, free,
glad, happy, likely, pleased, possible, simple, sure,
surprised.*
The recipe is simple *to follow.*

3 The gerund or the infinitive

Some verbs can be followed by the gerund or the
infinitive.

A With no change of meaning

The verbs *start, begin, continue* can be followed by
either the gerund or the infinitive, without changing
the meaning of the sentence.
Jeff continued *to smoke/smoking* despite the doctor's
advice.

B With a slight change of meaning

The meaning of the verbs *like, prefer, hate, love*
changes slightly, depending on whether the gerund or
infinitive follows them.
1 The gerund is more usual for general statements
when the emphasis is on the enjoyment (or not) of
the action.
Mary prefers *eating* out to eating at home.
2 The infinitive is more usual for more specific
statements where extra information is given.
Jane prefers *to eat* out because there's no washing-up to
do.

NOTE

With the verb *like + infinitive* there is often the added
meaning of a preferred alternative.

I like to drive there may imply 'I prefer that means of
transport to going by train or coach'.

C With a change of meaning

1 The verbs *try, stop, regret, remember, forget, mean,
go on* can be followed by the gerund or the
infinitive, but with a change in meaning.

Try

+ gerund = to experiment in order to achieve an
objective.
Try *going* to bed earlier and see if that helps.

+ infinitive = to attempt a difficult action.
Jill's been trying *to get* a job since she left school, but
with no success.

Stop

+ gerund = to finish an activity.
Stop *talking* and get on with your work!

+ infinitive = to interrupt one activity in order to do
another.
Roger stopped (what he was doing) *to have* a cup of tea.

Regret

+ gerund = to be sorry about an action in the past.
Many people regret *marrying* young.

+ infinitive = to be sorry about what you are going to
say.
Dr. Taylor regrets *to say* that she is unable to see patients
without an appointment.

Forget / remember

+ gerund = to (not) recall an action.
I distinctly remember *asking* them to come after lunch.
I won't forget *being* at the Olympic Games as long as I
live.

+ infinitive = to (not) do an action you must do.
Ann remembered *to lock* all the doors when she went on
holiday, but she forgot *to close* the bathroom window.

Go on

+ gerund = to continue an action.
I'll go on *applying* for jobs until I'm successful.

+ infinitive = to finish one activity and start another.
After seven years of study, Andy went on *to become* a
doctor.

Mean

+ gerund = to involve.
Dieting usually means *giving up* sweet things.

+ infinitive = to intend
I meant *to send* you a postcard but I couldn't remember
your address.

NOTE

The infinitive is only possible with *mean* in perfect and past tenses.

2 The verbs of perception *see* (*watch, notice*, etc.), *feel, hear, smell* have a different meaning when they are followed by the infinitive (without to) or a participle.
  a + participle = to experience part of an event
     I noticed a man *acting* in a strange way.
  b + infinitive without to = to experience the whole event
     I heard my sister *come* in at 1 a.m.

Unit 7

The passive

1 Verbs that can be used in the passive

Most transitive verbs can be used in the passive. A transitive verb is a verb which takes an object, e.g. *catch*.
  The police *caught* the thief.

Intransitive verbs cannot be used in the passive. An intransitive verb is a verb which does not take an object, e.g. *fall*.
  Rodney *fell* and hurt his leg.

2 Form of the passive

The passive is formed with the verb *be* in the appropriate tense + the past participle of the main verb. In the case of modals, e.g. *could*, and *must*, it is formed with the modal + *be* + past participle. See the table below.

3 Choosing active or passive form

In an active sentence, the subject is the person or thing that does the action.
  Liverpool *beat* Manchester United.

In a passive sentence, the subject of the verb is the person or thing affected by the action.
  Manchester United *were* beaten by Liverpool.

When we want to focus on the person or thing affected by the action instead of the performer of the action (the agent) we use the passive.

4 Including the agent (performer)

When we use the passive we can choose to include the agent or not. The agent is the person or thing who/which performs the action.
  The record is held *by Carl Lewis*.

We do not include the agent:
a when the agent is not important. So, we do **not** say:
   Trespassers will be prosecuted *by the landowner*.
b when we do not know who the agent is and so would have to use the words *somebody* or a *person*. We do **not** say:
   My car has been stolen *by somebody*.
c when the agent is obvious. So, we do **not** say:
   The thief was sentenced to five years imprisonment *by the judge*.
d when the agent has already been mentioned. So, we do **not** say:
   Some of Stephen King's books have been written *by him under the pseudonym Richard Bachman*.

NOTE

In informal English *get* can sometimes be used instead of *be* to form the passive. The agent is not generally mentioned.
  Nigel *got* stopped for speeding.

Tense	Subject	Verb 'be'	Past Participle
present simple	Letters	are	delivered twice a day.
present continuous	The suspect	is being	questioned by the police.
past simple	The programme	was	first broadcast in 1998.
past continuous	Our hotel room	was being	cleaned when we arrived.
present perfect	My car	has been	stolen.
past perfect	They	had been	warned about the danger.
future	You	will be	paid on Friday.
modal verbs	This meat	must be	cooked for at least an hour.

5 Verbs with two objects

A Some verbs can have two objects – a direct object (DO) and an indirect object (IO).

Lady Markham's late husband gave the painting (DO) to the gallery (IO).

Lady Markham's late husband gave the gallery (IO) the painting (DO).

B Either of the two objects can be the subject of the passive verb.

The painting was given to the gallery by her late husband.

The gallery was given the painting by her late husband.

C When one of the objects is a person, it is more usual for this to be the subject.

Bobby was given a new bike for his birthday.

rather than

A new bike was given to Bobby for his birthday.

6 Passive constructions with the infinitive

When we want to pass on information but we do not know whether the information is true or not, or we do not want to say where the information came from, we can use the passive form of these verbs: *think, believe, report, consider, know, say, expect* + the infinitive.

A When the information is about a present situation, we use the passive + infinitive.

The Queen *is thought to be* one of the richest people in the world.

Mr Smith *is believed to be* staying with friends.

B When the information is about something in the past, we use the passive + the past infinitive (*to have* + past participle).

The ship is reported *to have sunk.* Many people are thought *to have drowned.*

Have / Get something done (causative)

Have something done and *get something done* are both used to refer to actions which are done FOR the subject rather than BY the subject. Causative verbs are used instead of passive verbs to show that the subject causes the action to be done.

1 *Have something done*

I don't know how to repair cars, so *I'm having mine repaired* at the garage round the corner.

2 *Get something done*

I really must *get my eyes tested.* I'm sure I need glasses. *Get your hair cut!*

NOTE

1 *have something done* is slightly more formal than *get something done,*

2 *get* is more frequent than *have* in the imperative form.

3 Non-causative uses of *have* and *get*

Have and *get* are also used to refer to events which happened to someone, but were outside their control.

After being late for work every day for two weeks, *I had my pay reduced.*

I stood so close to the fire that *I got my legs burnt.*

Unit 8

Reporting speech

1 Direct speech

We can report what someone has said in two ways.

a We can report their actual words.

b We can report the idea they expressed.

When we report a person's actual words in writing, we use speech marks and an appropriate verb, e.g. *say, tell, ask.*

'I'll be late home tomorrow,' Bob said.

2 Reported speech

When we report the idea and not the actual words a person says we often make changes. These changes are usually to verb tenses, pronouns, word order, and time and place references.

3 Reporting statements

A Changes in verb tenses

When the reporting verb is in the past tense, e.g. *said,* we usually move the tenses in the sentence we are reporting one step back in time.

Direct speech		Reported speech
Present simple	➤	Past simple
'I'm a nurse,' she said.		She said she *was* a nurse.
Present continuous	➤	Past continuous
'I'm not going,' he said.		He said he *wasn't* going.
Past simple	➤	Past perfect
'Tony did it,' she said.		She said Tony *had* done it.
Present perfect	➤	Past perfect
'I haven't read it,' she said.		She said she *hadn't* read it.
Past continuous	➤	Past perfect continuous
'I was lying,' he said.		He said *he'd been* lying.
will future	➤	*Would*
'I'll get it,' she said.		She said she *would* get it.
Can	➤	*Could*
'I can speak French,' he said.		He said he *could* speak French
May	➤	*Might*
'I may be late,' she said.		She said she *might* be late.
Must	➤	*Had to*
'I must go,' he said.		He said he *had to* go.

NOTE

The past perfect and the modals *might, ought to, could, should* and *would* do not change in reported speech.

B No changes in verb tenses

1 When the reporting verb is in the present tense, e.g. *says*, we do not change the tense of the original verb. For example when we are reading what someone has said in a newspaper or letter:

Darren says *he's been* too busy to write before.

or when we are passing on a message:

Lucy says she'll be late.

2 When the reporting verb is in the past tense and we want to emphasise that the statement is still true we can keep the same tense if we wish.

'Bill is my cousin'   She said Bill *is* her cousin.

C Changes in time and place references

Some typical changes that may have to be made are:

Direct speech	Reported speech
today	*that day*
tomorrow	*the next day, the following day*
yesterday	*the previous day, the day before*
two days ago	*two days before, two days earlier*
now	*then*
here	*there*
come	*go*

Unless time and place words are reported at the same time and in the same place as they were originally said, they change.

'Marie phoned yesterday.' (said on Monday)

He said that Marie had phoned *two days ago/ on Sunday.* (said on Tuesday)

D Other changes

1 Pronouns may change when we are reporting speech. This depends on who is reporting.

'I'll give *you* a lift.' (Jack to Barbara)

Jack said he would give *me* a lift. (Barbara to someone else)

2 The determiners *this, that, these, those* may change to *the*.

'*These* jeans are too tight,' Cyril said.

Cyril said *the* jeans were too tight.

3 The pronouns *this* and *that* may change to *it*.

'Give me *that*!' Jayne said.

Jayne told me to give *it* to her.

E Reporting verbs

We can use the verbs *say* and *tell* to report statements. The structure after these verbs is *say (that)* + clause:

Richard said (that) he would be late.

and tell someone (that) + clause:

Richard told me (that) he would be late.

NOTE   *That* is frequently omitted in spoken English.

4 Reporting questions

A Changes

We make the same changes to verb tenses, time and place references and pronouns as we do when we report statements. We also change the form of the original question into a statement and omit auxiliary verbs (*do, does, did*) and question marks.

'When are you arriving?'

He asked me when *I was arriving*.

If there is no question word in the original we must use *if* or *whether*

'Do you understand?'

He asked her *if/whether* she understood.

B Reporting verbs

To report questions we can use the verb *ask* or the structure *want to know*.

'Are you enjoying yourself?' Mr Jones asked.

Mr Jones *wanted to know* if I was enjoying myself.

5 Reporting functions

A Reporting advice, commands, requests and warnings

We can report these kinds of speech using the verbs *advise*, *tell*, *ask* and *warn* + personal object pronoun + infinitive.

Advice
> 'You really should stop!'
> She advised me to stop.

Command
> 'Don't interrupt me!'
> He told me not to interrupt him.

Request
> 'Could you close the door please?
> She asked me to close the door.

Warning
> 'If you tell anyone, I'll ... !'
> She warned me not to tell anyone.

NOTES
1 The structure after *ask* is different depending on whether we are reporting a request or a question.
> 'Can you remind me please?' (request)
> He asked me to remind him.
> 'Can you come tomorrow?' (question)
> She asked me if I could come the next day.

2 The structure after *tell* is different depending on whether we are reporting a command or a statement.
> 'Come on! Hurry up!' (command)
> She told us to hurry up.
> 'It doesn't start till 8.' (statement)
> He told us (that) it didn't start until 8.

B Reporting suggestions

We can report suggestions with the verb *suggest* + clause.

For example, to report '*Let's stay in.*':
> She suggested that we (should) stay in.
> She suggested that we stayed in.
> She suggested staying in.

NOTE
> You cannot use the infinitive in this structure.

Unit 9

Relative clauses

A relative clause gives extra information. It is introduced by a relative pronoun: *who* (*whom*), *which*, *that*, *whose* or there may be no relative pronoun, Ø. The choice of relative pronoun depends on whether:

it is the subject or object or possessive of a relative clause.

it refers to a person or thing.

the relative clause is defining or non-defining

	A Defining		B Non-defining	
	Person	Thing	Person	Thing
1 Subject	who/that	which/that	who	which
2 Object	Ø/who(m)/ that	Ø/which/ that	who(m)	which
3 Possessive	whose	whose (of which)	whose (of which)	whose

NOTE
1 *who* and *which* are more usual than *that* in writing.
2 a defining relative pronoun is frequently omitted, particularly in speech.
3 *Whom* is formal and is used mainly in writing.

1 Defining and non-defining clauses

Relative clauses are common in spoken and written English. However, non-defining relative clauses are more common in written English than in spoken English.

A The information given in a **defining** relative clause is essential to the meaning of the sentence. It makes clear which person or thing we are talking about.
> The man *who/that* lives at number 36 has been arrested.
> The fingerprints *which/that* were found on the gun were his.
> The boy *whose* dog is missing is offering a reward for its safe return.

B The information given in a **non-defining** relative clause is not essential to the meaning of the sentence. A comma is put before the relative pronoun and at the end of the clause, unless this is also the end of the sentence.
> Mr White, *who* lives at number 36, is emigrating to New Zealand.
> We stayed at The Carlton, *which* is a five-star hotel in the town centre.

NOTES

1 In non-defining relative clauses, *which* can refer to a whole clause.

   He climbed the mountain wearing only a T-shirt and trainers, *which* was a stupid thing to do.

2 In non-defining relative clauses, after numbers and words like *many, most, neither, some*, we use *of* before *whom* and *which*.

   Dozens of people had been invited, most *of whom* I knew.

3 We usually use *that* (not *which*) after the following words: *all, any(thing), every(thing), few, little, many, much, no(thing), none, some(thing)*, and after superlatives. When the pronoun refers to the object, *that* can be omitted.

   It was something *that* could have happened to anyone.
   It was the most difficult exam *(that)* I'd ever taken.

2 *Where, why* and *when*

Where, why and *when* are used in place of a relative pronoun after a noun which refers to a place, a time or a reason.

A In **defining** relative clauses *why* and *when* can be omitted.

   I'd like to live in a country *where* it's summer all year round.
   Do you know the reason *(why)* Kate's changed her mind?
   June is the month *(when)* many couples get married.

B In **non-defining** relative clauses *when, where* and *why* cannot be omitted.

   Aileen was brought up in Scotland, *where* she was born, but she emigrated after her marriage.
   The town is quieter after lunch, *when* everyone is having a siesta.

3 Relative clauses and prepositions

A In formal English a preposition usually comes before the relative pronoun.

   The Hilton Hotel, *at which* we stayed while we were in New York, is expensive.

B In informal English a preposition usually comes at the end of the relative clause

   The Hilton Hotel, *which* we stayed *at* while we were in New York, is expensive.

C Defining

	Formal	Informal
Person	whom	Ø
Thing	which	Ø

The man to *whom* I spoke gave me different information.
The man Ø I spoke to gave me different information.
The car in *which* the robbers got away had been stolen.
The car Ø the robbers got away in had been stolen.

D Non-defining

	Formal	Informal
Person	whom	who
Thing	which	which

The hotel manager, to *whom* I spoke about my dissatisfaction, suggested I write to you.
The hotel manager, *who* I spoke to about my dissatisfaction, suggested I call you.

Unit 10

Wishes, regrets and preferences

1 *Wish*

We use *wish* to talk about situations we would like to change but can't, either because they are outside our control or because they are in the past. The tense of the verb after *wish* does not correspond to the time we are thinking about; it changes. The verb tense is one step back in time (as in reported speech.)

A A wish about a present or future situation is expressed with a past tense.

Situation	Wish
I am an only child	I wish I *wasn't* an only child.
I can't drive	I wish I *could* drive.
Rod isn't coming to the party	I wish Rod *was* coming.

NOTE

In formal English we say I/he/she/it *were/weren't*.

B A wish about a past situation is expressed with a past perfect tense.

Situation	Wish
I've lost my best pen	I wish I *hadn't lost* it.
I didn't remember	I wish I'*d remembered*.

C *Wish ... would*

We use *wish ... would*:

1 when we want to complain about a present situation.

Situation	Wish
A dog is barking.	I wish that dog *would* stop barking!
The road is icy.	I wish you *wouldn't* drive so fast.

NOTE

We can't say *I wish I would ...*

2 when we are impatient for an event outside our control to happen.

Situation	Wish
You're waiting for the bus	*I wish the bus would come.*

NOTE

It is not possible to use *wish ... would* with the verb *be* unless we are complaining. We say I *wish it were Friday* and not I *wish it would be Friday.*

2 Other structures to express wishes and regrets

A If we want a future event to happen or not happen, and this event is possible and not just a desire, we use the verb *hope* + present simple.
I *hope* I pass my exams.

B *If only* can often be used in place of *wish* with a slightly stronger sense of regret.
I wish Sue was here / *If only* Sue was here. She'd know what to do.

3 *I'd rather*

We use *would rather* to express a preference.

A about our own actions.

1 If we are referring to a present situation we use *would rather* + infinitive without 'to')
I'*d rather* be rich than poor.

2 If we are referring to a past situation we use *would rather* + perfect infinitive)
I'*d rather* have lived 100 years ago than now.

B about someone else's actions.

1 If we are referring to a present situation we use *would rather* + past simple)
I'd rather you *came* tomorrow / I'd rather you *didn't come* on Wednesday.

2 If we are referring to a past situation we use *would rather* + past perfect)
I'd rather you *hadn't told* me / I'd rather you *had kept* it to yourself.

4 It's time

We use the expressions *it's time* and *it's high time* to show that we think something should happen soon. We use the past tense to refer to the present or the future.
My hair is rather long. It's time I *got* it cut.
He's over thirty. It's high time he *settled down* and *got* himself a proper job!

We use the expression *it's time* + 'to' infinitive to show that the moment for something to happen has come.
It's 5 o'clock. It's time *to go* home. (We normally finish at 5 o'clock.)

Unit 11

Conditional sentences

There are four main types of conditional sentence. Each type has a distinctive pattern of verb tenses, and its own meaning.

1 Conditional 0

A Form

If + present … present or imperative

B Meanings

This type of sentence is used for conditions which are always true.

If *Mike reads* on the train, *he feels* sick. (Every time Mike reads on the train, the same thing happens: he feels sick.)

This type of sentence is also used for scientific facts.

If *you put* paper on a fire, *it burns* quickly.

It is also used to give instructions.

If the *phone rings*, answer it.

In zero or present conditional sentences *when* or *whenever* can be used instead of *if*.

2 Conditional 1

A Form

If + present simple … *will* future

B Meaning

This type of sentence is used to predict likely or probable results in the future, if a condition is met.

If *we don't leave* now, *we'll miss* the train.

If *we leave* now, *we won't need to* hurry.

First conditional sentences are often used to express persuasion, promises, warnings and threats.

If *you pass* your exams, *I'll give* you a job.

If *you don't turn* that music down, *you'll go* deaf.

C Some modal verbs can be used instead of *will*.

If we leave now, we *may* catch the train.

If you come to London again, you *must* call and see us.

3 Conditional 2

A Form

If + past simple … *would/could/might*

B Meaning

This type of sentence is used to speculate about imaginary or improbable situations; the implication is that the conditions will not be met.

You'd feel healthier if *you did* more exercise.

If *you went* to Africa, *you'd have to have* several injections. (It's not likely you'll go to Africa, but it is possible.)

Second conditional sentences can also refer to unreal situations.

If *people didn't drive* so fast, *there wouldn't be* so many fatal accidents. (Actually people do drive fast and there are a lot of fatal accidents.)

If *I were* taller, *I'd play* basketball. (Being taller is impossible for me.)

Second conditional sentences are often used to express advice.

If *I were* you, *I wouldn't drive* so fast.

C *Might/could*

Might and *could* can be used instead of *would* in the main clause of second conditional sentences to show uncertainty.

If you did more exercise, you *might* feel healthier.

4 Conditional 3

A Form

If + past perfect … *would/might/could have* + past participle

B Meaning

This type of sentence looks back at the past and speculates about possibilities which didn't happen.

If *I'd had* your address, *I'd have sent* you a postcard. (I didn't have your address, so I didn't send you a postcard.)
You might not have crashed into the bus *if you'd been driving* more slowly.

NOTE

When the *if* clause comes before the main clause, it is followed by a comma. When the *if* clause comes after the main clause, there is no comma between the clauses.

5 Mixed conditional sentences

A Form

If + past perfect … *would/could/might*

B Meaning

This type of sentence, which is a mixture of a third conditional sentence and a second conditional sentence, links a completed past action with a present result.

> If *I hadn't broken* my leg, *I would go* on holiday with you.
> *I'd have a better* job now, if *I'd worked harder* when I was at school.

6 Other ways of introducing conditions

A *Unless*

Unless can sometimes be used instead of *if not*.

> *Unless* we leave now, we'll miss the train. (If we don't leave now, we'll miss the train.)

B *As long as*

As long as is used to emphasize a condition.

> I'll lend you the money you need *as long as* you promise not to waste it.

C *Provided (that)*

Provided (that)… and *Providing (that)…* mean 'on condition that' and are slightly more formal than *if*.

> You can come on holiday with us *provided that* you do some of the cooking.

Unit 12

Probability and possibility

1 Expressing near certainty

If we are almost certain that something is the case, and this certainty is based on evidence, we can make statements using *must* or *can't*.

A If we are talking about a present situation we use *must* or *can't* + infinitive without *to*.

> My doctor *must be* married. She wears a wedding ring. (I am almost certain she is married.)
> Angus *can't be* English. He's got a Scottish accent. (I am almost certain he isn't English.)

We can also use the continuous form of the verb.

> Virginia *must be wondering* where I am. I said I'd be there at 3 p.m. and it's now 5 p.m. (I am almost certain she is wondering where I am.)

B If we are talking about a past situation we use *must* or *can't* + *have* + past participle.

> Sandra *must have passed* her driving test because I saw her driving a car on her own.
> (I am almost certain she has passed her test.)
> Fiona and Neil *can't have enjoyed* their holiday because they haven't said anything about it. (I am almost certain they didn't enjoy their holiday.)

We can also use the continuous form of the verb.

> I'm sorry I'm late. You *must have been waiting* for ages!

NOTE

The negative of *must* in this case is *can't*, not *mustn't*.

2 Expressing possibility

If we are not certain that something is the case but we think it is possible, we can make statements using *could*, *may* or *might*.

A If we are talking about a present situation we use *could*, *may*, *might* + infinitive without *to*.

> Paula *could/might/may be* on holiday. (Maybe she's on holiday.)
> Claude *may have* flu. (Perhaps/It's possible he's got flu.)

B If we are talking about a past situation we use *could*, *may*, *might* + *have* + past participle.

> Freda *might have overslept*. (It's possible that she's overslept.)

C It is also possible to use continuous forms.

> Julie *might be visiting* her mother.
> The missing girl *may have been wearing* a blue skirt.

NOTE

1 There is no real difference in meaning between *may*, *might* and *could*.

2 The negative forms of *may* and *might* are *may not* and *might not*. These are not usually contracted.
The defendant *may not be telling* the truth.
(It's possible that he isn't telling the truth.)

3 The negative form of *could* is *couldn't*. Its meaning is similar to *can't*.
He *couldn't be lying*. (I am almost certain he isn't lying.)

Articles

1 The definite article *the*

Three of the main uses of the definite article are to refer to:

A something that has been mentioned before.
Bill: I've got a dog.
Ben: What's *the* dog's name?

B something there is only one of in a particular context.
The Queen spent three days in Wales.
Soon after we'd taken off, *the* pilot welcomed us on board.

C something the speaker and listener both know about.
The film was really good – thanks for recommending it.

It is also used in these ways:

D with superlative constructions.
She's *the* fastest runner in Europe.

E with adjectives used as nouns referring to groups of people.
There's one law for *the* rich and another for *the* poor.

F with the names of oceans, seas, rivers, mountain ranges.
the Atlantic, *the* Thames, *the* Alps

G with the names of some countries and groups of islands.
the United States, *the* United Kingdom, *the* West Indies

2 The indefinite article *a/an*

These are the main uses of the indefinite article

A to refer to something for the first time.
I've got *a* dog.

B to refer to a person or thing (but not a special person or thing).
Can I have *a* drink please? Tea, coffee, beer, I don't mind.

C to refer to a person's job.
Alan is *a* telephone engineer.

E with numbers.
a hundred, *a* million

3 Zero article (Ø)

These are the main contexts in which no article is used:

A with plural countable nouns.
Ø International footballers are paid too much money.

B with uncountable nouns.
He used to drink Ø beer, but now he drinks only Ø water.
They fell in Ø love while they were in Spain.

C with the names of towns, cities, states and most countries.
Ø New York, Ø Texas, Ø Greece

D with nouns for certain places or situations.
Suzy went into Ø hospital yesterday.
on Ø deck, at Ø home, on Ø holiday, to Ø church, at Ø school

OXFORD
UNIVERSITY PRESS

Great Clarendon Street, Oxford OX2 6DP

Oxford University Press is a department of the University of Oxford.
It furthers the University's objective of excellence in research, scholarship,
and education by publishing worldwide in

Oxford New York

Auckland Cape Town Dar es Salaam Hong Kong Karachi
Kuala Lumpur Madrid Melbourne Mexico City Nairobi
New Delhi Shanghai Taipei Toronto

With offices in

Argentina Austria Brazil Chile Czech Republic France Greece
Guatemala Hungary Italy Japan Poland Portugal Singapore
South Korea Switzerland Thailand Turkey Ukraine Vietnam

OXFORD and OXFORD ENGLISH are registered trade marks of
Oxford University Press in the UK and in certain other countries

© Oxford University Press 2004

The moral rights of the author have been asserted

Database right Oxford University Press (maker)

First published 2004

2011 2010 2009 2008 2007

10 9 8 7

ISBN 978 0 19 438625 8

Printed in China

ACKNOWLEDGEMENTS

*The authors and publisher are grateful to those who have given permission to reproduce the
following extracts and adaptations of copyright material:* p10 'Distant space travel
better as family affair' by Cathy Keen, from UF News. Reproduced by permission
of John Moore. p17 'At home with Mamma' by Greg Burke © 1997 TIME Inc.
reprinted by permission. p22 'Maya Angelou' Usborn Book of Famous Lives.
Reproduced by permission. p26 'Trainspotting' by Regie Rigby, from
www.silverbulletcomicbooks.com. Reproduced by permission of Regie Rigby.
p34 'Are you a shopaholic? Quiz and facts on compulsive shopping' by Stephanie
Hall © 2001 by PageWise, Inc. Used with permission. p36 'Will Smith' by Alex
Blimes © GQ / The Condé Nast Publications Ltd. Reproduced by permission. p51
Information from Dr Martens website www.drmartens.com. Reproduced by
permission of R.Griggs & Co. p54 'Bad Habits' by Molly Parkin © Marie Claire/IPC
Syndication, Marie Claire, February 1989. Reproduced by permission. p60 'Anita
Roddick' Usborn Book of Famous Lives. Reproduced by permission. p62 'I flew to
Brazil – by accident' by Nigel Hughes © Woman/IPC Syndication, Woman, 11
December 1989. Reproduced by permission. p66 Discovery Road by Tim Garrett
and Andy Brown © Eye Books Ltd. 1998 www.eye-books.com. Reproduced by
permission of Eye Books Ltd. p76 'Emotional Intelligence' by Maureen Gaffney,
The Irish Times, 2 December 1995 (c) Maureen Gaffney. Reproduced by
permission. p86 'Telepathy' by Simon Hoggart and Michael Hutchison © The
Observer, The Observer 20 September 2002. Reproduced by permission. p88
'Down and Dirty' by Gavan Naden © Ganan Naden, Guardian Unlimited July 4
2002. Reproduced by permission. p91 'Guide to Inter-railing' from
www.theglobalvoyage.com. Reproduced by permission of Richard Tate. p95
© 2003 – Monster Worldwide, Inc. All Rights Reserved. You may not copy,
reproduce or distribute this article without the prior written permission of
Monster Worldwide. This article first appeared on Monster, the leading online
global network for careers. To see other career-related articles visit
http://content.monster.com. p101 Extract from Nineteen Eighty Four by George
Orwell (Copyright © George Orwell, 1949) by permission of Bill Hamilton as the
Literary Executor of the Estate of the Late Sonia Brownell Orwell and Secker &
Warburg Ltd. p107 Strange Places, Questionable People by John Simpson

(Macmillan:1998). Reproduced by permission of Lucas Alexander Whitley.
pp108–109 'Who's finger is on the button in your house' by Graham Thompson
© Woman/IPC Syndication, Woman, 12 February 1990. Reproduced by
permission. p117 Natural Disasters by Richard O'Neil © Parragon 1998.
Reproduced by permission. p121 Extracts from www.ecotourism.org.
Reproduced by kind permission of The International Ecotourism Society. p138 'I
know just how you feel' by Dea Birkett © Dea Birkett, The Guardian 3 September
2002. Reproduced by permission. p148 'Talk the Squawk' by David Alterton
© David Alterton, The Guardian 6 April 2002. Reproduced by permission. p150
Extracts from www.cjcj.org. Reproduced by kind permission of The Center on
Juvenile and Criminal Justice. p157 Information from www.comicrelief.com.
Reproduced by permission. p161 'Why do the eyes in some paintings appear to
follow the viewer around the room?' © 2003 Popular Science Magazine/
www.popsci.com. Reprinted by permission of Time4 Media, Inc.

Although every effort has been made to trace and contact copyright holders
before publication, this has not been possible in some cases. We apologize for any
apparent infringement of copyright and if notified, the publisher will be pleased
to rectify any errors or omissions at the earliest opportunity.

Sources: p24 gameloaded.co.uk; p27 www.scoop.co.nz;
p106 www.goodnewsnetwork.org p122 www.btcv.org; p160 www.bcentral.com

*The publisher would like to thank the following for their kind permission to reproduce
photographs:* Activision pp24l, 24r; Alamy pp12 (H. P. Merten/Robert Harding
Picture Library Ltd), 35tr (Jean-Philippe Soule/Around the World in a Viewfinder),
51 (Malcolm Freeman), 56tl, 56tr (Pictor International/ ImageState), 74 (foodfolio),
82, 87tr (Pictor International/ImageState), 101bl (Elvele Images), 101tr (Frank
Chmura/ImageState), 106 (Joe Sohm), 118bl (Phillip Carr/Photofusion Picture
Library), 118br (Charlie Newham), 125ba (Frank Field), 149br (Philip Wolmuth),
149tl (David Hoffman/David Hoffman Photo Library), 155l (Alex Segre), 155r
(Klaus-Peter Wolf); Allsport (UK) Ltd. p44l; BBC Picture Publicity p107; Bridgeman
Art Library p117 (Smithsonian Institution, Washington DC, USA); Camelot Group
Plc p158l (Adrian Brooks Photography); Comic Relief pp157b, 157l, 157r, 157t;
Corbis UK Ltd. pp9bc, 9bl, 9br, 9tl (Bill Varie), 9tr, 10r (Mendola/Attila Hejja), 13
(Lindsay Hebberd), 14, 15, 22 (Bettmann), 23br, 23c, 23tr, 27 (Michelle Garrett),
31bl (BarryLewis), 31br (Kit Houghton), 32, 35tl (Gail Mooney), 39 (Bettmann), 40
(Jamie Budge), 43, 46 (Patrick Ward), 53, 56b (Archivo Iconografico, S.A.), 57tc
(Philippa Lewis; Edifice), 57tr (Yann Arthus-Bertrand), 61tl (Dave Bartruff), 62, 66
(Charles & Josette Lenars), 67 (Michael S. Yamashita), 68 (Dave G. Houser), 69 (Carl
& Ann Purcell), 71bc (Bryn Colton/Assignments Photographers), 71bl, 71br, 71tl,
71tr (Liba Taylor), 72, 80 (David A. Northcott), 81 (Michael & Patricia Fogden), 87bl,
87br, 87c, 87tl (Wartenberg/Picture Press), 88/89 (Dewitt Jones), 90r (Owen
Franken), 91, 93, 97l, 97r (Martyn Goddard), 98l (Robert Holmes), 98r, 99 (Robert
Holmes), 101br (JackFields), 101tl (Bob Krist), 105tr (Gail Mooney), 112, 113br, 114
(Douglas Peebles), 118bc (Nick Hawkes; Ecoscene), 118tc (Richard T. Nowitz),
118tl, 118tr (Martin Jones; Ecoscene), 119l, 119r (Sally A. Morgan; Ecoscene), 121l
(VittorianoRastelli), 121r, 122b (Galen Rowell), 122c (CraigLovell), 122t (Galen
Rowell), 124 (Roger Ressmeyer), 125cl (Martin Jones), 125cr (Peter M. Fisher), 125tc
(Chris Hellier), 125tr (©LWA-Dann Tardif), 129 (Philip James Corwin), 130bl (Ed
Eckstein), 130br, 130tc, 137bl, 137br (Rick Gomez), 137tr, 144bl, 144br (Jeff
Zaruba), 144tl (HowardDavies), 144tr, 148 (Philip Gould), 149bl (Anthony Cooper;
Ecoscene), 155cr (Richard Hamilton Smith), 159, 161bl (Kevin Fleming), 161br
(Paul A. Souders), 161tl (Adrian Arbib), 161tr (Lester Lefkowitz); Empics p35br
(Tom Ward); Getty Images pp10l (The Image Bank), 17 (Frank Herholdt/Taxi), 61bl
(Simon Bottomley/Taxi), 97c (Werner Bokelberg/The Image Bank); Guardian
Newspapers p105b; Hotel Monna Lisa p90l; Hulton|Archive/ Getty Images p130tr
(Picture Post); iwantoneofthose.com pp132bc, 132br; Oxford University Press
pp19, 57bl, 57br, 102bl, 102br, 102t, 130tl; Paramount Zone Ltd. pp132bl, 132tc,
132tl, 132tr; Portsmouth News p57tl (Pete Landown); Press Association pp35bc
(European Press Agency), 60 (EPA Photo AFP/Manuel Ceneta), 158/159 (EPA Photo
DPA/Jan Nienheysen/jn-cl); Rex Features pp23bl (SIPA), 23tl, 29, 31tl (Mark Pain),
31tr (Richard Young), 35bl (Startraks), 36b (Richard Young), 36t, 42l (Action Press
(ACT)), 42r (Mark Campbell (MXC)), 44r, 48 (Sipa Press (SIPA)), 61br (Curtis Myers),
61tr (Steve Maisey), 71tc (Sipa), 76 (David Hartley), 105tc (Julian Makey), 110, 113bl
(Solent News (SON)), 113tl (Peter Heimsath), 113tr (Geoff Pugh), 134tr (c.Warner
Br/Everett), 136, 137tl, 149tr (Action Press), 155cl (Andrew Murray (AMU)), 158r
(Lehtikuva OY); Ronald Grant Archive pp9tc, 133, 134b, 134tc, 134tl; St Bride
Printing Library p130tl (Geremy Butler Photography); Volvo Car Corporation (UK)
p105b; St. Clare's, Oxford pp59b, 59t, 146b, 146c; Zooid Pictures pp16, 105tl,
125bb, 125bc, 125bd, 125be, 125bf, 125c, 125t, 125tl, 131, 146t

The greetings cards on p156 are reproduced by kind permission of Hanson White.

Illustrations by: Tim Davies p54; Emma Dodd pp39, 45, 52, 79, 96; Mark Duffin
pp41, 70, 85, 126, 150, 154; Spike Gerrell pp64, 86, 109, 120, 142; Tim Kahane
pp75, 92, 94; Ellis Nadler pp30, 50, 78, 95, 127, 143, 160; Andy Parker p153; Colin
Thompson pp25, 38, 63, 77, 104, 116, 140; Kath Walker pp18, 26, 34, 55, 84, 100,
128, 145.

Commissioned photography by: Steve Betts p.19 (exam scene); Chris King p. 138 (facial
expressions).